Death and the Moving

To Life, to Life,

For Ulele Burnham

Death and the Moving Image

Ideology, Iconography and I

Michele Aaron

EDINBURGH
University Press

Edinburgh University Press Ltd
The Tun – Holyrood Road
12 (2f) Jackson's Entry
Edinburgh EH8 8PJ
www.euppublishing.com

First published in hardback by Edinburgh University Press 2014

Typeset in Monotype Ehrhardt by
Servis Filmsetting Ltd, Stockport, Cheshire,
and printed and bound in Great Britain by
CPI Group (UK) Ltd, Croydon CR0 4YY

A CIP record for this book is available from the British Library

ISBN 978 0 7486 2443 0 (hardback)
ISBN 978 1 4744 0275 0 (paperback)
ISBN 978 0 7486 7776 4 (epub)
ISBN 978 0 7486 3047 9 (webready PDF)

Part of Chapter 3 was originally published as 'From Complacency to Culpability:
Conflict and Death in Post-9.11 Film', in Priscilla Roberts, Mei Renyi and Yan Xunhua
(eds), *China Views Nine-Eleven: Essays in Transnational American Studies* (Cambridge
Scholars Publishing, 2011). Part of Chapter 3 was originally published as 'Looking
On and Looking the Other Way: *Hotel Rwanda* (2004) and the Racialised Ethics of
Spectatorship', in James Walters and Tom Brown (eds), *Film Moments: Criticism,
History, Theory* (Palgrave, 2010).

Death and the Moving Image is supported by

Arts & Humanities
Research Council

Contents

PART III AFTER – RESPONDING TO DEATH

Figures

Acknowledgements

The completion of this book was supported by an Arts and Humanities Research Council (AHRC) research leave grant as well as a study leave from the University of Birmingham. In our age of the ever colder, ever more oxymoronic, educational institution, I count myself extremely lucky to have such warm, wise, and 'agitating' colleagues–friends in American and Canadian Studies at Birmingham. In particular, Danielle Fuller, a model academic, has steered me back on track at crucial moments and reminds me, as the rest of our small team does, of why we bother. I owe a debt of thanks to the, by now, hundreds of students who have taken my Death and the Moving Image class since I first started teaching it in 1998. At Brunel University and then at Birmingham, they have consistently enriched my thoughts on the subject. I'd especially like to acknowledge John Horne, who has been the model postgraduate student of recent years, and to thank him for providing countless additional resources for this project.

My work on this book has benefited enormously from the careful and generous feedback I have received from such astute readers as Anat Pick, Ulele Burnham, Sara Wood and Monica Pearl. A special thanks goes to the last for her generous scrutiny of the entire typescript as well as her enduring friendship. Thanks are due, too, to the research seminar audiences at King's College London and Keele University with whom I first tried out some of these ideas. My life has benefited enormously from the friendship and irreverence of my Birmingham crew, in particular Steve Hewitt, Jules Wright and Lindsey Myers, as well as from the enduring love and support of my parents and 'older' friends and colleagues.

This was not an easy book to write. Dwelling with death for too many years, however academically, is arduous and especially so to those who have had to put up with it and me during this time. My sharpest appreciation and love go to Vita and Ulele who have borne the brunt. For Vita, who has always exuded, and never just in name, this project's essential counterweight, I am eternally and humbly thankful. To Ulele, my *provocatrice*, and to whom this book is intellectually indebted, I send this swell of gratefulness. *Death and the Moving Image* has evolved since I started writing it, and changed course as I have. In the end, its waning cynicism is, I hope, where the next one will start. Here, uncharacteristically, is to life after death.

. . . what we call, by a somewhat corrupted term, love, is *par excellence* the fact that the death of the other affects me more than my own . . .
Emmanuel Levinas, *God, Death, and Time*, p. 105

The imaginative and historical terrain upon which American writers journeyed is in large measure shaped by the presence of the racial other . . .
Toni Morrison, *Playing in the Dark*, p. 46

Everywhere and Nowhere

Death is everywhere and nowhere in contemporary Western culture. Corpses litter Hollywood film; vulnerability or violence propels most mainstream fictions; the recently recovered or slowly dying make bookshelves groan. But the pain or smell of death, the banality of physical, or undignified, decline, the dull ache of mourning, are rarely seen. Cemeteries move further from the city, approach obsolescence as well as capacity, and hospitals hold dying at bay and far from the public eye. Yet our film and television screens are steeped in death's dramatics: in spectacles of glorious sacrifice or bloody retribution, in the ecstasy of agony, but always in the promise of redemption. This book is about these dramatics or, more precisely, the staging of these dramatics in mainstream film, and the discrepancies that fuel them and are, by return, fuelled by them.

The foregrounding of discrepancy, of the gaps or inaccuracies that characterise death's mediation in its restless departure from lived experience, has always accompanied its sociocultural study. Since Ernest Becker's Pulitzer Prize-winning bestseller of 1973 announced *The Denial of Death* – that the human condition is characterised by a fear of death which funds our actions but evades our consciousness – debates on the topic have negotiated this question of repression and of death's faux nowhere-ness in contemporary life.[1] Philippe Ariès provided the historical context to this death denial in his groundbreaking study of 1975: *Western Attitudes towards Death: From the Middle Ages to the Present*.[2] In it he traced death's social role from medieval to modern times: its long and slow journey from being familiar to becoming forbidden. Until the eighteenth century, death was an everyday event: an individual would die at home, surrounded by a steady stream of family, neighbours and children. With modernity, industrialisation and secularisation, things changed: death became an increasingly private or domestic enterprise and more about the loved ones looking on than the dearly departing themselves. Death shifted, in other words, from its function as public but banal ritual, to the intense, private, and even expressive performances of mourning in Victorian times, and then again to the conventions of 'acceptability', constraint, and solemnity, attending death in the subsequent period and since.[3] Such conventions segregate the dying into hospitals, regulate the excesses of grief but still redirect attention away from the body in decline or exanimation: 'Death, so omnipresent in the past . . . would be effaced, would disappear. It would become shameful and forbidden'.[4] The manifestations of this inter-diction would take somewhat different forms in different centuries and in different countries in the West but its modern entrenchment as taboo was universal.

This is a grand simplification of Ariès's historical cartography: its details are debated with erudition elsewhere but its prevailing themes, such as the romanticisation of death or its conservatism, will be addressed and updated throughout this study.[5] What the summary reveals, however, are several important, and enduring, displacements going on within death and mourning practices in modern times and within the entrenchment of taboo. These displacements hold particular significance for any study of modern culture but especially so for mainstream cinema which trades more than most on the diversionary promises of lavish fantasy. Freud's remark on attitudes towards death that we 'seek in the world of fiction, in literature and in the theatre compensation for what has been lost in life', achieves its most vivid realisation in this medium.[6] When Ariès connects responsibility for death's interdiction to an emphasis upon the preserva-tion of 'happiness, born in the United States around the beginning of the twentieth century',[7] we gain a clear mandate for the significance to this project of the Dream Factory, of the Hollywood system, which was consolidating socially and industrially at just this time, and its part in pro-moting the 'American/ised' way of life and way of death that preoccupy us here.

Journeying ever further from the truths of the body in decline, Ariès's historical displacements in the cultural role of death can be broadly conjured thus: from the public to the private; from the person dying to the person mourning; from the everyday to the extraordinary; and from ritualistic to romanticised remonstration or self-restraint. These new emphases, upon what can be usefully encapsulated as the exceptionalism of death, will prove to be very important to its cinematic treatment, and to my analysis. At their heart, for Ariès, was a certain denial, though he didn't call it that. Whether it was eroticised, sensationalised or simply unmentionable, death from eighteenth-century Western culture onwards was increasingly cordoned off from the natural and healthy functioning of society. In this book, I pursue the bifurcated or ambivalent place of death in twentieth- and twenty-first-century culture: the ongoing split between its over- and understatement, between its cold, bodily realities and its fantastical, transcendental and, most importantly, strategic representation.[8] Its cultural expression will be shown still to support the natural and healthy functioning of society but this sense of well-being is, I have found, highly contingent upon social factors that far exceed a *universal* fear of death. Popular culture, specifically mainstream cinema, will prove the privileged site for scrutinising such strategies' nurture of the welfare of 'Western society'.

For Geoffrey Gorer, an early voice in the study of death and dying and to whom Ariès pays tribute, the twentieth-century interdiction must be understood in terms of a specific historical displacement, and one that also renders a universal death *fear* an inadequate explanation. His seminal article of 1955, 'The Pornography of Death', argued that in its taboo and titillating status – as forbidden-but-with-frisson – it held the same role that sex did in Victorian times.[9] Death became the new obscenity, to be sequestered and repressed but also, tangentially, indulged, at least in those tawdry spaces that afforded it. A split occurred. Medical developments and the progressive control over the wages of the body caused a separating out of natural and unnatural death in society: 'While natural death became more and more smothered in prudery, violent death has played an ever growing part in the fantasies offered to mass audiences'.[10] This is where mediated death and cultural artefacts gain such prominence within the debate. Repressed in real life, death returns and returns extravagantly in representation. This split, and developing gulf, between sanitised natural and spectacular unnatural death will prove apposite, and even telling, in filmic translation. Not only will cinema's dramatic display of death contrast with its inconspicuousness in real life but both natural and unnatural death migrate to the screen, albeit in different proportions. Crucially, however, this book will demonstrate that the 'fantasies offered to mass audiences' by cinema depend just as much, *if not more*, upon the niceties of natural death as the blood fests of its special events. Death's critical importance here will hinge upon its salubrious, rather than lurid, spectacles. Prudery proves the most revealing still.

Since its inception, cinema has provided an ever more dominating forum for society's depiction of, and dealings with, death. It provides a rare site for representations of illness or grief, of wounded bodies or souls, or of the fringes of life. It is prolific in imaging death by stupefying risk, tragic misadventure or unpalatable crime. This pervasive staging of violent death proves not only gratuitous, or the flipside of repression, but psychologically strategic as Becker might have it: it serves our avoidance of mortality, distancing death from the self. Becker drew on the work of Otto Rank who put it thus: 'through the death of the other, one buys oneself free from the penalty of dying, of being killed'.[11] In crude terms, others suffer instead of us: the more we watch the death of others, the more we master it and are reassured of our own survival. For Alfred Killilea the aesthetic dimension of what we're watching is vital: the more violent or graphic the representation of murder, the more clearly Western culture seeks to avoid the subject of death: 'We continue to hide from the reality of our natural and unavoidable mortality', he says, 'by exposing ourselves to the more bizarre and violent manifestations of death'.[12] More than just an 'instinct to mastery',[13] or channelling of the 'death drive' in Freudian terms, we become inured to the place of death in our lives, hardened to it, precisely through the *graphic* visualisations of death and dying. And the more fantastical or discrepant such representations are, the stronger the guarantee of our distance from them. The individual might test and strengthen the death drive through these encounters with mortality, then, and culture, especially cinema, might offer a compelling platform for occasioning such thrills but psychoanalysis is insufficient to explain death's rich role on-screen. Instead, what is emphasised here is the aesthetic and psychosocial – the compulsory interchange between psychic and social factors – import of these representations and, crucially, their codependence.

Mainstream cinema abounds with such bizarre and violent manifestations, and numerous studies of action, thriller, gangster and horror films have pointed us to both their entertainment and ideological values.[14] Pleasure in, indeed especially in, fear or suspense is pivotal here: mainstream cinema, lest we forget, is above all else an entertainment industry. Similarly, as Joel Black reminds us, '[o]ur customary experience of murder and other forms of violence is primarily aesthetic, rather than moral, physical, natural, or whatever term we choose as a synonym for the word real'.[15] Though this study dwells on sombre topics and ethical suppositions, it is underwritten by the visual and visceral allure, or downright delight, these depictions promise their vast audiences. *Death and the Moving Image*, however, is not explicitly about murder or violence, monsters or villains, or such films' sensational depictions of ever less natural death. Instead, innocuous or poignant representations, the seemingly more seemly fantasies about mortality, take centre stage. These, I argue, are far more potent as indicators of the distancing devices that surround death's place in mainstream cinema and of the wider cultural needs such devices serve or betray. These distancing devices are about our fear not only of death but of our implication in others' deaths. Indeed, the discrepant depiction of mortality, I argue, stems from a set of other fears, cares or unconscious attitudes that are met and satisfied by the death dealings of mainstream film. The principal aim of this study, then, is to pursue and pin down these broader social attitudes and anxieties and, more precisely, what it is we are persuaded of, hardened to, or 'buy ourselves free' from in these moving representations.

These innocuous or poignant filmic images of death also provide far more meaty testimony to life's worth, to, that is, the unerring valuation of individuals' existence that takes place in the medium. This is *not* to privilege existential angst or a philosophical approach, far from it. Rather, it isolates how mainstream cinema works to bestow value upon certain lives, specific sociocultural identities, in a hierarchical and partisan way. So, where the blood fests of the blockbuster might speak to the cheapness of life, these moving images of death divulge also what is held sacred and which lives are sovereign in cinema. It is niceties, then, that populate this study. Whether as the nobility of dutiful sacrifice (Chapters 1 and 3), the beauty of dying (Chapters 2 and 4) or the 'progressiveness' of post-racism (Chapter 5), mainstream cinema's redemptive fantasies of death preach a corrective that masks what I will reveal as far more cynical, and sinister, mortal economies. By mortal economies I mean that film's structuring logic or systems of exchange or encounter are underwritten by life's worth, and by its, albeit imaginary, 'capacity to dictate who may live and who must die'.[16] Mainstream cinema is, in other words, an intrumentalisation of the politics of death or, after Achille Mbembe, 'necropolitics'.[17] The aim of *Death and the Moving Image*, then, is to unveil these mortal economies and thus the necropolitical frame to the outrageous fortune conjured by Hollywood and some of its best friends.

Film's primary corrective, or drive towards resolution or cure, belongs, to a great extent, to narrative itself. Mainstream narratives often end in death. This has as much to do with the *Bildungsroman* traditions of the feature film, the life journeys it has classically captured, as with the symbolic potential and flexibility of death.[18] Death resolves the problems or themes of the text, in its punitive, profound or just finalising effect, but its functionality is not limited to films' close. It plays a structural part throughout the narrative, whether or not it even occurs, or occurs only at the end. It provides, in other words, 'a mechanism rather than a subject of representation'.[19] At the same time, the shape and vibrancy of its part will be genre specific. Cinematic death has a particular relationship to narrative and genre, then, and though it remains subordinate to other issues in this book, its functionality animates the discussion throughout.

In pursuing the paradox of the 'paucity of experience and surplus of representation' of death in current times in the West, John Tercier turns his focus on CPR (cardiopulmonary resuscitation) to its depiction in television's medical dramas.[20] Pervasive, theatrical and uncommonly successful, television's CPR skews statistical and other facts. But, for Tercier, it is obscene in that '[t]he traumatic realism of the resuscitative scene is meant to arouse us . . . it demands an emotional response not to the life that was lived, but to the spectacle of death'.[21] Contemporising Gorer, Tercier expresses well the gratuitous pleasures of sensational immediacy here, of the 'frenzied' visuals of high-budget drama.[22] He also, unwittingly, points to its ethical import.

Making invisible or sequestering the dead and dying raises one set of ethical issues about the dismissal or 'abjectification' of vulnerability and the body in decline. But a sense of popular culture, channelling our capacity to be moved away from the human who is suffering and towards the dramatic effects of watching, raises yet another. Ethics will be a major theme in this study of death, as it has been for others, but my contrasting commitment to mass culture welds the concern for human relationality and its violent frame for encountering difference to popular entertainment and to the everyday fantasies of the majority.[23] This is not to erect impenetrable barriers between mass and marginal artefacts or media, between high or low culture, or between real and fabricated suffering – quite the opposite. As I have previously argued of ethical spectatorship, a continuum operates between these.[24] Real and imagined depictions of suffering, which can look alike and fill the same screens, command similar reactions and, therefore, connected theorisation. Part of the ethical landscape is a reckoning with precisely this, with the frame of entertainment for the news, say, or necropolitics for cinema. Similarly, a continuum of ethical reflection operates between the more rarefied or lowbrow images or texts. Where mass culture lends itself to moralism, 'ethical reflection', which is prioritised here, contests rather than cohabits with a state-sponsored prescription of right and wrong. *Death and the Moving Image* divulges the morality to mortality in cinema but it does so to point to something more dynamic, inherent, and even hopeful, in the relationship between film culture and human vulnerability.

Returning to Tercier's comment, and the parameters of this study, it is not just the grandeur of dramatic effect that lures us away from ethical reflection but the magnetism of affectivity itself. Interest has heightened in the spectators' emotions, via film studies' affective turn, or in their trauma, via the 'cottage industry' of its theorisation, since the 1990s.[25] It is superseded here, however, by the question of how spectators' reactions to these moving images extend film's mortal economies. The valuation of some lives over others in mainstream cinema, so central to this study, takes place on-screen and off, in the text and in its context. It is, in other words, embedded in the film's visual, visceral and narrative content but also in privileging the responses and conscience of the assumed audience. The Western spectator of mainstream cinema is woven into its necropolitics which affect and trauma theory don't adequately cover.[26] After all, as Vaheed Ramazani asserts, 'the notion of trauma has become a privileged cliché of American, if not Western, culture in the new millennium'.[27] On-screen suffering remains a fundamental coordinate to the moving image of death and dying but sustains complexity, politics and scepticism in this study. This is because, on the one hand, 'the logic of vulnerability is a vast web of interconnecting vulnerabilites': suffering always operates within, and compensates for, other systems of privation or stricture.[28] On the other, the image is *moving* in that it here always depends upon the production of sentiment for its power; it always forces or reinforces channels of feeling and of 'valuation' regardless of one's abilities to resist. So, while the moving image cannot but nod to film's status as time-based media, and to Barthian concepts of photographic immortality, my use of it in the title of this book, and throughout, prioritises this different emphasis.[29]

When Tercier writes that '[i]n the twentieth century death abandoned real life for representation', his pithy remark rings true in the context of his study but directs us to a central concern of mine: the way in which 'real life' so frequently stands for Western experience. It is, after all, only for some that death has abandoned real life.[30] This book, in other words, contests the universality, and apolitics, of cultural interpretations of death and dying. Indeed, it infers they are unethical. 'Identity' influences, if not determines, how and where we expire or, as David Field, Jenny Hockey and Neil Small put it: 'Worldly inequalities are in no way levelled at the time of death but persist, permeating every aspect of death and dying.'[31] Identity is even, as Cornell West clarifies, a 'matter of life and death'.[32] More than this, geography, race, class, gender, age and so on determine our proximity to death and are crucial to what Walter Benjamin called our status as 'dry dwellers of eternity': whether we revel in the fantasies on the screen as our only, or primary, contact with mortal constraints or remain mired in the problems of malnutrition, disease, civil war or occupation.[33] Context is everything. Though this book is fixed on mainstream Western culture and a 'majority' audience, it tries to keep the privileges and contingencies of this site and focus uppermost and seeks to resist the common if not ceaseless return to their concerns only, in other words, to their solipsistic thrall.

Ariès's work has proven to be a launch pad for much recent thinking on death and culture. Certainly his tendency 'to assume that the dead are white, wealthy and male' and his defining of culture via 'educated and wealthy elites' have been instrumental here.[34] Meanwhile, the polarities inherent in his conclusions – the healthy past versus the unhealthy present, for example – proved resonant, if contentious, as did the favouring of loss over desire as the governing trope of culture's treatment of mortality.[35] Jonathan Dollimore, in particular, speaks extensively to the misdirection of theorists of death who look only to loss and denial, rather than to the erotic binding of desire and death.[36] Elsewhere, I've privileged the erotic and ethical economies of spectatorship, and masochism's primacy within it.[37] Here, however, need and even perversity are oriented away from the self and towards a landscape or geopolitics of inequity and the deathly dealings of alterity that popular culture illuminates. The individual is crucial to this landscape but must not remain exceptional within it. That 'I' in this book's subtitle, then, points to the importance of identity, subjectivity and sovereignty to the meaningfulness of film and to the (Althusserian) triangulation at its heart: of the sociopolitical, the aesthetic and the personal/psychological.[38] Most importantly, that 'I' foregrounds the pattern and practice of privilege, the vortex of exclusivity and the tension with the 'other' upon which it depends.

The major revision to Ariès's argument is, of course, that death in contemporary Western society has not retreated into the private realm completely or convincingly at all. Rather, as Chris Townsend for one points out, culture is suffused with 'engagements with death – literary *and* visual, musical as well as philosophical'.[39] Scholarship has not been immune. There has been a steady but marked growth in interest in death and related topics, with an explosion in the twenty-first century, all at a time when death's 'recognition has become more publicly controlled and defined'.[40] The question of film's, or even film theory's, place in such control and definition will haunt this book. Within film studies, death-*related* topics dominated at first and leant towards the broader themes gaining traction in the arts in the 1990s. Queer readings of AIDS and mourning, millennial analyses of mass culture and apocalyptic mythology, and the continuing, and related, postmodern debate on the death of film itself supplemented the escalating interest at the time in cultural history, memory, but especially trauma whose 'star [was] rising within the academic firmament'.[41]

Marita Sturken, Suzannah Radstone and later Paul Grainge argue that cultural forms become important sites for the reflection *and* generation of individual and national loss and memory.[42] The enduring and hyper-mediation of atrocity or disaster underlies the burgeoning critical interest in cultural trauma that Wheeler Winston Dixon, Kirby Farell, Vera Dika and Mikita Brottman, among others, have written about in various ways in relation to film.[43] Characterised by repetitiveness, redundancy, pessimism and, at times, prurience, these cultural productions, and their viewers, seemed to suggest Western culture's *growing* hold on practices of death, and cinema's distinction as a principal forum for fulfilling this. Certainly, the films that stage catastrophe, whether real or imagined, perform, or provide a public platform for, a cultural practice of death and mourning and, in so doing, they load death with historical and national meaning that cinema is perfectly positioned to impart. According to these theorists, they also work in different ways to displace fear, to offer catharsis, distraction or redemption.

Led by the multifarious place of death in film, rather than the broader and emergent themes it animates, this study nevertheless pivots on its conservative functionality which these earlier works inform in explicit and implicit ways. Informed by the multidisciplinary trajectories of academic debate on the topic, first and foremost, *Death and the Moving Image* provides a survey of the representation of death and dying in mainstream cinema from its earliest to its latest renditions. In pursuing this range, it traverses narratives and genres fuelled by the prospect or promise of death, films filled with 'actual' death, and also grief-stricken tales of loss, fewer in number but more searing in effect. Its 'before, during, after' span takes into account this manifold presence – its expression or function as, say, structural charge, necessary spectacle or immobilising sorrow – and reflects this pseudochronology and figurative scope. That said, the three parts are neither discrete nor equally balanced: the brevity of the last is indicative of my turn away from trauma. But it is the benefits and price of death's abiding conservatism in culture, of that 'buying oneself free', and its historical and technological contexts, that will be pursued most relentlessly here: the politics and aesthetics, ideology and iconography, of death in cinema perpetually troubled by 'my' part in it.

How, then, do the various roles that death performs in the moving image – as something flirted with, embodied or responded to – determine the structural, aesthetic and political exchange between cinema and death? How do such variables as gender, sexuality or race, nation or narration or film-making practice have impact upon the representation of death and its sociocultural import? How does the fact that death 'moves' – in being filmic but especially in being emotive – render the study of the cinematic representation of death distinctly coercive or collective or ethically entangled?

Part I, flirting with death, considers the precedence of self-endangerment, of the individual risking his or her life, in mainstream cinema. The first chapter addresses the action genre, the second suicide films, and the third looks at sacrifice in post-9/11 Hollywood. Moving from the timeless to the timely, from the recuperative to the absolutory, the section progresses from the structural role of flirting with death in film, its 'recovery momentum', in Chapter 1, to its detailed historical and geopolitical contextualisation in Chapter 3. In Chapter 2, film's limited but highly symbolic representation of suicide, of the individual's witting or self-willed self-killing, affords the distinction of cinema's mortal economies. These, the death-dealing visual and narrative logic of film itself, depend upon the interplay of identity and power, of, more immediately, gender, nation and race. This complex interplay, animated through the discussion of an Oscar-nominated Palestinian film, will remain in tension throughout the study and its identification of mainstream cinema as necropolitical.

Part II addresses dying in cinema. Elaine Scarry's seminal work on the unshareability and inexpressibility of pain provides the framework for exposing and exploring the rich cinematic language for bodily decline. It is a language of metaphor and of idiom; of the longhand of narrative and the shorthand of genre, but it is pre-structured in mainstream cinema by a grammar that seems irredeemably ideological. Chapter 4 maps out this language via the terminal illness film, its rigidity and its room for manoeuvre beyond Hollywood. The political underpinnings, and especially the racial unconscious of this language, preceding and determining it, are pursued in Chapter 5. Emerging steadily throughout, the ethical dimensions of the moving image of death are most fully explored in Chapter 6. The unshareability but connectivity of watching others die on, and through, film proposes a more radical cinematic language of human vulnerability. The last part contains a single concluding chapter. Drawing together the various discussions of the book, I locate, finally, this more radical relationship to human vulnerability within a Hollywood feature film about the Mexican–US borderland. In so doing, the book ends with the possibility of a more hopeful future for mainstream cinema's dealings with death.

Mainstream cinema is epitomised by Hollywood, by, that is, 'white Hollywood' where, as Mantha Diawara clarifies, 'Blacks exist primarily for White spectators whose comfort and understanding the films must seek'.[44] Hollywood provides most of the case studies here, and African American history a recurring setting for questions of race. This recurrence is inevitable given the pre-eminence of North American cultural history for any study of mainstream film and the primacy of black–white race relations within that history. But the relativity of social value, or the mortal economy of representation, as it gets played out to such vivid or veiled extremes in cinema, is always more than the seeming binary of this black–white relation.

As Michele Wallace reminds us, 'black stereotypes have become only the most visible symptom of the problem – the easiest thing to pick on'.[45] Yet it is the broader dynamic of colonialism and subalternism that yields the intellectual frame to the study, that introduces its necropolitical approach to film in Chapter 2 and seals its wishful thinking in Chapter 7. I hope to keep that broader dynamic in play throughout. Though the place of gender within all this is, as always, of vital consideration, its significance is constrained. White Hollywood is invariably male, or at least masculinist, just as the non-white-authored films discussed below are directed, and populated, by men as well, but the double layer of women of colour's erasure should not go unsaid. This erasure, this invisibility at the level of content and production, is an unavoidable feature of the terrain this study covers. The wishful thinking with which this book leaves off, that more hopeful future of Hollywood's dealings with death, should be tempered accordingly.

The North American emphasis is augmented by a comparative, as well as longitudinal and latitudinal, approach throughout. Non-Western, non-fiction and early examples expand the scope of this study, pointing to related concerns within film studies at the same time as complicating and, I hope, deepening our understanding of mainstream cinema and its (racialised and sexualised) normative consciousness. There is disproportionate attention to contemporary examples, but forceful reasons for this. Most obviously, there are simply more films of historical atrocity, terminal illness, bloody violence and so on, in this period due to well-known industrial and technological shifts. There was also that surge of scholarship on the topic. But there have been significant social and demographic changes that have had an impact on representation as well. Firstly, as Mary Bradbury acknowledges, 'people live longer and take more time to die'.[46] More narratives, or genres, about aging and dying would arise naturally, therefore. At the same time, the 1980s' AIDS crisis resulted in a proliferation of texts about bodily vulnerability and dying in the West, as writers and other artists set their experiences to page, canvas or screen, enhancing this 'era of autopathography'.[47] The premillennial context occasioned another cause for the surge in apocalyptic narratives and, for Nancy Berns, 'closure emerged so prominently' in this period too, but the 1990s also witnessed a major increase in the representation of cancer.[48] According to Robert Clark this occurred because the 'leading edge of the "baby boom" generation . . . reached 44 years of age in 1990'.[49] Such films, he continues, 'were now relevant to this generation', but were also reflective of how 'health care costs became a significant economic and political issue in the late 1980s'.

Death and the Moving Image is then very much of its time: of the cultural, critical and historical location from which I write; of the urgencies surrounding the world's economic crises, continuing and emerging conflicts, depleting resources and aging populations, and of the global expansion of film/digital cultures notwithstanding their enduring inequities.[50] For Alessia Ricciardi, death's proliferation within contemporary culture is down to the predominance of technologies, not least of the screen, providing new forums for death's 'basic, if problematic, ubiquity as a signifier' as well as 'new modes and constellations' for mourning and, we might add, for that 'frenzy of the visible'.[51] While new screen technologies and the expansion of film cultures widen the field for death's sombre or more extravagant return, such forums, as Margaret Gibson reminds us, inevitably widen the 'gap between "real death" and its imagined or simulated forms'.[52] Death, which is repressed or inaccessible in real life, returns in culture in various forms, genres and guises but still we must, as Sandra Gilbert puts it, 'reconcile death denial with death display'.[53] Such reconciliation underpins this book too, even as I seek to expand the context, to impose the politics, and to refuse the solipsism of death's discrepancies. More than this, the specificities of the technology or media that manage this return, and their mass, niche or otherwise imagined audience, remain key to understanding film's repetition of entrenched patterns of dealing with, taming, or even curing death in mass entertainment, or even its potential to break free. Indeed, this study traces another course, its own recuperative path perhaps, in pursuing this sense of the potentiality of film, even of mainstream film, to do death differently.

For Leo Bersani the reassurances and redemptiveness that characterise culture can be shattered only by the radicality of art.[54] *Death and the Moving Image*, however, seeks out some kind of shattering of the salvific impulses of Western culture from within its most popular forums. Film or, better still, film culture is taken here as a principal conduit of mainstream Western culture, of its import and, in fact, its exportation. Dedicated to the popular, to the political implications of mass culture's themes and imperatives, this book's abiding aim is to take the mainstream to task for its mortal economies but also ultimately to disinter the capacity for film, and film criticism, to engage with life and fragility more productively. Judith Butler, articulating a hope for a global community in the midst of the divisive inhumanity to others' suffering, post-9/11, and the United States' 'war on terror', prioritises the representation of vulnerability:

One would need to hear the face as it speaks in something other than language to know the precariousness of life that is at stake. But what media will let us know and feel that frailty, know and feel at the limits of representation as it is currently culti-vated and maintained?[55]

It is to the power of the moving image to let us know and feel that frailty, to coerce but also to commune with human vulnerability, that I now turn.

Part I

Before – Flirting with Death

CHAPTER 1

Self-endangerment and the Subject of Film

Legend has it that, when the first moving images were shown to the public in Paris in 1895, the Lumière brothers' *Train Pulling into a Station* had the small audience running for their lives. Though this is a telling tale of the remarkable potential of the new technology – especially its capacity to harness perspective and illusion in the service of the sensational – more interesting, for our purposes, is how, almost immediately, 'cinema going' meant a brush with danger.[1] Of course, it is rarely the case that cinema is truly dangerous, that it actually involves risk or causes death, though its strong ties to propagandist and to subversive expression evidence its power and have restricted its use across historical and national contexts. But this primal scene of cinema history and of the media's imperilling potential usefully delineates the main interests of the first section of this book. I want to argue that the moving image still involves, if not depends upon, some kind of encounter with what might be called self-endangerment. On the one hand, this is an argument about film content, on the centrality of risk to narrative and to genre, and to the set pieces, spectacles and character arcs that constitute them. On the other hand, it is an argument about the experience of watching film, specifically how it involves some kind of surrender or abandon, albeit a thrilling and temporary one.

Cinema is about self-endangerment, then, in terms of both content and spectatorship. Part I's task is to illustrate this claim. It will show how self-endangerment is both rife and central to narrative pleasure but also, crucially, how 'safe', ultimately or unconsciously, it is made to be. The representation of self-endangerment, not least in its murky distinction from suicide, will be shown to be only temporary, and in Hollywood, at least, conservative: its perilous promise cushioned by irreality or failed realisation. Its protagonists, and the spectators who share in it, are 'saved' in the end. The danger was all part of the fun: the journey's thrills and final reassurances. As the title – 'Flirting with death' – suggests, such a dalliance with danger, by characters and by spectators, is a staged and managed affair, and one that lies at the heart of the medium's potential (and prestructured) conservatism: its self-limiting playfulness, its 'first base'-only ethos. A number of trite distinctions emanates from this, not least those pertaining to the differences between, say, mainstream and independent film, and between Western and third cinema: the conservatism of the Hollywood model, for example, versus what is authentic, subversive or free about others. The comparative conservatism of Hollywood will be a recurring question in the book as we position its texts, and those closely related to it, against other contexts, in order properly to gauge the meaning of the mainstream.

In this first chapter I shall argue for the pervasiveness, and productivity, of self-endangerment, and of the narrative's 'prospect of death' in mainstream cinema. But what purpose might such an argument serve? What does reframing cinema in these terms reveal about cinema or, indeed, about its relationship to death? Where, in the introduction, I rehearsed various answers to this question more generally, what is disclosed here, quite vividly, is the significance of self-endangerment to explaining mainstream film's pleasures and politics. How can the prospect of death be entertaining? How can it structure and determine narrative pleasure, and what, therefore, might this tell us about the sociocultural, aesthetic, or psychic, function of self-endangerment in cinema? In what follows I consider how self-endangerment – as self-risk that references death – is structured into film content in broad terms before moving on to specifics in order to build a more detailed answer to these questions.

There are two sets of films that can be distinguished for their centralisation of self-endangerment, for their perpetual reference to the prospect of death. That is not to say that numerous other groups of films, or genres, don't depend upon such a prospect. They do. Indeed, one of the aims of this book is to show how pervasive death and its cultural accoutrement are in film. Horror, for example, is characterised by the imminence of violent death. The narratives of film noir and melodrama are driven by the fatalism of their protagonists. While all these genres, however, are populated by characters who are reckless, often in their disregard for the warnings of others or their inability to control their passions, their relationship with death is irrational or frequently fantastic and, for now at least, not our concern. Our focus here is, instead, on self-endangerment as logical, as willed, as known: as an expectation both of the protagonists and of the audience.

The first set of films, and the main focus of this opening chapter, represents the 'genre' most replete with death and most shaped by self-endangerment: the action film. With its numerous subgenres, and constant hybridisation, the scepticism of those scare quotes attends its dubious status and definition as genre (indeed, it seems the paradigmatic post-genre genre) though, for ease, I shall continue to use the term. Intimately tied to the development of the blockbuster, and epitomising recent industrial trends, the action film has come to dominate what is thought of as mainstream cinema as well as its exportability. In this way, self-endangerment is an ever-proliferating feature of film content. The second set of films lies at the opposite extreme. It represents the rarest image or theme, that of suicide, of self-endangerment for its own sake and the embrace, rather than proximity, of death, and it will be the focus of Chapter 2. Where the action film comes to define the mainstream project, the suicide film seems antithetical to it. And yet both, as will become clear, have much in common.

Before I turn to the action film, I want to establish a more general principle: the place of peril in narrative per se. To do this, I'll look briefly at two Hollywood films, *Mr Jones* and *Fearless*, both produced in 1993. Despite star protagonists (Richard Gere and Jeff Bridges) and directors of note (Mike Figgis and Peter Weir), *Mr Jones* and *Fearless* as male melodramas, and those dealing with suicidal tendencies and mental illness to boot, were hardly remarkable in their critical or financial impact.[2] They do, however, encapsulate the broader structural function of self-endangerment in mainstream film, and distil some of the key issues for the emerging discussion. Primarily, they reveal how self-endangerment's place within, and punctuation of, the text dovetails with the conservatisms of mainstream narrative (and spectatorship). They also introduce, in what will become a familiar refrain, the ideological and aesthetic coordinates activated through it. These will prove increasingly important as the chapter, and the book, progresses.

Mr Jones and *Fearless* have a striking image in common: they both emphasise a scene in which the male lead stands upon the ledge of a tall building in a mortality-testing, death-defying, and martyr-invoking moment. It is a recurrent image in *Mr Jones*, framing the narrative – it is where the film starts and where it ends – and in *Fearless*, as well as being pivotal to the plot, it provides the advertising picture; it represents the film. While the similarities between these two films run beyond this shared image, so contrary an image of a male lead in a Hollywood narrative, they do not, however, stray far from their association with self-endangerment.

Having been rescued from the ledge of the house he was working on as a carpenter, Mr Jones (Gere) is admitted to a mental hospital, but soon released. When readmitted, he is confirmed as suffering from manic depression. He wins his competency hearing and is discharged rather than involuntarily committed. This displeases his psychiatrist Dr Bowen (played by Lena Olin) to whom an attachment continues to develop until he 'crashes' and agrees to remain in hospital as her patient. Bowen uncovers the roots of his problems partly through investigating his story. Taking this as betrayal, Jones leaves the hospital. The doctor pursues him, they are reconciled and their relationship becomes sexual. Bowen eventually resigns, having had Jones transferred. Jones, again feeling betrayed by her, gets released and returns to his earlier manic ways. Warned of his potential suicide attempt, Bowen follows him to the original ledge. Because of her presence he does not jump. The film ends with them reunited, sitting on the roof.

In *Fearless*, an aeroplane has crashed. Max Klein (Bridges) is one of the few survivors and leads the others to safety. Suffering from post-traumatic syndrome, Max keeps proving his invincibility to himself by acts of self-endangerment. These include eating strawberries to which he had previously been dangerously allergic. Having befriended another traumatised passenger, Carla (played by Rosie Perez), he 'cures' her feelings of guilt for her baby's death by re-enacting the impact of the plane through a car crash. She is restored to herself but Max ends up in intensive care. Recovering, he goes home with his wife (Isabella Rossellini) from whom he had separated earlier. He 'reacts' to a strawberry but returns from the edge of death.

Self-endangerment and Narrative Structure: the Recovery Momentum

In both *Fearless* and *Mr Jones* the climactic final scene involves a self-endangering situation founded upon revisiting the 'primal' one: the opening one of the film. Max mentally revisits the plane crash while he is asphyxiating on a strawberry; Jones returns to the ledge from which he was about to jump at the beginning of the film. Cure, especially in *Fearless*, hinges upon the revisitation or repetition of the original trauma: a highly therapeutic pattern akin to the psychoanalytic process. In this way, the films offer themselves as healing processes and invoke 'madness' as illness but especially as the 'disequilibrating' force in the narrative: adversity temporary and contained.

In Freud's early writings and practice of hypnosis, the talking cure involved the recalling and reliving of the suppressed feelings that originally caused illness, which *'permanently disappeared when we had succeeded in bringing clearly to light the memory of the event by which it was provoked and in arousing its accompanying effect'.*[3] This re-enactment, or 'abreaction', undid or cured the original trauma. The importance of re-enacting to recovery remained central to psychoanalysis as it developed, even as the talking cure was dismissed in its simplicity, in its inability to account for the repetition rather than disappearance of trauma-inspired symptoms. When emotions caused by the original psychic trauma are suppressed, the patient is destined to repeat them, or rather repeat situations that provoke them:

> ... the subject deliberately places himself in distressing situations, thereby repeat-ing an old experience, but he does not recall this prototype; on the contrary, he has the strong impression that the situation is fully determined by the circumstances of the moment.[4]

In this way, the 'compulsion to repeat' allows the patient to dwell within his or her trauma, rather than to expel the traumatic emotions: 'the patient repeats instead of remembering, and repeats under the conditions of resistance'.[5] The repetitive compulsion is undone only through its interpretation (by way of analysis) and working through (by the patient). In this way, as Freud stressed, cure is not as simple or immediate as the moment or act of discharge, or abreaction, implicit to his and Breuer's earlier work.[6]

The narrative in *Fearless* is a variation of this curative process, of the 'remembering and working through' of Freudian therapy.[7] The life-threatening situation of the aeroplane crash is the origin of Max's trauma. He represses the anxieties it produced in him, such as his fear of death or will to live, feeling himself instead to be fearless if not immortal. The film follows his repetitive, 'fearless' self-endangering activities as revisitations of these emotions of resistance. It is only when his self-endangerment, in the final scene, allows him to submit to the original anxieties that he is cured. That the curative process is inscribed within the social and domes-tic space, rather than within the medical realm, makes it more accessible to the viewers (while reifying the normative, the family). Cure operates only through Max's own processes of self-awareness and not directly as the result of therapy. In fact, *Fearless* takes itself out of, or at least diminishes, the medical discussion of mental illness, and the therapist is postured as something of a buffoon.

Rather than the plane crash being forgotten by Max, it is a constant presence in the film: in his dreams, memories and drawings – those areas where the unconscious slips through.[8] The heavy presence in the film of Max's thoughts or, rather, memories – what could be called his 'mindscreen'[9] – both signifies subjectivity and intensifies identification for the spectator who is strongly aligned with the protagonist during these periods of heightened subjective experience. In this way, the curative process is not only available to the audience but also confirmed as the governing experience of the film. The spectator shares in the trauma but also in its discharge. This position for the spectator, and 'purpose' for the film in confronting trauma – expelling, displacing or indulging it – will resurface throughout this book.

The initial life-threatening experience of Jones is not meant to be the origin of his 'illness' but a symptom of it. The narrative of *Mr Jones* can also be seen, however, as an episode in illness and cure, in that this original scene, while not the originating trauma for the character, serves as the original trauma for the viewer which is then revisited at closure. In fact, narrative itself could be seen to follow this path, so that recovery is always precisely about a form of repetition, a repetition of equilibrium. Where cure in *Fearless* involves the resurrection of the past and rejection of self-endangerment, in *Mr Jones* it incorporates balance which necessarily extends beyond the protagonist alone. Jones comes back from the edge and Bowen comes up to meet him, as an answer to his earlier question: 'what would you risk everything for?'

While *Mr Jones* might be seen to offer a less conventional path or representation of mental illness, the mutuality of its ending seems more reflective of the heterosexual momentum of the piece, the union of the man and the woman fundamental to Hollywood narrative, than the machinations of transference that it nevertheless plays out. Where *Mr Jones* subsumes self-endangerment within the romance narrative and the rather lame but popular plea for moderation, *Fearless* closes off self-endangerment with the grand and unrealistic gesture of the final curative moment, so that it seems, ultimately, a point of plot. Where *Mr Jones* has been reduced to the status of 'conventional melodrama',[10] Max's return from death at *Fearless*'s end 'smacks of a loss of nerve'.[11] In both cases, again truer to the conventions of Hollywood narrative cinema than to the treatment of mental illness, the men are saved by the women who love them, and the films trace the passage back to, and recovery of, the lost or self-endangered self. This quest for identity is confirmed by the final scenes in which the women call the men back from the edge of death by shouting their names: they are literally saved by the assertion of their identities, through interpellation.

It isn't just melodramas, or mental illness films, that follow this curative trajectory. Mainstream cinema has a particular narratival relationship to self-affirmation. Broadly put, narrative closure is traditionally marked by the triumph of the protagonist's self over adversity (even though, of course, closure can involve the death of a character, even the protagonist).[12] This trajectory, then, can be recast as a narrative investment in recovery; a formulation that proves especially meaningful for the analysis of filmic representations of illness, and Chapter 4 will take this further. Classical Hollywood cinema is the defining system at the base of mainstream film production, and has become synonymous with its principle characteristic, the traditional narrative: the succession of events in a *'cause–effect relationship'*.[13] Closure is a key feature, the ultimate expression of narrative intent, confirming the meeting of expectations, the answering of questions and the stilling of movement. Narratives of illness often follow traditional paths of bravery and triumph but narrative itself can be seen as a passage to the resolution of problems, to the recovery of harmony as, in fact, quintessentially about cure. So cure, as illustrated in *Mr Jones* and *Fearless*, embodies both the conservatism of the text and the implicated viewer's therapeutic investment, and coheres usefully into what I'd like to call the recovery momentum of narrative.

The will to closure is a formidable force and crucial to mainstream film. It is condensed, most frequently, into the happy ending and its gestures of conventional love: unification, domestication and marriage. As we look further into the recovery momentum of mainstream narrative, as a psychic and social passage to self-reaffirmation, we find strategies not only for maintaining the status quo but, more explicitly, for maintaining and policing normative identity within it. While both *Fearless* and *Mr Jones* suggest this reinforcement (both end with the bonding of the romantic couple), at this juncture it is not the meaning or ideology of narrative that is key but its structuring, the idea of closure as a return following disruption. Both Vladimir Propp and Tzvetan Todorov, the key theorists of narrative, speak to this sense of recovery. Todorov turned Propp's conception of the narrative's struggles between, for example, good and evil (as hero and villain),[14] into the equilibrating path of a narrative: the opening state of social harmony suffers a disruption, usually in the form of a villain's intervention, before order or, as John Fiske puts it, 'another, preferably enhanced or more stable, state of equilibrium' is restored.[15]

The recovery momentum proves a useful analogue for mainstream cinema's (conservative) investment in cure and self-affirmation, or, and as we shall see later especially, cure *as* self-affirmation. *Mr Jones* and *Fearless*, with their male protagonists and their emphasising, even mythologising, of recovery – their depictions are underwritten by messianic themes and images – allow the men to overcome fully their self-endangering condition. They integrate these seemingly oppositional characters into their mainstream projects and, in so doing, negotiate the interplay between an emphasis upon self-endangerment and conventional reassurances.

Though repeating and even reiterating Hollywood's narratival favouring of the male existential experience, *Fearless* and *Mr Jones* are suffused with self-risk and, as such, offer the fascinating incidence, and management, of contrary motivations. As we turn to action cinema, a genre that depends, at least superficially, on duty rather than on trauma to fund its pervasive spectacles of self-risk, we find, nevertheless, a similar play-off. This genre's preoccupation with self-endangerment surpasses the recovery momentum to reveal something ambiguous but resounding about 'flirting with death' itself.

Mavericks and Martyrs: Action Cinema and the Marvellous Anticipation of Death

Action cinema, as its name suggests, prioritises action sequences over the intricacies of storytelling, spectacle over narrative, surface over depth. This is, at any rate, how it has been theorised and how, for some, it encapsulates profit-led, dumbed-down Hollywood. Various writers have sought to recover the genre, or rather the critical value of the genre, from arguments fixated on those simple oppositions, or, rather, they have extricated from these oppositions important arguments on the play-off between, say, high and low culture, mainstream and marginal production, male and female visual pleasures or consumer affinities.[16] Gender has proved to be a recurring priority of such criticism, and industrial and technological trends of increasing interest.[17] These critical issues will infuse our analysis too: reframing action cinema as about self-endangerment tends to support the various arguments advanced about how the genre is meaningful, especially in terms of the maleness, and the commercial and ideological currency, of the subjectivity it expounds. That the genre in which death is most expected is also the one seen as least capable of profundity, nods immediately to the odd place of death within culture.

Action cinema is characterised by the fast-paced, adrenalin-fuelled, depiction of pursuit or competition and, invariably, of combat. The nature of the pursuit and/or combat – whether on horseback, on foot, or as the oft-obligatory car chase – depends on subgenre and social context. What I mean is, the western, the war film, the Japanese samurai film, or the various waves of the Hollywood gangster or disaster movie, all provide different settings for 'action'; all wage different forms of battle with era-specific degrees of graphicness based on national production codes as much as on the special effects available. The amount of blood we see, or the body count, depends not only upon issues of censorship or cultural practice but also upon technology, though, as will become evident, it is not graphic realism that provides death's key indexes here.

What action films share, and what makes them so popular and in such primal terms, is the thrill of showing one individual or group pitted against another individual or group or, as in the sci-fi action movie, against some external threat to his or their existence. This is our modern coliseum. 'Life or death' is invariably what is at stake in this pitting, and what makes it so thrilling. This is as true of Akira Kurosawa's *Seven Samurai/Shichinin no Samurai* (1954), the urtext of action cinema, as it is of Guy Hamilton's *Goldfinger* (1964) or Tony Scott's *Top Gun* (1988) or the Wachowski brothers' *The Matrix* (1999). Action ensues through the need to compete, to win out, to survive. It ensues from the dangers integral to the plots of the films but also to the job specifications of the central characters, and it ensues, most importantly, as self-risk. The warrior, the secret agent, the fighter pilot . . . the messiah, must, by definition, confront death. And death must pervade the films to prove the status of the central characters and, with it, their value(s), valour and, often, patriotism. In this way, tied up in the self-endangerment of the action figures is a host of qualities that perform the films' ideological work but also find self-endangerment, the individual's life-risking, straying ever further from its 'actual' presence in society. You don't have to be David Blaine (or Harry Houdini) or 'Men on Wires' either to realise that spectacular acts of self-risk are rarely witnessed by the masses or to acknowledge their marketability.[18] Such acts, however, further obscure the self-destructive or suicidal behaviours of a not insignificant proportion of the population. Heroin addicts, the morbidly obese or depressives join extreme sports junkies in a catalogue of private hazards. Cinema, then, creates and indulges a fantasy of self-endangerment, and it is this fantasy, while acknowledging the gap between it and the real, that is also coming under scrutiny here.

It is important to emphasise that action cinema, though saturated with the death of others, frequently nameless and faceless others, centres on *self*-endangerment. This distinction is crucial: it places the onus on the self, on the machinations of subjectivity, which is a main focus of mine. It also represents the turning inward of outward aggression, of sadism, which Freud termed secondary masochism.[19] Rather than stress the masochistic economy of cinema, as I have done in previous work, psychoanalytic understandings of this turn or return are less important here than other things.[20] Indeed, in later chapters, Levinasian understandings of it will more fully take their place. For now, though, this emphasis on the self reminds us that film is a self-centred medium, a key exponent of Western individualism and individuation. Though hardly news, given the medium's developmental domination by Hollywood, cultural and national coordinates will become increasingly pertinent. We shall move on to the ideological work of self-endangerment in film later but, for now, let us explore its more formal qualities.

Action cinema is centred on self-endangerment in three main ways. Firstly, the films are underwritten by the prospect of death that emerges immediately and is referred to throughout the text in both vocal and visual terms: as spectacles and within dialogue. This expectation of death is also created extracinematically through pre-sell strategies and the audience expectation accompanying such high-concept genre films. Film content, then, is framed by the likelihood of fatal consequences and punctuated by death-dealing events. Secondly, this expectation coalesces in the numerous 'actual' self-endangering activities of the main protagonist, activities that 'he' invites, confronts but also generates. Crucially, this self-endangerment exceeds the dangerous or death-dealing events and any fatalistic ambience, and takes on greater meaning. So, thirdly, the dangers of the job, the dutiful self-endangerment, is joined by, indeed it affords, self-endangerment of another sort: self-endangerment as non-conformity but also, often, as recklessness. This sort brings with it a host of other, related conditions – self-loathing, trauma, suicidal tendencies and acts – it is, in other words, a version of self-risk that is much closer to its 'real' presence in society. It is this third area that is the most telling for our purposes for it moves beyond the superficial allure of the spectacle of heroism that characterises the genre to reveal the individual's and the collective's fragile ego beneath.

Top Gun epitomises the genre both in its focus on mortal combat and in its instigative role in the growth of action cinema in the late 1980s and 1990s. It was also the 'first VHS title to ship more than one million copies'.[21] But, more than this, it epitomises the genre's three-pronged relationship to self-endangerment, just outlined, through its central character Pete 'Maverick' Mitchell, played by Tom Cruise. The film starts and ends with spectacles of self-endangerment to which Maverick is both incidental and central but, as will be shown, his self-risk exceeds the notions of duty that underwrite them. Maverick is a fighter pilot with a reputation for remarkable skill, for disregarding authority and even for recklessness. The film is structured around various aerial combats and, or mostly as, training exercises in which fighter pilots display their derring-do pursuing the 'enemy' across the sky. These extended sequences powerfully simulate the high-speed, perilous encounters and the urgency, bravery and bravado implicit in the men's actions. With the camera 'in the cockpit', the action unfolds through close-ups on the pilots or as their point-of-view shots as they pursue the alien MiGs, and this thrilling intimacy is intensified by the raspy voices of their headset exchanges as well as by the melodramatic cadences of the rock music soundtrack. In other words, there is a major investment (in cinematic and financial terms) in heightening the spectator's alignment with the self-endangering experience.

The film starts with just such a sequence: the dangerous spectacle that establishes the risks of the job and the high stakes that underpin all subsequent action to underwrite the film with the prospect of death. Maverick and Goose (Anthony Edwards) and Cougar (John Stockwell) and Merlin (Tim Robbins) are in two planes engaged in battle with an unidentified enemy that has crossed into United States airspace. The US planes win the showdown: they become 'locked on', their missiles' target centred on the enemy plane. In the lexicon of aerial combat, to be locked on means 'you're dead'. The enemy retreats as a result. While we see almost no dying or dead bodies in the film, we know that a plane exploding means death, and that being 'locked on' causes it. Becoming 'locked on' is the goal of aerial combat and of the training exercises, and it means that the prospect of death is ever present, and constantly referred to, without 'actual' death ever needing to happen.[22] Indeed, in this opening sequence, the equation is enough for the combat to conclude. This does not conclude the opening scene's exposition of self-endangerment, however. Cougar, thrown by the encounter, has some kind of panic attack while returning to the aircraft carrier and is unable to control his plane fully to land safely. Maverick ahead of him, and dangerously low on fuel, defies the order to land and heads back to talk Cougar down, thereby risking his own and Moose's life.

If what fighter pilots do is dangerous, then Maverick's version of it is even more so. The danger of being a fighter pilot resides not simply in combat itself but in the extra high-risk activity of aerial combat.[23] What is established in this opening sequence, then, is death's proximity but also Maverick's particular flirtation with it. Self-risk is the norm in this environment but Maverick, as his name foretells, takes further risks by breaking the rules. It is not just his exceptional flying skills or contrast to weaker others (such as Cougar) that single him out, or even his arrogance, but his refusal to toe the line. He manages to defy various prohibitions: he is not court-marshalled for disregarding orders but awarded a place at 'Top Gun', the exclusive pilot training school, and he has an affair with a teacher there (Charlie, played by Kelly McGillis) and a teacher who originally rejects his advances. He even manages to evade 'you're dead-ness': despite being locked on to by another plane, Maverick's daring flying defies death and the previous logic of the equation. But there is a disturbing edge to his non-conformity: there is more to his self-endangerment than professional and patriotic obligation, or macho superiority. As Iceman (Val Kilmer) puts it: 'every time you go up in the air, you're unsafe'. Even Moose tells him that he feels scared as a result of Maverick's recklessness. When, shortly afterwards, Moose dies while ejecting from their out-of-control plane, this tragedy and Maverick's unavoidable implication in it, forces Maverick to reappraise his relationship to his reckless self-risk.[24] Within this reappraisal is a resolving of an older issue that, to some extent, is meant to account for his behaviour. His fighter pilot father's mysterious and 'classified' death – which threw into doubt the 'old man's' abilities – haunts Maverick as much as any psychological complexity could play a part in this shallow tale. When visiting his superior officer, Viper (Tom Skerritt), after his and Moose's accident, and being cleared of responsibility for it, Maverick hears the truth about what happened to his father. Viper explains that the secrecy surrounding the event was due to the fact that the combat that killed him took place on the wrong side of an international border and not, therefore, because his father had done something wrong. He then asks Maverick: 'Is that why you fly the way you do? Trying to prove something? Yeah, your old man did it right . . . His F-4 was hit, and he was wounded, but he could've made it back. He stayed in it, saved three planes before he bought it.'

While dutiful self-risk and, finally, self-sacrifice explain the father, other factors contribute to Maverick's wilful, nay suicidal, recklessness. In many ways he is simply, albeit temporarily, 'damaged' – his sense of self caught up in an endless, and necessarily destructive, testing of his own skill, of 'living up' to, but also surpassing, his absent father – and such damaged men frequent the genre. But a key factor to this tale is a masculinist proving of potency: an arrogant self-regard that militates against the necessary selflessness that defines a true hero. This isn't to say that, in coming finally to define true heroism, masculinist principles are dispelled by the film but rather that they are refined. Heroism, according to cinema, requires self-risk but self-risk for one grand purpose only: to save others. Heroism, and male potency here, is compromised, therefore, if self-endangerment is tainted by the ego, by narcissism, or by suicide. Such self-endangerment, such tainting must be temporary: it must be recovered to its ideal form. Following a period of shaken confidence, Maverick gets back in the saddle for a 'real' combat situation. Though he falters briefly, he saves the day: protecting his colleagues and his country. Only then, only through this lesson, can he truly qualify as hero, and be rewarded accordingly. In keeping with the paralleling of his potency as pilot and lover, this reward finds him taking up his rightful position as teacher at Top Gun, and as Charlie's lover once again.[25]

This structural, episodic and refined self-endangerment is absolutely typical of the action genre. If we turn to another seminal action film, *Lethal Weapon* (Richard Donner, 1987), we find the same thing. In its definition of heroism, it promotes, but then eschews, reckless self-endangerment by, or rather as, its end. This time it is Mel Gibson who takes the role of an exceptionally talented but maverick serviceman, the police officer Martin Riggs. This film is much more explicit about the significance of self-risk to its narrative, to the construction and appeal of its hero, and to the thrills of the action genre. Where *Top Gun* put the emphasis on male mastery, *Lethal Weapon* keeps displaying its hero in a state of compromise and stresses the proximity of death. The film is full of death-dealing scenes – it is a 'shoot-em up' after all – but the first death, the film's opening sequence, depends upon the lure and aesthetics of suicide to set the tone.

The film opens with a death which, typically for a mainstream narrative, establishes the themes of the film: drugs, the city, but also self-risk. A young blonde woman awakens mid-coke- and sex-induced reverie, writhing on a bed. She is wearing little: a negligee and knickers. After a little fingertip nibbling, she snorts a bit more coke and, with a smile on her face, takes a look at the view from the balcony of the high-rise apartment, her top blowing open in the wind. Next we see her mounting and then jumping from the railings. Her slow-motion descent is captured as a point-of-view shot and as long and side shots, and concluded with the camera inside the car that her fall crushes. Despite this car-crushing demise, she lands, oddly beatific on the roof. No blood spatter, no twisted limbs, just a beautiful and markedly feminine and sexualised corpse that has more in common with pornography, both soft core and snuff, than with any realistic depiction of a dead body. Just in case we should have missed how gratuitous this opening sequence is, we are told shortly afterwards that the woman was actually murdered, having been poisoned prior to her grand leap: 'If she hadn't have jumped she'd have been dead within 15 minutes'. Ludicrous and trashy though this is, it makes clear something I will keep coming back to in this study: the way that death in cinema is not simply about the slaughtering of enemies but a pervasive aesthetic of self-risk too.

This 'wasted' experience contrasts dramatically with the other suicide scenes in the film. Indeed, we receive at least three in the first thirty-five minutes: 'at least' because our introduction to Riggs's self-risk is somewhat more ambiguous: it sees him striding past colleagues sheltering from bullet fire, to egg on a lone and evidently unskilled gunman to shoot at him. When, unsurprisingly, the gunman misses, Riggs aims, fires, and takes him out. Again non-conformity combines with recklessness and self-endangerment to amplify heroism. As the commanding officer present

Figure 1.1 The temporarily Falling Man.

says: 'You're a psycho son of a bitch but you're good'. Called to the scene
of a suicidal man atop a building, Riggs joins him on the ledge and, rather
than talk the man down, Riggs forces him to jump to the inflatable crash
pad below, and jumps with him.

What is more, any ambiguity attending Riggs's self-risk is thoroughly
cleared up in an unusually graphic and rare depiction of male suicidal
intent. Riggs, slumped on the floor in front of the television and empty
beer cans, a photograph of his dead wife and son on his lap, weeps as he
places his loaded gun, his lethal weapon, into his mouth. He is unable
to fire, however. This inability to fire, here, contrasts sharply with his
utter lack of hesitation, his trigger-happiness, elsewhere and clarifies
the different stakes of the two versions of his self-endangerment: how
the former, the 'psycho son of a bitch' scenario, can constitute heroism
and the latter compromises it. Though these two work in opposition,
and are rendered distinct, they are absolutely entangled. While Riggs is
unable to pull the trigger, his proximity to death underwrites all of his
actions as his new partner recognises immediately. Murtaugh (Danny
Glover) is well aware of Riggs's reputation for a reckless disregard for
his own safety, for being, as well as using, his 'lethal weapon' but clarifies, as *Top Gun* did, too, how such self-risk is antithetical to dutiful self-
endangerment for it imperils the lives of others, not least that of Murtaugh
himself who is 'too old for this shit'. The gun, Murtaugh says, is for
control and incapacitation, not killing, though he'll come to moderate this
view.

In action cinema, a self-risking protagonist is a genre requirement, and a hero with a 'death wish' is the stuff of film legend. While self-endangerment in action cinema has a formulaic, and profoundly conservative, function, and there will be more on its ideological conservatism later, the genre's use of it, and its broader implications for our cultural understanding of death, are not adequately explained either by the curative logic that is closure (the recovery momentum) or by the grandeur of the high-stakes spectacle: in other words, neither by its structural nor its sensational roles. Clearly, enacting and resolving self-endangerment enable numerous opportunities to prove the dimensions of the hero's fearlessness and the film's budget (and Hollywood's investment in the status quo) and self-endangerment's formal and spectacular endowments are obvious. But self-endangerment itself is neither singular nor straightforward. As *Top Gun* and *Lethal Weapon* reveal, there are, at base, two seemingly simple types at play here, one 'bad' one 'good'. While the move from bad to good self-endangerment represents that curative logic or conservatism, the move is hardly linear and the two types are far from discrete.[26]

When dutiful, professional, even non-conformist, self-risk slips into, or becomes, framed by suicidal recklessness, then self-endangerment is tainted. It must be restored to its 'purer' form for conventional closure to be achieved. Curious, but significant, conclusions arise from this. Firstly, action cinema but, more specifically, its definition of the dutiful self-endangerment of heroism, contains, even depends upon, reference to suicide or, at least, to a reckless, unnecessary or gratuitous self-endangerment. Put another way, in the action film, dutiful self-endangerment *always* slips into suicidal or gratuitous recklessness. Heroic self-risk, it would seem, cannot exist without reference to its shadow. Secondly, this gratuitousness often represents a stylisation, an aestheticisation of self-risk. Such stylisation exceeds the required audience appeal of the high-stakes spectacle – the special-effects-enhanced life-'n'-death battle is lure enough already – and, instead, functions to bestow value upon the life that is imperilled, a function that becomes increasingly important in this book. Thus, the construction of dutiful self-endangerment, that is, of heroism, is ambiguous, it is muddy, both in its entanglement with the 'psycho' or non-heroic version and in the inevitable, if dubious, visual pleasures that accompany its aesthetic renderings. In what follows we'll look more closely at these conclusions and thus to the complexity of self-endangerment's relationship to the 'subject' of cinema, by which I mean not just its recurring content, its favoured stories, but its favoured version of self-hood.

Favourite Subjects

The action film – the most exportable, that is globalised, and most popular, that is lucrative, film genre – is replete with risk-taking protagonists but, as I've suggested above, their practices mean more than just a ready audience or return. The depiction of heroic self-risk is tied to its shadow, to its darker side, though the shape and weight of this connection vary. Films filled with dutiful self-endangerment – action films and their associated subgenres and precursors – are, perhaps surprisingly, framed by reference to suicide. I say surprisingly because both logic and faith – as religious or patriotic fervour – dictate that the aggrandising of 'cause' does not sit well with the doubt or despair associated with suicide. But therein lies the rub: religious and secular notions of self-risk have longstanding, though oft-ignored, antinomy. Self-risk and self-sacrifice are deified in Judaeo-Christian tradition, revered in 'legitimated' nationalist practices – that is, those associated with this tradition, rather than Islam say – but prohibited, policed, and criminalised within society. No wonder things get muddy in their cultural expression. Increasingly apparent, of course, is the need to define what suicide means, and this will come, but for now the emphasis on the gratuitousness of these depictions, on an indulgence in charisma- or crisis-oriented self-risk, serves us well in understanding the thrills of the action film and the import of its central characters. To return, then, to the first of those curious conclusions: looking in any direction from *Top Gun* and *Lethal Weapon* reveals a repetition of heroism's odd connection to its underside.

Robert Aldrich's *The Dirty Dozen* (1967) is a war film about twelve convicts who are trained as soldiers and given a high-risk mission behind enemy lines. Should they succeed in the mission, their crimes and sentences will be pardoned. The men are chosen because of their expendability – they all have long or life sentences – and what that credential lends to the task (and, of course, to the genre). The flimsy tie the men have to their own mortality, 'we're all dead anyway' one says, clearly provides the proximity to death required for an action-based narrative. The film opens with a hanging in the military prison, however, and then goes on to emphasise the suicidal tendencies of the men. A close-up on laceless shoes and a comment about how a prisoner's guitar is without strings confirm that the men are 'high suicide risk' and have had removed from their cells anything that could be used by an inmate to take his own life. The tone that is set for the film is not of self-sacrifice in the glory of combat but that of a narrative baptised in the iconography of stage-managed deaths. Heroism will be excavated from some of these men but, though their circumstances amply commend them to the requisite risk-taking, heroism here remains haunted by self-killing.[27]

The Great Escape (John Sturges, 1963), another classic war film, is set in a German prisoner-of-war camp during World War II. It tells of a mass escape by the Allied forces imprisoned there. Early on, their ranking officer, Captain Ramsey (James Donald), has a meeting with the German Kommandant who advises him to ensure that his men, who've a reputation for break-outs, stay put and stay alive. In this film, however, rather than self-risk being the way in which one does one's duty, self-risk *is* one's duty itself. As Ramsey explains to the Kommandant (Hannes Messemer), self-risk is the logical, the only, expression of soldierly obligation. To be a soldier is to keep resisting. The men imprisoned have no choice but to risk their lives trying to escape. Again, the narrative and thematic investment in self-endangerment – in the depiction of heroism, in the seeding of action and suspense – is writ large but, more than this, the contiguity between duty and self-abandon is exposed in its full force. In *The Great Escape* the contiguity is seamless – the two are, in fact, conflated – whereas, elsewhere, there is far more of a tension between them. Indeed, this tension is rife in the action film, and fraught with, while mediating, 'life's worth': profundity indeed.

This same conflation of duty and self-sacrifice occurs at the end of a more recent film, *Black Hawk Down* (Ridley Scott, 2001). In it, Hoot (Eric Bana), having refreshed himself briefly following the most traumatic of battles, heads straight back out to the front line stating to his incredulous but awestruck brother-in-arms: 'that's just what we do'. The nobility and paternalism on display in this extreme (overblown and thus more laughable than laudable) performance of heroism are consonant with the sensibility of *The Great Escape*, not least in conjuring the exceptional qualities of the United States/Allied forces: their selflessness as saintliness. The propagandist function and 'soft power' of the conflation of duty and self-sacrifice are clear. Though this ideological reserve is not simply about the United States, it is its primary domain.

The fundamental attachment of national or humanistic duty to self-risk, common to both *The Great Escape* and *Black Hawk Down*, also morphs into a more spectacularly, rather than sentimentally, gratuitous signature trope of the post-modern, high-gloss action movie. *Lara Croft: Tomb Raider* (Simon West, 2001), for example, opens with a typical scene of the protagonist embroiled in a death-defying encounter with an aggressive foe, here a robot. But Lara (Angelina Jolie) hasn't simply invited or generated this situation, she has actually commissioned it. Having 'killed' the enemy machine, Lara flips open its control panel and we see that she had it programmed to 'Kill Lara Croft'. Physical, and frequently national, superiority is proven through the protagonist's excessive proximity to death: excess which exceeds necessity. Nowhere are the framing and punctuation of the narrative by death-dealing episodes *as gratuitous self-endangerment* more elegantly or excessively rendered than in the James Bond series, from Terence Young's *Dr No* in 1962 to the present day. To be Bond, and therefore *On Her Majesty's Secret Service* (Peter R. Hunt, 1969), are not just to invite, suavely to flirt with, danger but to find oneself amid elaborate set pieces of imminent death. Bond films are studded with such scenes. Most memorable perhaps is *Goldfinger* (1964), in which 007 is strapped to a table, legs splayed, as a laser burns a slow but steady path between his thighs heading up towards his . . . torso. The sexual, even masochistic, implications of this spectacle are clear, but what we have here, again, is the mounting iconography of the action genre in its nascent form.

Unlike the other protagonists mentioned, except perhaps Lara, Bond historically has lacked even shallow psychological causation for his maverick and self-risking behaviours: all is enacted in the line of duty. Both Bond's and Lara's acts represent a constant testing and proving of the characters' extraordinary talents. Their imminent death scenes, their spectacular self-endangerment, are all surface. Visual pleasure is grounded firmly in the thrill of high-stakes action coupled with, or rather intensified by, the physical and erotic allure of these characters. If Maverick and Riggs recklessly self-risk out of grief, desolation or narcissism, Bond's flirtation with death is, or at least was, without (need of) explanation. In later Bonds, especially Daniel Craig's incarnation, this ceases to be the case: his derring-do is tinged with traumatic effect. Indeed, the current call and response of the Bourne and Bond franchises, find Bond, like his American partner, self-loathing, heart-broken and out of control.[28] As this longstanding franchise trains itself again to the contemporary, it is the masculine and masculinist psychology of Hollywood heroism that gives it shape.[29] It is important to note that Lara's enduring lack, despite Jolie's ample presence, finds her emblematic of heroines of old, of the very different story for girls. In her study of the action genre and gender, Yvonne Tasker traced the characteristics of North American films' 'fighting heroines'. She found that they possessed the caricatural sexualisation of comic book fantasies, were played for laughs in their novelty (especially within 1970s 'Blaxploitation') or, particularly in the late entry of the Hollywood action heroine in the mid-1980s, had their self-risk footnoted by maternal duty.[30] Crucially, such women's acts and breaks with male tradition were '*explain[ed] away*', rather than explored psychologically or otherwise, and another 'common device has the heroine explicitly taking over her father's role after his untimely death'.[31] While Lara gets to save the world without reference to maternal instinct, she is still 'doing it for daddy' who disappeared many years earlier but inspires her actions directly and indirectly. Gloriously refreshing though her invincibility is, her mournful duty to his memory and his instruction propels the narrative just as her Barbarellan pose commands the gaze. Self-endangerment in mainstream cinema remains highly gendered.

In all the films discussed above, heroism is being defined through the melding of duty and self-risk, and often in highly stylised terms. Always, however, there is reference to a more intimate, or psychic, flirtation with death which cannot help but complicate patriotic or personal responsibility even as it seeks to clarify it. Before we consider what those stylised qualities shore up, ideologically speaking, let us confront the issue of this complication, and begin to suggest why self-endangerment gets so muddied.

A primary reason for the muddiness is that self-risk for its own sake – that is as charisma- but, especially, crisis-led recklessness for the individual alone rather than for anyone or anything else – is seen as antithetical to society and the social project. (This is not exactly the same as saying that suicide is taboo – which, of course, it is – for suicide is too limiting a term: its distinction will be discussed in the next chapter.) This selfish self-risk is the unthinkable and, of course, the undoable. But it is clearly not the unrepresentable in as much as I have found the action genre to depend upon its spectacular, emotive and narrative renderings. Its pervasive presence is harnessed, however, to offset and ultimately venerate dutiful self-risk and with it other socio-cultural coordinates that are to be venerated too. 'Selfish' self-risk, then, is there to be firmly and familiarly rejected but must be entertained (and entertaining) to render the protagonist fallible but able to recover, human but always also exceptional. Let's not forget, though, that selfish self-risk is also essential to the social project in broader terms: if there was no propensity for individuals to self-risk, even dutifully, out of ego-oriented reasons, then few would ever 'serve'. In this way, the wall between the selflessness and egotism of self-risk is necessarily porous. We shall never know whether a soldier's ultimate sacrifice was the product of depressed resignation (despite the medical diagnosis of post-traumatic stress disorder [PTSD]), if the martyr has 'his' eye too firmly on the rapture of heaven, or if the suicide victim thinks only of the benefit to those left behind. What we do know is that we do not call the warrior altruistic, or associate suicide with heroism, for powerful and powerfully policed social reasons.

At the same time, the call to duty itself is not so simple. In our liti-gious, oil-led or info-saturated times, at least in the West, the purity of 'causes', even for the most military minded, has weakened. The new visibility of war demystifies its content and expands anti-war sentiment. Multiculturalism, meanwhile, messes with both the glory of God and the state, not least because it denies them their monology and their singular-ity. This is, of course, about now, and now is not all we are dealing with. Ridden with class and race issues historically, 'signing up' has always had its bitter pills, inner conflicts, and material advantages. Action film navi-gates these truisms: the everydayness and extraordinariness, appeal and danger, of its focalising men; their rampant individualism must be tamed in the service of both the self and of others.

Clearly, what is at stake in these spectacles of self-endangerment is the vicarious thrill of confronting and surmounting certain death, and the pleasure of both watching suffering and watching it ease. It is a journey of heightened alignment with the self-endangering character to resolution which, as I've suggested, recovers the excesses of self-endangerment for the sake of defining heroism while also restoring the status quo: the *raison d'être* of the Hollywood machine. While I have stressed the universal and structural qualities of the narratives, the self that is endangering has certain specifications and so we come back to mainstream films' favourite subject: the white 'American' male. This cliché and this mantra of mainstream Western identity depend upon the interdependence of its three parts. In this chapter's closing pages I want to return to how self-endangerment in mainstream film bestows, and entrenches, individuals' value along racial, national and gendered lines.

The United States has long celebrated its independent spirits. Both the self-made man of the American dream, and the self-ruled pioneer of the great journey west, are characterised by their non-conformity as well as their bravery. The Hollywood action film, like the western before it, venerates this maverick sensibility. Its rule-breaking loners epitomise Americanness but they also render recklessness sexually alluring. Where in *Top Gun* sexual and professional prowess converge early on as the alpha-male fighter pilot proves his potency both in the cockpit and in his cocky wooing of Charlie, in *Lethal Weapon* things don't come to a head quite so soon or so superficially. Indeed, Gibson's sex-symbol status is purely part of an external economy, for spectators, rather than an internal one, at least in the first film. After the soft-core aesthetic of the opening 'suicide' scene, Riggs is immediately sexually objectified.[32] Crossing his trailer naked, we're introduced to our protagonist through the infamous 'butt shot'. Unlike Maverick, no live romance will footnote Riggs's self-assurance in this film, though the nuclear values of heterosexuality and home underpin the *Lethal Weapon* series nevertheless, as they did the late 1980s action film.[33] Rather than celebrating masochism, say, or any illicit sexuality, the sexiness of the self-endangerer in mainstream cinema exalts the American hero and the conservatism of his recovery. *His* eroticisation gains this emphasis as we move towards Chapter 2 which will show how different things are for women, as does his *recovery* as the non-white, non-American self-endangerer is shown not to gain the same liberty.

The sexualisation of self-endangerment operates more widely than the action genre. In *Mr Jones* the protagonist's exceptionalism conflates his sexual allure and flirtation with danger. The trailer shows Jones withdrawing a large sum of money and directing an attractive bank teller to keep one of the hundred dollar bills because 'you're taking me for lunch'. Impulsive indeed – which is how the trailer describes him – he kisses another woman on the street and runs off as her boyfriend gives chase. He tells a (female) judge he's 'a big personality', and asks his (female) doctor if she wants to make him ordinary. The allure and excitement of Jones, at least in his manic phase, are offset further through contrast to the sane and solid Howard (Delroy Lindo) who deals with his rooftop antics at the film's start and appears his only friend over its course. Here, as in *Lethal Weapon*, a dependable African American sidekick enhances the white protagonist's grandiosity. This is not to overstate the place of race in these films as I've discussed them here – though the racial dynamics of the American dream, or nightmare, are not forgotten, nor is their role in the buddy film[34] – but to suggest its unconscious or grammatical presence nevertheless, something that will become increasingly important as this book continues.

It is important to entertain the idea also that this sexy or scary aspect of self-endangerment is specific to North American characters or Hollywood alone. While this issue exceeds the parameters of this study, a few points are worth raising not least because they'll resonate in later discussions. Maverick, Riggs, Bond, and Croft – and Jones and Max – wear their extraordinariness on their sleeves. What is exceptional about these characters, what makes their reckless acts so admirable or compelling, so 'psycho but good', are externally validated or seek external validation, as with Mr Jones above. Their exceptionalism is, in this sense, egoistic. It is expressed in terms of public acknowledgement in all the films discussed in this chapter, whether as the various competitions in *Top Gun*, the pardons granted in *The Dirty Dozen* or Max's reportage as the 'Good Samaritan' in *Fearless*. This egoistic self-endangerment contrasts with the representation of the hero's dutiful self-risk in other national contexts.[35] In Japanese traditions, for one, the warrior is still extraordinary, and still in terms of self-endangerment, but the defining of honour is more internal.[36]

Seven Samurai, for example, opens with the generic events of the hero confronting a deadly situation, and self-endangering scenarios punctuate the film. Crucially, however, its opening scene involves the hero having to cut off his topknot in disguising himself as a monk. The topknot marks the samurai: it is the outward marker of his identity and to lose it is to be debased.[37] Through self-diminishment, rather than self-assertion, the warrior is established in this film. What become most important are the inward markers of the samurai identity, of self-risk neither for status nor reward. This is not to idealise Japanese traditions of dutiful self-sacrifice or ennoble them unproblematically: not only is *Seven Samurai* about the strict caste system of sixteenth-century Japan but the history of seppuku and the related practice, kamikaze, is fraught with thorny issues of class, gender and nation.[38] Instead, where egoism characterises the Hollywood films, the Samurai are distinguished not just for their ability but also for their modesty about their ability. Where Maverick, as the prime example, is led and misled by his ego, the Japanese warrior must not be.[39]

According to Michael DeAngelis, Riggs, like Maverick, represents the 'classic Reagan-era hero' in his invulnerability, and epitomised the 'outsider/rebel [role] emerging at the forefront in [*sic*] American culture in the transition from the 1970s to the more politically conservative 1980s'.[40] Rather than connecting them only to the 'hard bodies' of the Rambos of post-Vietnam film which, according to Susan Jeffords, recuperated American might after the inglorious defeat, I'd like to suggest that Riggs and Maverick herald a softer 1990s masculinity. In place of muscle-bound invulnerability, the new man of 1990s cinema was flawed, fragile and certainly weedier than his predecessors. Yet, as both *Fearless* and *Mr Jones* demonstrate, he could prevail. In this way, invulnerability becomes attached to psychological triumph, to, in fact, 'soft power' which was coined as a term at just this time.[41]

The battles that are won in the films discussed in this chapter are ideological ones, and the representation of self-endangerment proves an integral part of this. For all its testimony to the grandeur of spectacle and the cheapness of life, the action film foments enduring principles of the valuation of life in nationalist and gendered terms. This mortal economy – this dynamic between one's identity and one's worth – is not limited to the favourite subjects of the action genre alone. Indeed, it will come eventually to apply to mainstream cinema itself. For now, however, we leave behind the 'psycho son of a bitch' and turn to the other set of films in which self-endangerment is structured into film form: the suicide film.

Seemingly adversative to popular entertainment and, with their protagonists *not* stepping back from the ledge, to the recovery momentum of mainstream film, such narratives nevertheless share and progress the deathly stakes of cinema already revealed.

CHAPTER 2

Cinema and Suicide

Death is everywhere in film but suicide is not. As the last chapter showed, the most successful and exportable genre, action cinema, thrives on the self-endangerment of its predominantly male protagonists. While a certain recklessness appends the portraiture of some of Western cinema's best-loved heroes, from *The Great Escape* (John Sturges, 1963) to *Lethal Weapon* (Richard Donner, 1987) to Jason Bourne (2002, 2004, 2007) – confirming non-conformity, celebrating the maverick and with it both masculinity and Americanness – once recklessness serves this purpose, it must be dispensed with, it must come under control. Self-risk for its own sake, or for unclear, ignoble or unknowable reasons, seems antithetical to the mainstream project, antithetical, that is, to the ideology, iconography and 'I' of the stories it trades in.

According to cinema, the most likely way for people to die is through criminal assault. Suicide, which far outstrips murder statistically – responsible for roughly double the number of recorded deaths each year in the United States, and much more in (all other) countries with fewer homicides – is nevertheless rarely represented.[1] There are obvious reasons for this – the financial and psychological benefits of escapist entertainment among them – but it is mainstream cinema's emphasis not just upon happy or uplifting endings but upon the strengthening of certain notions of the self that tends to make it shy away from the more morbid and nihilistic versions of self-endangerment. It is no surprise, then, that where suicide is most often or most fully dealt with is outside, or in reaction to, Hollywood traditions. This is not to say that suicide doesn't appear in Hollywood film, or tokenism in other cinemas, but to recognise that the relationship between cinema and suicide varies both quantitatively and qualitatively according to formal and cultural parameters.

This chapter will argue two general points: that mainstream cinema, while rife with the spectacle and functionality of self-endangerment, cannot entertain suicide, albeit that it might render suicide entertaining, and, that where suicide is dealt with in mainstream film, it is almost always about something else. In broad terms, suicide in Western cinema is an act of varying, and sometimes climactic, importance but is not what the story or plot is ever truly about. By suicide, I mean self-willed self-killing: an individual wittingly electing to take his or her own life and then achieving that end. As the previous chapter suggested, there is a fuzziness to this definition; such 'witting election' is, after all, hard to ascertain or to record. Statistics on suicide are considered unreliable, masking, for example, the tendency to favour other causes of death.[2] At the same time, suicide is inherently mysterious. As Steve Taylor asserts, it often fails and must be thought of as an act of which the outcome is not known.[3] While I am concerned with suicide as a result as well as as an act, or an act implicitly linked to a particular result, namely death, Taylor in his study of suicide chooses instead to emphasise the 'acts of risk-taking'.[4] The fuzziness of risk-taking fuelled my discussion of film's dutiful but damaged men in Chapter 1, and their determination of mainstream film's 'favourite subjects'. In this one, I want to bypass the taboo of suicide and the careful tread that limits even the use of the word, and home in on its specific presence and use in Western cinema. I am emphasising 'Westernness' here for a number of reasons. Film is, I believe, always to be shown to be absolutely bound up with cultural context but this emphasis reflects the particular remit of this book: despite gesturing beyond the Western frame, it is Western and particularly North American film culture that is under scrutiny here but never as a self-contained, sealed or impermeable entity or as totally homogeneous. While using non-Western culture to enhance our understanding of the West might smack of precisely the kind of self-serving or narcissistic practices this book wants to critique, I hope that it will not prove to be purely solipsistic.

The chapter is split into two unequal parts. In its bulk I focus upon a small group of films that are *about* suicide – are preoccupied with and foretell it – rather than those that use it as some kind of plot device or peripheral character detail. These films, and I will analyse two in detail, will be shown to encapsulate what I am calling the mortal economies of cinema. First, however, in a shorter opening section I survey the use of suicide in mainstream film in order to distinguish the various forms and functions it takes and the key tropes of its representation. I start with this survey because the ways in which suicide has been understood thus far within the tomes of suicidology are not immediately or ideally relevant to cinema. Suicidology was born in the analysis of statistics by Émile Durkheim and developed through an alternate emphasis on case studies. Yet cinema never *depends* on fact for its fantasies.[5] Where Durkheim's seminal work 'fails to distinguish between deaths which are undertaken because death is believed to be desirable in itself, and deaths which are achieved in the pursuit of some other end, as in the case of martyrdom', this chapter concerns itself with the manner in which, and the process by which, cinema mines the unfathomable desires and mythic roles of its suicidal figures.[6]

The Forms of Cinematic Suicide

There are, roughly, six forms of suicide in Western cinema: roughly, because these forms are neither discrete, for they overlap, nor fixed, for this is a preliminary rather than conclusive framework and, of course, coverage is, invariably, partial. While these forms represent a range of narrative and thematic investments for suicide, and vary in the centrality or symbolism of the act to the story, what can be discerned is a continuum of meaning. All cinematic suicides lie somewhere along a line from their agents' heroism to their nihilism, all negotiate its ennobling and ignoble implications with various degrees of consciousness or ideological fervour.

The first form of suicide in film – what I'd like to call *professional suicide* – is the most pervasive. Dutiful, often soldierly, it involves sacrificing one's life as a condition of one's profession, as the nature of the job. In war films, the prime example, individuals participate in high-risk operations: they allow, with varying degrees of consciousness, their lives to be taken within the conflict in which they are engaged. Distinct from the casual self-endangerment of the police officer or fighter pilot – in which the potentially fatal outcome of risk-laden service goes unacknowledged or, at the very least, unacknowledged as in some way desirable – here the suicidal act is elected. The individual makes a conscious choice to sacrifice him/herself to save others or, at the very least, for the 'cause'. This is not the same as being 'killed in the line of duty' – a default, euphemistic or metaphorical suicide – or flirting with death like Maverick in *Top Gun* or Riggs in *Lethal Weapon*. It is, instead, the individual exacting a choice to give his or her life in an, albeit extreme, fulfilment of a role. Such acts are rarely acknowledged as suicide at all, except when their logic is being questioned usually with reference to the madness of war. Suicide, thus, remains a purely negative description or ascription. Heroic self-sacrifice, 'giving one's life' in service, is rendered utterly logical. Indeed, often these films are preoccupied with precisely this issue of choice or consent, with reflecting upon the need and logic of the act. Through this they, too, work to polarise heroism and suicide further and lay bare their ideological coordinates.

In *The Dirty Dozen* this polarisation is striking. The pathologisation and criminalisation of suicide and its association with the imprisoned men at the start of the film, contrast sharply with their moments of glory when they give their lives in battle at the end.[7] In *Saving Private Ryan* (Spielberg, 1998), especially in its much-lauded opening scene – with its verisimilitudinous extended sequence of the Normandy landing, as a frenzy of involuntariness – the question of consent seems almost to predominate. The professional suicide of the central characters hinges upon their increasing acceptance of their fate, and its distinction of the value of a good life. In contrast, Clint Eastwood's *Letters from Iwo Jima* (2006) lays bare the national specificity, as well sociocultural factors, of professional suicide through the Japanese military's explicit demand for dutiful self-killing. Hell-bent on heroicising the white American male, Edward Zwick's *Glory* (1989) is preoccupied with aggrandising the choice of professional suicide. Indeed, the 'career death' of Colonel Robert Gould Shaw (Matthew Broderick) in taking charge of the first all-black volunteer company during the Civil War, reaches its apotheosis through his leading their charge into the firing line at the film's close. Their ultimate sacrifice for honour and country, for tragedy most noble, is underwritten by Hollywood's racial politics that will be taken further in the next chapter and centralised within the language of dying in Part II.

Professional suicide, then, most commonly represents the ultimate sacrifice of the war film, and the soldier who fends off the enemy single-handedly while his comrades escape. It also covers a range of other characters: the minister who propels himself on to a wheel, with no hope of return, to clear a path for others' escape from a sinking ship, as in *The Poseidon Adventure* (Ronald Neame, 1972); the pilot/father who uses his plane itself as the final weapon to stave off disaster, as in *Armageddon* (Michael Bay, 1998) and *Independence Day* (Roland Emmerich, 1996); the scientist, guilt- and loss-ridden, who distracts the alien enemy while the other survivor escapes, as in *I am Legend* (Francis Lawrence, 2007). Suicide, in these contexts, is the final fulfilment of a social role and of a commitment to one's country, family or loved one/s. The stakes are high and there's no surprise, then, that the disaster genre, especially its millennial apocalypticism, depends upon it.

Professional suicide in cinema is fringed with political import. Indeed, this form could be seen to represent the ultimate consent to the state apparatus and to both the repressive and ideological practices Louis Althusser described.[8] I've dwelt longest on this type for precisely this reason, because it is the most closely attached to the power of the state. This, the state's deathly coordinates as exacted through culture, is a primary concern of this book. Born of honour, love and pride, professional suicide is always shot through with notions of duty and citizenship, of national or religious allegiance and obligation. It forgoes rather than indulges self-reflection, and staves off more problematic implications by never being called suicide. This, in turn, sharpens the divide between the actions performed by these American heroes and those of 'non-American' suicide terrorists. The abiding theme, then, of professional suicide is national, social, religious duty and it is, invariably, associated with men.[9]

The second type is related but distinct: *honourable suicide*. It is frequently attached to 'professional' groups, outside the social set-up of service, which operate by an alternate set of codes and, in particular, by an alternative code of honour. Such films often belong to the gangster or mobster genre, where individuals take their own lives rather than betray others, or as the apotheosis of personal integrity. The suicidal act epitomises their (countercultural) duty; it is an extension of their code of honour. Many movies about the Mafia include, if not exploit, this form, from *The Godfather: Part II* (Francis Ford Coppola, 1974) to *Bound* (Wachowski Brothers, 1996). The British film *In Bruges* (Martin McDonagh, 2008) makes climactic use of honourable suicide while also exploiting it for its comic, existential and even intertextual resonance.[10] When Harry (Ralph Fiennes) realises he has accidentally shot a little boy while trying to kill one of his hit men as punishment for accidentally killing a child, he turns the gun on himself saying 'You've got to stick to your principles'. The abiding theme of this type is personal integrity. Again, it is men, largely, who enact it.

The third type is *dishonourable suicide*: a speedy exit taken as a result of dishonour, as an admission of guilt and evasion of punishment or public or professional humiliation. This group involves various men killing themselves when they realise they have been discovered in their 'crimes'. This popular trope of punitive cinema is not about honour so much as about cowardice and admission of wrongdoing, laden with a broader ideology of punishment. Frequently, the men, and it is men who invariably shoot themselves, are already in positions of power. A fine example of this type and character is Sandy Woodrow (Danny Huston) in *The Constant Gardener* (Meirelles, 2005) not least because of how his suicide works in contrast to that of the hero of the film, Justin Quayle (Ralph Fiennes). There are numerous other examples. The abiding theme of this type is guilt and fear and, again, its actors are men.

The fourth type is suicide *as avoiding dying*, as a solution or resolution primarily to illness and debilitation. Such films tell of assisted or pre-emptive dying, of euthanasia, that is, or mercy killing, and include: *Ich Klage an/I Accuse* (Wolfgang Liebeneiner, 1941); *It's my Party* (Randal

Kleiser, 1996); *The Event* (Thom Fitzgerald, 2003); *The Life of David Gale* (Alan Parker, 2003); *Son frère* (Patrice Chéreau, 2003); *The Sea Inside* (Alejandro Amenábar, 2004); *The Hours* (Stephen Daldry, 2002) and *Million Dollar Baby* (Clint Eastwood, 2004).[11] Their protagonists choose to die a 'better' death than the one that is fast approaching or to stop prolonging their physical suffering or the emotional pain of others. There is a shift in the identities, especially the gendered identities, of the self-killing figures in these films. Where, in the previous categories, they were almost exclusively male, here they are female (*The Life of David Gale* and *Million Dollar Baby*) or homosexual or associated with a compromised masculinity (all the others). It is as if there is something inherently divergent in terms of manliness about evading pain. Certainly, for Ron Brown, a 'violent "masculine" death [has historically] contrasted to notions of a "feminine" death, which signifies an easy way out'.[12] What is more, Brown's remark that female suicides 'predominantly appear in high art' corresponds to the 'art-house', auteurist or aesthetic bent of this group.[13] These films are not condemnatory of their men but an attachment to gendered normativity attends and complicates their representation of suicide. The true-story-based *The Sea Inside* is extraordinary in trying to eek out the difference between euthanasia and suicide, and fervently to restore virility to its paralysed protagonist. In it the main character, who is petitioning the Spanish government to allow him to die with dignity through euthanasia, becomes embroiled in a discussion with a paraplegic pastor who has opposed his petition on various grounds. The pastor requires that Ramon (Javier Bardem) call his 'elected death' what it is – suicide. In so doing, it would be relegated to the sacrilegious and criminal status that it deserves, according to the pastor. This Ramon relentlessly opposes. Consequently, the film is committed to rendering him far from irreverent or depraved. It inscribes his wisdom, sanity, care for others and his obsession with legality. At the same time, the film expends both a lot of energy and cinematic licence to construct his fantasies of walking as inherently heterosexual: he walks along the beach and into a woman's arms. It is not just morality that is at stake in defining suicide, therefore, but masculinity too. The abiding theme of this type is avoidance of suffering.

The fifth type is suicide *as avoiding living*, as the willed ending of life. The act here is prefigured and predetermined, and examples from this group provide the main interest of this chapter. Examples include: Louis Malle's *Le Feu Follet* (1963); Michael Haneke's *The Seventh Continent* (1989); Mike Figgis's *Leaving Las Vegas* (1995); Sofia Coppola's *The Virgin Suicides* (1999); and Gus Van Sant's *Last Days* (2005). Where all the previous types provided clear justification for the act, this one does not. The reason goes unspoken but the desire for elected death is declared openly and often repeatedly. These films wear their suicidal aesthetics, their voluntary, and sometimes romanticised, flirtation with death on their sleeves: the actual suicides are prefigured in the films which are replete with references to it. There is also a subset to this group of films about mental illness where suicide, though more functional, is avoiding living as the result of depression or other conditions: from *One Flew Over the Cuckoo's Nest* (Milos Forman, 1975) to *Girl Interrupted* (James Mangold, 1999). The latter film sets the suicide attempt of its protagonist, Suzanne (Winona Ryder), against those of her fellow patients, especially Daisy's (Brittney Murphy) successful hanging. Suzanne's recovery is more than cure, it is the parabolic rite of passage of the white American middle-class girl.[14] There is no abiding theme to this type, though alienation describes many of its characters well. Men as well as women commit suicide in these films.

A final category is worth mentioning if only because of its heightened place within the cultural emphasis upon the 'madness', threat, and fear of suicide, and its appeal to mass entertainment and media scandal. The sixth type then is mass, group or cult suicide: in other words, those suicides that do not involve one individual alone but many. This type, it should be noted, can overlap with professional suicide, in that the war film frequently involves the 'elected' deaths of a group, but also with the other forms too. This type includes the true-story-based films and documentaries, some made for television, about the mass suicides at Jonestown in 1978 or Masada in AD 73,[15] and *Downfall* (Oliver Hirschbiegel, 2004) which tells of those who died alongside Hitler in his bunker in 1945. In Jonestown, Guyana in 1978, 909 members of the religious cult, the Peoples Temple, took their own lives rather than be forced to give up their community, as they saw it. In some ways, they acted out of personal integrity though it is generally accepted that they were the victims of their charismatic and pathological leader, Jim Jones. In Masada in the Judaean desert in Israel, a community of 960 Jews were believed to have killed themselves to avoid dying at the hands of their attackers during a Roman siege. This type also includes the euthanasia programmes appearing in sci-fi narratives such as *Soylent Green* (Richard Fleischer, 1973) and *Children of Men* (Alfonso Cuarón, 2006). It has also been used in recent Japanese films such as *The Manual* (Osamu Fukutani, 2003).[16] Though its sensationalism might be obvious, it is worth noting the belief, as articulated in *Taste of Cherry* (Abbas Kiarostami, 1997), that there is more than the individual's soul at stake in one man's suicide. The collective stake in the taboo of suicide might qualify the opprobrium it receives.

The seismic proportions of suicide's affront to society when it is not *for* society, on society's terms, mean that cinema keeps suicide at bay, relegated and reduced to these six types of cinematic suicide, to their very specific social, moral and narrative uses. These are frequently infused with conservative sentimentality and determined by ideological factors. The barriers between the different forms of suicide are often fiercely defended in film as elsewhere, despite, or rather because of, their supposed impermeability. The discussion of action cinema in Chapter 1 suggested how much more entwined professional suicide and suicide as avoiding living might be than the expectations of the genre would allow. Other films explore the supposed or imposed impermeability explicitly. Hany Abu-Assad's *Paradise Now* (2005), which I discuss at length below, and other films depicting suicide terrorism, such as *The War Within* (Joseph Castelo, US, 2005) and *Theeviravaathi: The Terrorist* (Santosh Sivan, India, 1998), confound all six types with their traumatised but dutiful, persecuted but religious, brothers-in-arms.[17] The Durkheimian emphasis on the individual's alienation *or* altruism, as motives for suicide, seems especially inadequate then to capture the breadth, interrelatedness and complexity of motivations that cinema can suggest for suicide.[18] More in sync with mine, then, are the broader, and more film-friendly categories provided by Jean Baechler of escapist, aggressive, oblative (religious or sacrificial), and ludic suicides.[19] The latter's emphasis on play, on the place of quests or tests and the egoic, resonates for the action film in particular. The most rarely represented in cinema, and least covered by my types, is 'aggressive' suicide: suicide that aims to punish, or appeal to, someone else. It is, of course, 'suicide as avoiding living' but part of the release it offers the individual is revenge upon, or a lesson for, someone else. Michael Haneke's film *Caché* (2005) includes this kind of suicide, as Majid (Maurice Bénichou) kills himself on camera and has that film sent to his childhood oppressor. This act, however, is part of a much longer lesson being exacted upon George (Daniel Auteuil) and, supposedly, upon the wider French community for its colonial past.[20] This sense of suicide functioning as part of a dynamic and as a lesson is especially relevant for cinema, based as it is on an engagement with others and commonly judged for the messages or values it imparts. It is, or must, of course, be, of particular relevance to this book, attentive and attuned as it seeks to be to the aesthetic, political and ethical import of watching death. It is, then, with our eye to the bigger picture of suicide's impact – and the 'lessons' in its representation – that we move on from this survey.

Cinema *about* Suicide

Let us now turn to the films, few though they are, that take suicide as their central and abiding concern. My aim here is to demonstrate that while films *about* suicide tell us little of the emotional and psychic realities that give rise to, and result from, the act itself, they tell us a lot about cinema and, ironically, what makes it tick. Suicide's taboo or totemic status in Western society – the extraordinarily potent and often over-valued prohibition against it – is retained by mainstream film, translating into suicide's anathematic, symbolic or even metonymic roles. These roles or functions, and their ideological and geopolitical import, are my primary focus in what follows. The unreachable or unspeakable of cinematic suicide, however, that such translations or displacements represent – how it gestures towards the impossible distances between us, and the incommunicability of personal despair – haunt this discussion nevertheless.

The small group of films *about* suicide includes examples from European and what is often (though dubiously) termed World cinema and from the ever-blurring fringes of North American production. It is composed of the following: Louis Malle's *Le Feu Follet* (1963); Hal Ashby's *Harold and Maude* (1971); Michael Haneke's *The Seventh Continent* (1989); Mike Figgis's *Leaving Las Vegas* (1995); Abbas Kiarostami's *Taste of Cherry/Ta'm e guilass* (France/Iran, 1997); Sofia Coppola's *The Virgin Suicides* (United States, 1999); and Hany Abu-Assad's *Paradise Now/al-Jannah al-ān/* (Occupied Palestinian Territories/France/Germany/Netherlands/Israel, 2005). The historical and geographic spread of this clutch of films is less contrived than it might appear: these are simply the 'major' films – within the 'international' marketplace, that is – a fact that testifies both to the rarity of the representation of suicide and to its inherent resistance to definition and to genre-fication and the finance- or zeitgeist-fuelled trends propelling it.[21] These films are about suicide in the sense that their narrative and cinematic preoccupations with this otherwise illusive topic are striking as is their lack of interest in rendering the causation of their principal acts transparent or discrete. Nevertheless, they are also very much about the directors, the national cinemas and sociocultural context from which they arise.

Seventh Continent and *Taste of Cherry*, for example, resound with auteurism – the evocative stylistic and thematic preoccupations of their directors – and even 'autourism': the propensity for such films to travel well. Kiarostami, especially, is often thought to have perfected his films' exportability. On the one hand, this has been crucial to his success vis-à-vis Iran's pronounced censorship practices; on the other, it is emblematic of his emphasis on universal concerns or, as some have it, his Westernised aesthetic intent.[22] Kiarostami has commented of all his films that '[t]heir roots are intertwined . . . The underlying concept is life against death,'[23] and more specifically that it is the 'preciousness of life' that binds *Taste* to the two works preceding it.[24] Certainly, the focus on suicide in *Taste* is consistent with Kiarostami's fascination with alienated individuals elsewhere. What is more, the film has much in common with Kiarostami's other work in terms of his recurrent use of the car,[25] and with recent Iranian films more broadly in their repeated '"quest" through a realist location'.[26] Suicide, in *Taste*, seems subsumed within the wider aesthetic and metacinematic preoccupations of Kiarostami's *oeuvre*. Even the film's aesthetic and thematic stress on alienation, through a visual decentring of the protagonist and an emphasis on the unsaid, becomes a powerful comment on the auteur rather than on suicide. According to Chris Lippard, the director's repeated play upon what is 'hidden' operates in his films and his public persona both: Kiarostami 'keeps not only his story veiled from his audience – partially hidden behind a concern for (the cinematic) form – but also, in a sense, himself'.[27] The film is primarily, then, an extension of the director's signature.

In the end, *Taste* doesn't actually give us suicide achieved: one of the conditions for membership of the small group of films distinguished here. The fate of the protagonist, Mr Badii (Homayoun Ershadi), is left unknown and a more poetic and self-reflexive conclusion is privileged instead. The film cuts from a head shot of Badii in his self-dug grave to a grainy image of crew and cast in a pre/post-shoot scene, and thus '[his] suicide is both evoked and evaded through cinematic means'.[28] The film is fascinating for confounding expectations – and it opens in a similarly ambiguous way[29] – and for associating cinematic suicide with a number of stylistic, self-conscious and antisentimental tropes which will resurface in the case studies below. For all that, it is too much an auteur film, too much about Kiarostami rather than about suicide, to form my primary focus here.

The same is true of *Seventh*. It concludes with the graphic depiction of self-killing. As in *Taste*, the intensity, claustrophobia even, of the tight focus on the suicidal characters, a mother, father and child in this case, yield nothing of their emotional back stories. The result is blank and, in the case of *Seventh*, bleak too. We do not know until about an hour into the film that the parents have decided 'to leave' – revealed when the husband remarks that he must cancel the newspaper. Though *Seventh* does not meet this particular criterion for the films about suicide, deathliness pervades the film from the first. It inhabits the banal, repetitive gestures and journeys of the three, the sterility of their intimacy and flatness of family life. For Peter Brunette, '[t]he static, artificial, perfectly balanced framing, along with the family's expressionless faces, conveys an impression of death-in-life'.[30] Alienation, Haneke admits, is his primary concern but mass culture, which it emerges from, is far from benign and is his abiding 'antagonist'.[31] *Seventh* sits squarely within Haneke's ongoing obsession with the emotional bankruptcy of post-capitalism and its principal tool, television culture, which 'anesthetize[s] violence'.[32] At the same time, such 'themes of modernity, commodification, emptiness – present in the work of many counter-cinematic film-makers – are prominent throughout the film', and in this way, *Seventh* is again more about Haneke – and, for Catherine Wheatley, about modernist or countercinema, or, for Libby Saxton, about ethics – than it is about suicide.[33]

Seventh shows what no other film does, however: the sheer physical difficulty and discomfort of suicide. Ben (Nicolas Cage) in *Leaving Las Vegas* may wince and splutter on route to his long last gasp but all others render suicide painless or invisible and, again, not abject, which is especially problematic for such politicised fare as *Paradise Now*.[34] The vivid enactment of swallowing pills by the mother in *Seventh* has been seen as 'an extraordinary and upsetting acting tour-de-force [*sic*]',[35] and is typical of Haneke's assaultive fare, but such a rarity underscores the mythic role of suicide in cinema in general, and this dimension will be of increasing concern below.

There are intriguing things about all the films mentioned, too many to pursue fully here. The nihilistic preoccupation with post-capitalist ephemera and decadence is found in *The Devil, Probably* and *Seventh*; one man's sense of his own impotence or futility leads determinedly to suicide in *Le Feu Follet* and *Leaving Las Vegas*. *Harold and Maude*, while framed by suicide, is actually about the sweetness of life, the taste of cherries, and *Taste of Cherry* doesn't actually depict a suicide. I have settled upon *Virgin Suicides* and *Paradise Now* for reasons that will become obvious. Though conspicuously dissimilar beyond their narration of the elected deaths of their main protagonists, the two films are obsessed with suicide *and* very much in dialogue with Western culture and, especially, with Hollywood. Both fulfil all the conditions for membership of the group that I distinguished above, and do so in an uncomplicated way. While *The Virgin Suicides* and *Paradise Now*, like *Taste* and *Seventh*, carry additional circuits of meaning – are, to a meaningful extent, about 'Sofia Coppola' or 'Palestinian Cinema' as well – these do not overwhelm their treatment of suicide or, more importantly, its critical significance. Instead, the two speak loudly to, they even come to epitomise, the prin-

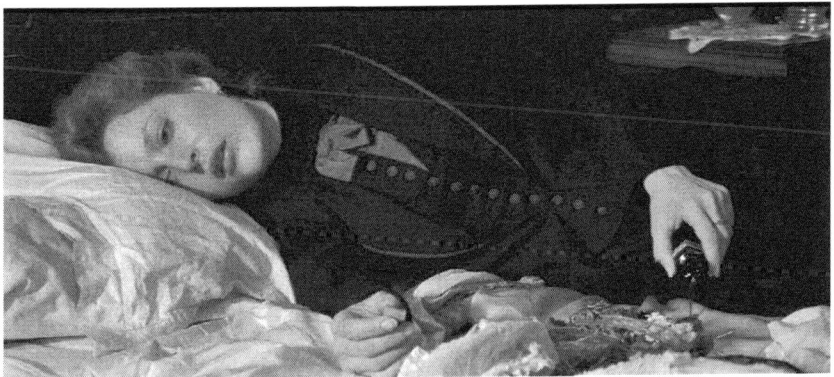

Figure 2.1 Lily Bart (Gillian Anderson) expires in *The House of Mirth*.

cipal dynamics between cinema and suicide, and their ideological and geopolitical coordinates. In pursuing these dynamics, it is my aim to broaden our understanding of the cultural expression of suicide and, in so doing, to reveal the myths that it depends upon, if not trades in: myths that cannot be removed from the prism of gender or geography or race.

The Vanishing Point I: Femininity, Suicide, Cinematicism

At the end of Terence Davies's *The House of Mirth* (2000), Gillian Anderson's Lily Bart takes several fraught but grateful sips from a sleeping draught. Reclining upon a bed, the potion, bloody and potent, drips from her increasingly slack grip, pooling upon the white sheet below; a vignette of abjection and decadence. In contrast, the frozenness of woman's beauty – at, in, or rather as death – and rarely more tellingly or tangibly captured.

This scene, this literal vanishing point of a life extinguished, revives various closings of seminal literary texts, beyond Wharton's herself that is, in which defiant and doomed heroines fulfil the tragic inevitability of their stories by taking their own lives – Anna Karenina, Edna Pontellier, but especially Emma Bovary whose self-poisoning is reconjured here but whose slow and ugly experience of it contrasts so strikingly with Lily's.[36] Such is the lot for a certain brand of 'awakened' woman in the annals of modernist fiction; such is the romance with death haunting the Western imagination in its depiction of self-sacrificial femininity. But while this image echoes within a literary history of fatal constraints, and an art history of sexualised death, especially martyrdom, it is to cinema's aestheticisation of suicide that I turn, and the role of gender, ideology, but also inevitability, within it.

In the following discussion we will draw out the connections between the representational logic of visual pleasure, that is, of post-Mulveyian understandings of cinema's unconscious, and the persistence of a cultural 'necromanticisation' of femininity. By necromanticisation I mean not only how woman is figured as beguilingly and prophetically ethereal (and this ethereality, as conjured by Hollywood, will recur throughout the book) but, more simply, and neo-logistically, how she embodies a romance with death. In this way, I'm putting the romance into necromancy and taming necrophilia's hard core. Our focus here, then, is on the enduring – and recycling – erotic economy of the to-be-dead woman as beloved spectacle, muse and, or rather as, inevitable projection of male desire and despair. The vanishing point, then, of our title, combines the literal – the frame of woman's disappearance – with the more figurative: the representational and perspectival logic that renders that disappearance hard to avoid.

Sofia Coppola's debut feature *The Virgin Suicides* (1999) presents itself as the ideal case study here not only because it announces its preoccupations with the subject matter from the word go and is so thoroughly borne of Hollywood, literally as well as stylistically, but because its cinematic and necromantic self-consciousness pervades the film. In many ways *The Virgin Suicides* takes the cultural legacy of the feminisation of 'literary' suicide, with which I opened this discussion, and laughs at it or, more precisely, winks at it, for there is far more irony than humour in this dizzyingly knowing tale.

During the film's title sequence, Lux, luminescent, Lolita-esque, superimposed on a wispy sky, winks at the spectator. This sequence follows the film's Lynch-like opening: summer hues of suburban America interrupted sharply by inharmonious death. Away from day's warm glow, Cecilia (Hannah Hall), the youngest Lisbon sister, has slit her wrists. Her young limp body is carried from bloodied bathwater to the ambulance but there is no 'blue velvet' here: no cops nor crimes, none of the high drama of social or sexual perversity. Neither is this the grotesque, or what is cordoned off or lies hidden or lurks, building, behind, as in Lynch's imaginary and its stress on the unconscious. Instead: the accumulating cliché of the all-too-sun-dappled suburb – of basketball and barbecue, lush gardens and dog walking – runs, albeit jarringly, alongside and commingling with something more sinister. Instead: Cecilia's childlike beauty, stilled in its watery frame, her eyes open, vacant, her long hair pluming around her head in a scene strongly reminiscent of John Everett Millais's

Figure 2.2 Knowing Lux (Kirsten Dunst).

1852 painting *Ophelia*. Hoisted up by the ambulance men, a (bogus) tarot card of the Virgin Mary falls from Cecilia's hand and the iconicity of self-sacrifice, in all its female and sacred glory, is reiterated. That the card has '555 Mary' upon it melds this iconicity of visual culture to the contrivance of cinema: 555 is the fictional phone number prefix used in North American film and television. Coppola's close-up on this calling-card-cum-suicide note-cum-direct-dial-to-mom ensures we take none of this as gospel.[37]

Where Cecilia is Ophelia, Lux is Lucrece. These are far from perfect fits but Coppola is emphatic about the semantic echo. Lucrece or Lucretia, another Shakespearean heroine subject to various incarnations, committed suicide after being raped. The moral codes at play in *The Virgin Suicides* are contrasted to this parable of female honour. Despite her 'ardent fidelity' to Eugenides's original novel, they part company in key ways.[38] He stages the opening suicide thus: Cecilia '[slit] her wrists like a Stoic while taking a bath . . . afloat in her pink pool, with the yellow eyes of someone possessed and her small body giving off the odor of a mature woman'.[39] Though no less rich in intertextual detail (horror movies; Ancient Rome) or female mystique, this extract, like the entire novel, is broadly referential and even multisensorial, where Coppola tightens her focus on the necro-mantic legacy: here through these classical icons of female self-killing.

Cecilia survives this first attempt and instead fulfils an alternate trope of female suicide: defenestration. She jumps from her bedroom window and is impaled on the railing beneath. Defenestration, like 'watery deaths', has a particular visual history: it, too, was repeatedly represented in Victorian times as the period more openly confronted, albeit with lurid interest, the fact of suicide.[40] On the one hand, these Victorian images 'confirmed statistical knowledge', on the other, they *embalmed their symbolism and with it the feminisation of suicide*.[41] As Ron Brown argues, '[t]hat so many of these images are of women indicates the visual representation of suicide is less about self-killing than it is about Woman'.[42] Now, Coppola isn't simply reckoning with the fact of suicide here. Though the film points to its practice and prevalence, it does so tongue-in-cheek. The television news report, for example, might stress how Cecilia's death 'has increased the awareness of a national crisis' but the caricatural excess of the reporter is followed by a ludicrous vignette: the sobering tale of a suicidal teenager's poisonous pudding which accidentally killed her sweet-toothed grandmother instead of herself. Neither is the film concerned with the devastating impact of suicide upon family and friends. This goes, and therefore remains, unsaid. Instead, the focus of the tragedies' trauma falls upon a small group of neighbourhood boys who provide the film's principal narration, as the non-specific, unidentified voice-over, the 'multiple male narrator' who opens and leads us through the film's retrospective tale.[43] For these boys the Lisbon sisters are so overdetermined – so unattainable, so unknowable, yet worshipped – that they remain eternally haunted, trapped even, by the girls' symbolism; by their own necromantic obsession. This overdetermination is all: Coppola's close-up on necromanticism doesn't just repeat or nod to the symbolism of female suicide but shows up how, precisely, this symbolism gets embalmed, gets preserved through time, through the solipsism and perversity of the male imaginary. Crucially, this male imaginary is a necromantic imaginary, and it is what underpins visual culture: it is, I'd suggest, the patriarchal unconscious of narrative cinema that Mulvey speaks of.

The film unearths this necromantic male imaginary in three connected ways. Firstly, through emphasising the symbolic legacy: the film, as already suggested, is steeped in the iconography of feminised death. Secondly, through a cinematic knowingness that transposes this legacy to film: the erotic allure of the to-be-dead girl is framed, if not suffused, by a meta-filmic consciousness if not confidence. Thirdly, through mindfully centring the male existential experience: the girls function as muse, spectre and siren for the boys, and little else.

Despite the defenestration, we see neither Cecilia, nor any of her sisters 'plunging through the air from a height',[44] yet the film does allude to the symbolism of 'soaring', of freedom and agency, that came to be associated with the Victorian version of this act and its protofeminist expressions.[45] At the end of the title sequence, the apparitional Lux is in the sky – an angel, a vision, a ghost – but how did she get there? The sequence started with an image of her standing in the middle of the road, sucking a lolly looking around and off-screen, and ended with her winking from those celestial heights. Prior to this, and following Cecilia's admission to hospital, the film cuts to the middle of the road again, only this time the camera is looking up at the houses as it tracks along the centre of the street. The slight low angle of the slow-paced movement then changes: seemingly released from the tracks, the camera speeds and rises, taking off as it were. Craning to the leaves of the trees, we soar upwards. The shot of the sky is superimposed on this shot of the leaves, the latter dissolves and the sky dominates. Up there, Lux rematerialises. '[S]oaring is – for a moment – an act of autonomy or self-assertion.'[46] Female freedom and agency are illusive and allusive here but, crucially, not elusive: it can be made tangible. Fantasy is heaped upon fantasy, yet with direction. The girls are trapped by what precedes and determines them, not simply by the constraints of their current situation. Coppola, of course, is not. The sisters' family life may be suffocating, but 'notice for removal' has already been given. Lux is not Lucrece: she responds to her despoiling with promiscuity not martyrdom.

Coppola's film depicts the whole gamut of suicidal acts, at least those that are especially 'feminine': hanging, gassing, poisoning and, of course, wrist slitting and defenestration.[47] While the use of guns has come to dominate the league tables of suicidal methods of choice in the last three decades, it is, most commonly, a male practice.[48] Eugenides's narrator does mention 'gunshots coming from the ghetto' in his less mythic renderings of the teenagers' lives, and even that men 'top' themselves – they are 'found twisted in the shower, still wearing their work clothes' – but there are no shootings, or ghettos or racial issues in Coppola's more exclusive revisioning.[49] The film's final scene is a veritable checklist of checking out though, and this is important, without the money shot. We are shown neither a death bed, nor on-screen expiration, nor even a full-length corpse. Only partial visions of the virgin suicides, limbs alone, are given: Bonnie's dangling lower half behind Buzz in the Lisbon basement; Mary's stockinged legs that the boys jump over in the kitchen. Lux, the American dreamer, the prom queen, dies in the family car: the police open the garage door to reveal just her arm dangling from the open window in the exhaust-filled room. Each girl is shown purely in the context of the boys and men. These are neither our, nor their, intimate spectacles. There is no Lily Bart here; no decadent spectacle of death for our contemplation, erotic or otherwise. Various critics found this suicide fest excessive.[50] But that is, to my mind, to miss the point. The overkill isn't here. The excessive triangulation of 'femininity, death and textuality' long predates this film: it is its precondition as much as its preoccupation; indeed, its precondition is its preoccupation.[51]

When Elisabeth Bronfen describes Western culture in terms of this triangulation, she is speaking primarily of art and very much of literature. I am suggesting that through Coppola's film we can, and should, render this configuration cinematic. I don't just mean that the content links the three, which it does, or that her film is metacinematic, which it is, but, instead, that Coppola firmly locates it in the necromantic conditions of visual pleasure itself. Film is revealed here as the medium par excellence for embalming the to-be-dead woman for erotic contemplation, and an erotic contemplation that chimes precisely with how Western cinema, and feminist film theory, have interpreted her. (This is not of course to say that Western Cinema doesn't present women differently, or unnecromantically, or that feminist film theory hasn't disputed the dominance of this male imagery. It is to privilege, however, the resonance of these traditions for the understanding of this film in particular and of the relationship of cinema and suicide more broadly.) Indeed, in our introduction to the to-be-dead girls, we receive an almost clichéd enactment of Mulvey's formulations of the female spectacle. Bringing to mind Lisa's (Grace Kelly's) self-exposition in *Rear Window* – where 'she moves from one lamp in the room to another, giving part of her name as each is switched on . . . so that her identity rests upon our ability to see her'[52] – the quintessential love objects in *The Virgin Suicides* are similarly stilled and named and, crucially, via the universal male gaze of the boys looking on. Getting out of the car, having returned from the hospital, the image freezes on each sister in turn as the voice-over says who it is. The lepidopterist quality of this scene translates the novel's evidence-mounting, as the men 'piece it all together', into pure female spectacle.

Where the film starts with *Lolita*, it ends with *Vertigo*. Debra Shostak has summoned Faulkner as Eugenides's literary forebear, but Coppola's inheritance is so Hitchcockian.[53] The sick green haze which pervades the film's final set piece might be an apt accompaniment to the asphyxiation-themed prom party the boys attend – a making-good of the algae-altered air in the neighbourhood – but its connection to the girls' suicides, the boys' longing and their reconjuring of their love objects twenty-five years on, cannot help but recall Madeleine's reincarnation and Scottie's unabashed desire for the dead woman in *Vertigo*. Changing into Madeleine's (Kim Novak) grey suit, to complete her restyling by

Scottie (James Stewart) into the guise of his lost love, Judy steps out of the hotel bathroom bathed in the green neon light of his necrophilic fervour.

Though it depends on it aesthetically and narratively, Coppola's film is not about suicide at all but about Western culture's necromantic obsession with women and cinema as its ideal expression. The girls are harbingers more than heroines: symbolic, referential from the start. When Lux and her wink fade fully into the blue sky at the end of the title sequence, the male voice-over launches the movie proper, bridging into, and returning us to, the street where the sisters live:

> 'Everyone dates the demise of our neighbourhood to the suicides of the Lisbon girls. People saw their clairvoyance in the wiped-out elms, the harsh sunlight and the continuing decline of our auto-industry. Even then as teenagers we tried to put the pieces together. We still can't . . . After all these years, we can't get [them] out of our minds.'

The Lisbon sisters, prophetic, figurative, dead, with Lux, their metonymic star, are, as A.O. Scott puts it, 'sacramental, sacrificial figures, more like creatures of fantasy or legend than American teenagers'.[54] While, for Bert Cardullo, the tale is odorously superficial, the one dimensionality of the girls is purposeful.[55] The girls remain abstract spectres, purely referential, and in this way, the film is not about suicide but rather about how suicide within culture always betrays something else. They remain myths, objects of erotic contemplation and epistemophilic obsession.[56]

Cardullo finds Lux's 'dishwashing detergent' name emblematic of the film's banality but, for me, it is its 'cleansing' properties that reverberate (though its commercial traits should not be forgotten). In the final rinse, what must be noted is just how 'white' this film, these suicides, and these critical frameworks are. Coppola's 'ardent fidelity' to the novel did not stretch to keeping Eugenides's, albeit peripheral, reference to racial unrest in the film. Though there is, undoubtedly, a knowingness to her omission and to this final rinse, the richness and reverberations of the film's dialogue with the male imaginary cannot help but leave silent, all too familiarly, questions of race. At the same time, why does Victoriana provide the natural frame for the film's iconography of suicide? Why is there this aesthetic tradition or deathly history rather than something more local, more distinctly American? While this discussion has provided a productive evaluation of the role of suicide in Hollywood cinema, in the final part of this chapter, such effervescent Eurocentrism, and its place in film culture, will be taken to task.

The Vanishing Point II: Blind Spots and the Dead-already

In the previous discussion it was the representational logic of sexual difference that rendered woman as 'vanishing point', as required illusion sustaining the erotic economy that underpins visual pleasure: Hollywood's modus operandi. This particular representational logic or perspective does not fit all, however, and, more importantly still, it doesn't fit all for critical reasons. For one thing, it is a Western and decidedly white model: the erotic or, at least, aesthetic economy of suicide is part of a Eurocentric imaginary which is immediately undone as one looks beyond the mainstream or to the suicide or death of racial or ethnic others even within Hollywood.[57] For another thing, and perhaps of yet greater import, as we move away from this geographic context and its solipsistic thrall, different economies and logistics fuel and determine films' aesthetic and ideological perspectives on suicide.

In what follows I consider self-killing within an Islamic frame. Hany Abu-Assad's *Paradise Now* (2005), which I will focus on here, is a Palestinian film about a suicide terrorist mission. Its title refers to the fundamentalist belief in gaining heaven or nirvana upon sacrificing one's life for Allah, a belief that has gained in prominence since the second intifada and '9/11'. It contrasts sharply with Kiarostami's necessarily apolitical *Taste of Cherry* (1997) which placed its central character's quest to end his life within the Islamic prohibition against suicide. Its title refers not to the joys of death but, instead, to the simple pleasures of life. These two films could not be more different in their ideological aspirations: while they share a religious theme, it is marginalised in both with varying degrees of, and stakes in, self-consciousness. At the same time, their iconographic and metacinematic similarities speak to a Middle Eastern aesthetic as well as how this is tempered by, and a product of, the demands of the global marketplace.

Let's begin with *Paradise Now*'s vanishing point. Set in Nablus in the West Bank, Said (Kais Nashif) and Khaled (Ali Suliman), friends since childhood, work in a garage fixing cars. The day we meet them they find out that, having volunteered to become martyrs some years earlier, they have been chosen for a mission together, as requested, and must leave their homes the very next morning. Various obstacles will delay the mission's fruition but, at the film's conclusion, Said is seated on a Tel Aviv bus, explosives strapped to his torso, about to fulfil his destiny. Initially peripheral and partly obscured, he comes increasingly to dominate the frame. Through what is a recurrent technique in the film, the camera moves slowly towards him; it then comes to settle on an extreme close-up

Figure 2.3 The first shot of Said on the bus.

Figure 2.4 The camera tracks towards Said.

of his impenetrable gaze. Preceded by a montage of head shots of the other main characters, this longer take ends with the explosion: represented by the film cutting to white.

This vanishing point is remarkably literal. Not only is it the moment when Said dies but this is depicted on-screen by a cut to white. He dies, departs, but also the image disappears. More than this, however, the view of him seated on the bus offers a graphic depiction of the perspective- and depth-of-field-generating scene that originated the vanishing point: where parallel lines appear to move towards each other, to converge and disappear on the horizon. Here, the straight-on camera shot, down the middle of the inside of the bus, shows its two lines of parallel bars moving closer together into the distance. A 'real' vanishing point is not visible, however – the bars do not go on that long – though the structure gestures towards it: no confluence, nor the necessary illusion of it, are achievable. Depth of perspective is foreshortened, thwarted, curtailed, much like the Palestinians' restricted movements and the reach of their land: the unattainablility of a vanishing point, of the horizon, resonates further still.[58] Back to the literal and the bus: at the meeting of the two rows, in the centre of the frame, is the Israeli soldier. Rather than the illusion of harmony, or the harmony of illusion, integral to classical art (and Western neo-liberalism), *Paradise Now*'s visual field is structured, or originated, by the occupying force, by occupation. Said is decentred accordingly.

Paradise Now and, specifically, the frame of Said's disappearance are determined then not by the representational logic of visual pleasure (nor by the cultural 'necromanticisation' of Western femininity beneath it) but, instead, by an *imperialist economy*. In other words, *Paradise Now*'s representational regime, here as its perspectival structure, is governed by the logic and legacy of occupation which locate the Israeli soldier at its hub. The to-be-dead figure is, here, the dead-already Palestinian, not as a condition of Western fiction and its erotic economies but as a condition of life in the occupied territories, and its political realities. Such realities are, according to Achille Mbembe, necropolitical: they are grounded in the terror and exercise of death through which sovereign power is enforced. Indeed, for him, Palestine's colonial occupation represents 'the most accomplished form of necropower'.[59] Necropower creates what Mbembe calls 'the living dead', but which I find more productive to call 'the dead-already'.

Paradise Now's imperialist economy pertains to the Palestinian experience but also to cinema more broadly. In this way, the dead-already figure is to be revealed as a condition both of cinema and of colonialism, and the correspondences between them. By this I am referring to the medium's imperial legacy: how technology and early film, both as anthropological ventures and Hollywood narrative, developed as 'Europe constructed its self-image on the backs of its equally constructed Other – the "savage", the "cannibal"' so that, historically and persistently, as Robert Stam and Louise Spence concluded in 1983, '[t]he spectator is unwittingly sutured into a colonialist perspective'.[60] Thus, this legacy – how the Eurocentric imaginary assumed and reinforced the centrality of the white subject – gives rise to what E. Ann Kaplan would later summarise as the ongoing 'imperial gaze'.[61] In addition to this, the inherent or prestructured imperialism of the apparatus, the economic, narrative and aesthetic influence of Hollywood upon film-makers and film industries and, of course, audiences around the world has meant that cinema or world cinema is caught, forever, in relation to the urtext of Hollywood. The difficulties that national cinemas have faced in competing with Hollywood's market dominance, and in having their own stories chronicled, could be likened to a 'vanishing present', along Spivakian lines.[62] In *Paradise Now* there is just as much the sense of time's and capitalism's relentless movement, with its emphasis on the banality of everyday life, as of native histories under erasure. And it is these two realms that Spivak speaks of in her *Critique of Postcolonial Reason: Towards a History of the Vanishing Present*. When Ian Boucom expands upon Spivak's word choice, our vanishing points echo on, he writes:

> the vanishing present in the subtitle of Spivak's text might thus be understood less as a flickering present constantly disappearing before our eyes than as a long present . . . that has repeatedly attempted to constitute or solidify itself by what it abjects or causes *to* vanish.[63]

Paradise Now's imperialist frame translates the to-be-dead character – the narrative or dramatic hook of the suicide film – into the dead-already, the captive, stifled figure of the colonial long present.[64] While *Paradise Now* is determined by this frame, it is very much in dialogue with it too. Its representational regime is, thus, the product of, it brings together but also resists, both film's imperialist legacy which it works with and, inevitably, within, and the Palestinians' colonised present. The translation of the to-be-dead figure into the dead-already represents a negotiation, and a necessary one at that, of the margins and the mainstream, of political intent and universal appeal, of documenting injustice while captivating the widest audience, but most succinctly, of imperialism's past and present which have particular resonance for national cinemas as well as for the Palestinian plight. It is a negotiation that the doubly exiled Abu-Assad – as diaspora-dwelling Palestinian and as Palestinian per se, that is, as inherently dislodged – is well placed to make.[65]

Such a negotiation, and the representational regime or logic determining it, are, of course, what underpin exilic or postcolonial cinema more broadly.[66] Speaking of the 'accented cinema' of diasporic film-makers, Hamid Naficy defines it thus:

> Although it does not conform to the classic Hollywood style, the national cinema style of any particular country, the style of any specific film movement or any film author, the accented style is influenced by them all, and it signifies upon them and criticizes them. By its . . . subversion of the conventions of storytelling and spectator positioning, its critical juxtaposition of different worlds, languages, and cultures, and its aesthetics of imperfection and smallness, it critiques the dominant cinema. It is also highly political because politics infuses it from inception to reception.[67]

This definition serves *Paradise Now* very well as I hope to demonstrate below. As well as brushing against 'conformity' or convention on various levels, stylistic and otherwise, the film is infused with politics textually and extratextually – politics is in the before and after but also in the during of the film. *Paradise Now* makes the imperial frame explicit, immediate and 'live', and reveals the high stakes involved in it. The film lays bare not only the logic and legacy of Israeli occupation but also, in its subversion of film convention and its aesthetics of the broken and the banal, its persistence. Such a negotiation also underpins political or 'third' cinema, especially as Mike Wayne described it in terms of its dialectical relationship to dominant (First) cinema and art (Second) cinema.[68]

Let us turn, then, to *Paradise Now*'s representational regime and how the logic and legacy of occupation determine, or rather predetermine, the look of the film and, more specifically, construct Said and Khaled as dead-already rather than suicidal. 'Dead-already-ness' is a pervasive theme: not just denoted by these characters but, as I suggest, attached to the state of occupation itself. Indeed, it operates on various levels from the literal to the figurative: as the iconography of the broken say or the apparatus of decentring.

First and foremost, there is an equation of the occupation with death or, at the very least, with contesting life. Various characters remark on how difficult living is in terms of an absence of freedom of movement – we're told of closed checkpoints, we see numerous roadblocks – and of life's basics, such as clean water. 'Life here', Said says, 'is like life imprisonment.' Khaled stresses the direct equation of the occupation with death. He responds to Said's doubts about their mission with: 'Under the occupation we're already dead.' Later, Suha (Lubna Azabal), the film's notional 'love interest', who is against suicide bombing, expresses profound opposition to the men's plan, saying how there are other ways to live and to resist, to which Khaled replies: 'In this life we're dead anyway'. The equation of the occupation with death, of Palestinian life with death, pervades the film and is always gesturing beyond it. Palestinians, as Ibrahim Kira puts it, 'perceive that the denial of their statehood reflects their annihilation as a group'.[69] The film also makes clear the link between life in the territories and broken-ness. Primarily, this takes place through the constant reference to broken cars: from the garage where the film starts and the two men work, to the faulty doors and windows of the numerous cars that follow. For Nadia Yaqub this reflects the breakdown in 'the social and economic fabric of Palestinian society'.[70] The first scenes at the garage consolidate immediately the link between cars and the land or life itself. A customer complains that his bumper is not fixed for it is not level, and Khalid and Said set about proving that it is. Finally, in a perfect portrait of inequity as inbuilt, as always already, they discover that it is not the bumper that is uneven but the ground itself.

The prevalence of cars and driving in the film points, inevitably, to the genre of the road movie. For Kay Dickinson this

insinuation of a Palestinian participation in the traditional preoccupations of the [genre] – rebellion and freedom – not only democratizes these aspirations, [but] exposes how Western ideals (as embodied in the car and road mythologies) are often founded, as we have seen, on extreme exploitation.[71]

It also intensifies the impotence and futility of the Palestinian quest for liberty. It is not irony that drives its dialogue with genre, however, for, like the film's car chases that nod to action cinema, *Paradise Now* exploits such genres' universal appeal and mass audience. Some criticised *Paradise Now* for collapsing into such conventional tropes, yet, as well as being emblematic of the exilic/dialectical experience of negotiation, the film remains in an active, outspoken, and self-conscious dialogue with Hollywood, with Israel, and with the West.

The occupation is also equated with suicide bombing itself, as its involuntary response. Said's impassioned final speech in the film, in which he attempts to restore the terrorist group's faith in him, to fulfil his mission, makes very clear how suicide bombing is the only available response to Israeli violence. 'If they take on the role of oppressor and victim . . . then I have no other choice but to also be a victim . . . and a murderer as well.' For Said it is the only and inevitable and appropriate way to resist. But the direct link between occupation and suicide bombing is borne out by statistics and their analyses which measure such terrorist activities against political events. As Robert A. Pape and James K. Feldman have argued in their study of the practice: '*military occupation is the main factor driving suicide terrorism*' so that, in the end, '[o]ccupation causes suicide terrorism'.[72] In this way, Said's statements give shape to the statistics but this is no crass cause-and-effect tale. The film refuses to give only one side of the story, just as it refuses to give a singular or clear reason for Said's desire to die: the occupation is at the root of all problems, suicide terrorism isn't simply endorsed. Instead, *Paradise Now* problematises it and, specifically, Said's subjectivity, much like Spivak's problematising of Sati and the subaltern woman's overdetermination.[73] Said's plight is realised through suicide but not at the expense of his cultural and psychic specificity.

The equation of the occupation with death is most powerfully manifested through Said's lifelessness, his characterisation as a broken man. Relentlessly morose, he is unwilling, if not unable, to smile despite, for example, the coaxing of a photographer taking his picture or Suha's flirtation. His rejection of romance is established early while the impossibility of it is conveyed throughout. At the start of the film, Said dismisses Khaled's talk of Suha, getting up to leave as his friend starts to tease him. The would-be couple's one patently romantic scene occurs only in the context of no future: with Said's body strapped with explosives. The two are seated in her parked car talking in what could otherwise appear as a conventional scene of romance.

When they finally kiss, the pink-tinged sky beyond their silhouetted figures invokes the iconic sunset of the love narrative. But this is the end of days far more than it is romantic convention. Indeed, the scene is self-conscious in its relationship with such film tropes or rather with their entertainment value. Having told Suha his father was a collaborator, she encourages him to speak about it. Said says 'Why talk? To get your pity? To entertain people whose life is a bit better?' It is only then that they kiss, only after a rejection of the sentimental, and the sensational, and of genre (reads Hollywood's) expectations. That the kiss simultaneously fulfils such expectations – is both their rejection and embrace – is emblematic again of the film's dialectical relationship with conformity and mass (reads Western/ised) audiences, as well as with its own self-conscious self-defeat.

What is more, Said's comment on 'entertaining people' joins various other metacinematic scenes. As with the mention of the collaborator and martyr videos, available for purchase or rental by the photographer, and the making of the latter by Khaled and Said, *Paradise Now* keeps pointing to the audience for the spectacle of tragedy as eager and suspect, subject to ridicule and disapproval. When Khaled is asked to rerecord his martyr film, because the camera didn't work the first time, the profundity of what was his final speech is unavoidably undercut with humour but also inauthenticity. Perhaps this inauthenticity, and the various contrasts between him and his friend, explain why Khaled, in the end, chooses not to fulfil his mission. Unlike Said, Khaled laughs and jokes and loves. Where Said rejects mass culture – he even blew up a cinema once – Khaled embraces it. The allure of being a hero for him is clearly connected to the representation of them: he practises pulling the bomb's cord, as a cowboy might draw his gun. Khaled is also the only one of the film's main characters for whom family appears generative. Elsewhere it is death-bound rather than life-giving.[74] Said's and Suha's fathers are literally dead already. Said is so haunted by his father's acts, by the fact that he was a collaborator, that he shares his death sentence. He also, as his mother points out, looks 'so much' like him. When the mission goes wrong – when an Israeli patrol causes them to run back across the border – Said goes AWOL while Khaled makes it back to the terrorist group. Once night has fallen, Said, lost and scared, goes and lies on his father's grave, seemingly to pull the trigger. His suicidal-ness is removed from its religious and political intentions and becomes absolutely tied to his legacy and internal psychology. His alignment with his dead father, his lining up on his grave, his odd filling of his shoes, suggest that dead-already-ness is his inheritance.

There is another symbolic vanishing point in the film which comes when Said's mother 'reads' his coffee cup. Seeing the hole in the middle of the stain, she say's 'Oh my God – your future is blank'. Said had made the hole with his thumb, he is the author of his own 'no future'.[75] 'Will you ever grow up?' his mother says, and, of course, as we know, he won't.

The denial of romance and intimacy in the film is concomitant with its denial of the male gaze, that is, with desire-bound structures of looking.[76] The film is determined by something else. Despite the frequency with which the imperial and masculinist frame of cinema overlap *Paradise Now* avoids any overvaluation of sexual difference, of the body as source of desire, of this particular aspect of the cinematic apparatus. An alternative aspect is at play instead, as Roy Brand notes 'Abu-Assad seems to enjoy showing the cinematic apparatus involved in the making of a suicide bomber'.[77] While he is referring to the making of the martyr videos in the film, and *Paradise Now* as a martyr video itself, as the film's metacinematic spotlight on the market for the macabre, I'm emphasising how the pre-structures of looking – the making of the spectacle – are grounded in an imperial, rather than erotic, economy.

There are no 'conventional' objects of desire or of identification in the film. While Suha is our first sight, her introduction contrasts sharply to Lux's for example. Where the latter's first frame is brim full with the spectrum of suburban comfort and seasonal colour, Suha's is barren and blunt: she stands at a junction of roads looking towards the checkpoint she's about to approach, dusty hills in the distance, a truck or two some distance behind. Similarly, the extreme close-up on Said's dirty fingers – our first sustained gaze at him – is an unlikely introduction to the romantic lead. The resistance to exhibitionism, much like Said's rejection of entertainment above, counters the conventions of dominant, that is, classical, cinema. It operates not only through the rejection of romance but through the decentring of the gaze. Crucially, this decentring is as much a question of spectator positioning – a prevention of objectification – as it is of conveying the Palestinians' compromised subjectivity. Indeed, it is compromised subjectivity minus the requisite sexualised othering that dominant cinema performs.

The depriveleging or decentring takes place cinematically in two ways: first, as the metacinematicism already mentioned that points to the complicity of the 'audience' (both internal and external to the film) in the 'making of martyrdom' and to a self-consciousness that undercuts dogma; second, as camera movement and framing, and it is with this that I wish to close this chapter.

An aesthetic or apparatus of decentring exists broadly in *Paradise Now*.[78] The film contains numerous long takes of single characters which are predominantly shot straight on but avoid both the direct gaze of the character and the symmetry of the frame. As mentioned earlier, the camera often moves slowly towards a character but he or she is very rarely centred in the frame. One of the very few times when this occurs is when Said is seated on a toilet wiping sweat from around the explosives. The absolute confinement of his circumstances is exacerbated by the tightness and symmetry, near unique to the film, of the space. When he then looks in the mirror, grey and wet with fear, the head-shot has him centrally placed in what appears as a direct gaze. Said is staring at himself in the mirror, however: it is only, finally, on the bus that he is centred and becomes subject to our gaze alone.[79]

Dead-already-ness is conveyed here through the denial of subjectivity and centrality, or rather of subjectivity through centrality, through that is, the conventions of dominant cinema. It is only in the explicit to-be-dead moments of the dead-already, in the convergence of to-be-deadness with dead-already-ness, that subjectivity can be regained. It is only through suicide that agency is realised. Said says just this in that impassioned final speech which Brand restates thus: 'in *Paradise now*, the way out of victimhood is not by resisting its oppression but by yielding to it completely'.[80] The impossible agency of the Palestinians is rendered cinematically through the negotiation of the inherent power dynamics, the loaded logic, of film. What results is a decentred-ness that resists objectification while complicating subjectivity (or, after Spivak, that respects the complicated subjectivity that is the subaltern's truer experience).

This seems a bleak conclusion, of course, that agency is achieved only through suicide. While it is not unfamiliar in terms of female literary suicide, and is entirely relevant to the plight of the Palestinians, I have striven to convey how it is that *The Virgin Suicides* and *Paradise Now* mediate the deathly subject–object terrain in very different ways, mythic or otherwise. They do so for crucial reasons. Coppola's emphasis on the excesses of female objectification and male longing in *The Virgin Suicides* erased a racialised history but its effervescent Eurocentrism lies not with this alone. Though inevitably dehistoricising, the omission confirms Coppola's singular focus on exposing necromanticism. Its white, 'American' and middle-class contours are unremarked upon by her even as they underlie the nostalgic recreation of 1970s suburbia. While there is irony in *The Virgin Suicides*, however, through which Coppola comments on this obsession of visual culture, ultimately she simply repeats and revels in the necromantic. She exploits it, critiques it, but resolutely embellishes it, seasoning it even with a pinch of paedophilia. This Coppola can do because her national, racial and class privilege affords her potential distance (actual, critical or aesthetic) from the sisters' suffocation.

Regardless of the endurance of woman's constraints even in 'advanced' nations, the denial of autonomy is not a given. Dead-already she is not here. This is not to dismiss the difficulties faced by the most disenfranchised women in the West nor to ignore those finding freedom through suicide. It is to distinguish Abu-Assad as exercising a very different, and far less agentic, relationship to the visual and mortal economies of cinema, to its imperial legacy and his death-bound subject. It is to distinguish necromanticism from necropolitics: the beauty inherent in the fantasy of the to-be-dead girls, dodgy or not, from the death-dealing immediacy of the most brutal exercise of sovereignty. As Abdul R. JanMohammed asserts of the death-bound subjectivity of slaves – and slave history is the urtext of contemporary necropower – suicide 'seizes the capacity to actualize death away from its monopolistic control by the Master'.[81] Said embodies this bleak but liberating conception: the dead-already but death-bound subject's only and ultimate mode of resistance. This bleak but liberating conception might also ring true for the urgency of accented cinema. Here, at least, and as I have argued above, Abu-Assad, like his film, and its protagonist, constantly and self-consciously negotiates monopolistic control, whether as 'Hollywood' film's visual economies, or Israeli occupation. As a Palestinian he lacks the distance to do anything else, at least in this film.[82]

The discussion of suicide in film provides profound insight into the self-sustaining frameworks of film itself, and the gendered and racialised mortal economies of subjectivity in cinema and beyond. It tells us less, however, about the reality of self-killing for those who undertake it and for those who are left behind. For that reality, we might look not to film *not about* suicide – these, where suicide is peripheral or a plot detail, fare little better – but to film which is not quite so much about 'film', so caught, that is, in relation to the Western/ised thrall of narrative and commerce which dominates cinema. Though heady with negativity by this point, it is, I suspect and Eric Steel's documentary *The Bridge* (2005) confirms, within film beyond the lure of fiction or Hollywood that we might evade the logic of the vanishing point and find, instead, some less illusive or divisive truth about the suicidal experience. Such a 'truth' might make good on the impossibilities of cinematic suicide that I alluded to earlier.

It might surmount the incommunicability of personal despair, of pain which cannot be shared not least because the law has required it – in criminalising assisted suicide – but mostly because film, this medium of vicarious pleasure, has trouble depicting the intensity, the untold depths, of this most profound and private experience. This is not just to echo the centrality of continuity to mainstream film – so that suicide is inherently antithetical and to be avoided – or even the 'unshowable' of trauma. Rather, this is to point to, and end this chapter with, cinematic suicide as a profound challenge *to* the paradigms of filmic representation and *for* an empathically wrought *necropowerless* cinema. The possibility of achieving the latter will haunt especially the final chapters of this book but such a challenge will be reckoned with in various discussions to come as I explore films' different attempts to evade or at least move on from these mortal economies. In the next chapter, the impact of the 11 September terrorist attacks in the United States will provide a particularly potent context for considering such attempts.

CHAPTER 3

Sacrifice and Spectatorship in Context

A certain 'timelessness' has characterised the representation of self-endangerment thus far. In the first chapter, the eternal struggle between the burdens of the self and the demands of society was waged within the action film and its glorification of heroism, of duty and, especially, of the American way. In the second, the enduring structures of phallocentrism and imperialism were revealed beneath some of the most noteworthy films about suicide. But the flirtation with death is, itself, a timeless theme: the thrill of survival, the allure of the flame, is an age-old conceit. For Freud this flirtation formed the cornerstone of his universal theory of the drives, as the pre-eminence of the death instinct.[1] As discussed in the introduction, the individual tests and strengthens the death drive precisely through these brushes with mortality, and 'culture' offers a compelling platform for occasioning such thrills. But the flirtation with death also provides the joy of mastery and the (perverse) allure of pain that Freud associated with masochism. Fears or frights are conquered, suffering indulged, and, most importantly, and however eventual its appreciation might be, there is pleasure in it. In this chapter's approach to film's flirtation with death, our attention will turn to 'what's in it' for the individual, both as imperilled protagonist and as witness to the prospective suffering, on-screen and off.

In previous work I have explored the 'pleasure of un-pleasure' in cinema, finding masochism to underpin film's, especially the erotic thriller's, threats and promises but also coming to describe spectatorship per se.[2] I don't want to repeat that discussion here but I do want to revive some of its most salient points for their resonance. The primary one of these is that there exists another pervasive form of self-risk in cinema and that is sexual self-endangerment: from classical melodrama to neo-noir, dangerous desire, rather than ennobling struggle, drives the narrative. There is, in other words, a libidinal charge to protagonists' propulsion to their own potential demise. Another, and related, point is that even this desire cannot be viewed in sexual or psychic terms alone:

the psychosexual and the social interpretations of self-endangerment are not discrete. Post-war film noir provided the most obvious version of this. Its reckless Romeos are not just lustful but, in many ways, lost: their newly disempowered status fuels their doomed attempts to take (on) the femme fatale. But previous chapters provide another version. The depiction of Riggs and Maverick, the Lisbon sisters and Said, demonstrated the interplay of psychic (all things sexual and internal) and social (all things external) factors. A final point to be taken from the discussion of masochism is that mainstream cinema, lest we forget, is an entertainment form. Whatever else it might provide, discomfort or even distress, we watch it for enjoyment, and any negative affects must be reconciled accordingly. Where sexual self-endangerment so instantly implicates pleasure, social self-endangerment must also be seen as gratifying.

To clarify, and carry over, then: the pervasive flirtation with death in film, whether stemming from duty or desire, speaks to the psychic and social interpretation of the 'needs' of characters and, crucially, to those of spectators too. Cinema's flirtation with death, or its relationship to self-endangerment, is to be understood in psychosocial terms as in some way beneficial. Certainly, we've seen already how it accomplishes, and models, bravery or beauty, say, and, though the questions and gratifications of politics or style, ideology or iconography, are never far away, they're not our principle interest in this chapter. Instead, we turn to this more dynamic understanding of the salutary encounter with, or embrace of, self-sacrifice, not for the erotic or imperial economies betrayed or wishes fulfilled through it but for the psychosocial benefits it affords.

This turn to the spectator does, I hope, recall the claim made at the very start of this section, that cinema is about self-endangerment in terms of content *and* spectatorship. The former zone has dominated thus far, and I have shown self-risk within film content to be a rife but temporary and conservative force, but here the question of the spectator's recovery momentum, as reflecting spectatorial rather than narratival investment, comes to the fore. Where psychoanalytic film theory has argued for the self-fortification and self-cohesion that comes with conventional closure among other things, such reconsolidation is, here, to be contextualised.[3]

A certain timelessness has characterised the representation of self-endangerment thus far but, in this chapter, we shall be thinking of self-endangerment as also timely. To do so is to stress again the importance of context, to put self-endangerment into its socio-historical surround, but it is, in addition, to see it as serving a more specific psychic function that can be mobilised in times of need. This is not just another nod to superstructure but superstructure in step with history and in league with social conscience. Cinema's flirtation with death is to be shown, then, as swayed by the times. It speaks to the human condition and on condition that there is profit from it. This profit is psychosocial in nature rather than ideological or commercial though inevitably these are involved.

Cinema's flirtation with death, like culture's more broadly, has always been historically impacted. Heroic genres, such as action or disaster movies, or tragedies, such as melodrama or film noir, surge or are reinvented in certain periods, much like their literary or pictorial forebears. Films are products of their times in a host of ways – thematic, stylistic, technological, commercial, and, of course, psychosocial – and to see them in isolation is truly to miss half the picture. But my point here is less generic. In asking 'what's in it?' for the individual, and putting that question and that individual in context, we are going to home in on a specific period in North American history and Hollywood cinema: after the terrorist attacks in the United States on 11 September 2001. Post-9/11 film has an intense relationship to self-sacrifice and self-risk and provides a potent context for understanding the full weight of the psychosocial rewards of cinema and for the role of ritualised violence and renunciation within it. In what follows I shall identify and evaluate an emerging and distinctly post-9/11 thematic that operates in the narrative, aesthetic and psychic economies of a group of mainstream films about self-sacrifice from the mid-2000s. These films are to be characterised by their ethical engagement, their capacity to stage and negotiate, with some profundity, the (Western) individual's complicity in the suffering of others. This ethical engagement, and its perspicacity, will come under increasing scrutiny as the chapter progresses.

Conflict and Complicity in Post-9/11 Film

9/11 has an intense relationship with self-endangerment: self-risk and suicide played a major role in its events, repercussions and interpretation. The events themselves were the result of suicide bombing and terrorists' kamikaze-like use of the body as weapon of mass destruction. But they also represented, as Jacques Derrida declared, 'two suicides in one: [the terrorists'] own . . . but also the suicide of those who welcomed, armed and trained them'.[4] This 'double suicide', or the United States's 'auto-immunitary' suicide, reflected that nation's complex part in the attacks, its creation of the terrorists in practical and political terms: through unwitting sponsorship but also through encouraging anti-Americanism via foreign policy and geopolitical intervention.[5] This double suicide, or double bind, will resonate below as we discuss the relationship of complicity to ethics.

Returning to the literal, the attack on the twin towers and the fire before their collapse, led about two hundred people to leap to their deaths from the roof, quasi-suicidally, rather than succumb to the flames. Such actions provided some of the most iconic images – real, remembered or remediated – of the day. Richard Drew's 'The Falling Man' was a photograph of one such jumping figure. Though the image was pulled from the media circuits within twenty-four hours, owing to concerns over taste, it became highly symbolic of the horror of the events. In terms of dutiful or professional self-risk, the war on terror, initiated by George Bush in the immediate wake of 9/11, would lead to the mobilisation of US and coalition forces (and insurgents and Taliban) in Iraq and Afghanistan, and thousands of soldiers risking and losing their lives.[6] This was for Derrida the ultimate phase of auto-immune crisis and 'the most obviously suicidal . . . because it describes the way in which, by declaring war against terrorism, the Western coalition engenders a war against itself'.[7] As well as resulting in extensive civilian injuries and deaths in these two countries, 9/11 and the ensuing war caused an increase in suicide terrorism, attempted or achieved, too.[8]

9/11 also has an intense relationship to cinema. When those looking on at the attack on the twin towers described it as being 'just like a movie', they confirmed both the centrality of Hollywood to the imagining of disaster and the blockbuster scale and ambition, the production values even, of the terrorist plot.[9] Not only did it look like a film, but it felt like one too. Stephen Jay Schneider 'found the video footage of the towers coming down . . . fascinating and devastating'.[10] Peter Bradshaw would note in discussing the realism of Paul Greengrass's *United 93* (2006), how the duration of the events from the first to last plane crash 'fits with horrible irony inside conventional feature-film length'.[11] But 9/11 had a more direct impact upon American film culture. A month after the attacks, an 'Arts and Entertainment Task Force' was created which aimed 'to help align Hollywood's money and talents with the Bush administration's need for films appropriate to this new era of 'terror'.[12] This task force would have a number of instant effects on scheduling and on the green lighting of certain projects. As well as this concrete impact, there was a broader range of ways in which mainstream film reflected and responded to 9/11.

There were those 'Rescheduled' films: the war/hero movies whose releases were rushed forward after 9/11, such as *Black Hawk Down* (Ridley Scott, 2001) and *We Were Soldiers* (Randall Wallace, 2002), or pushed back as was the case of *Collateral Damage* (Andrew Davis, 2002).[13] Such alterations furnished the fearful with triumphant narratives, 'recuperative of American valor', or reflected an, albeit time-sensitive, imposition of respect and good taste.[14] There were the 'Re-enactments': the numerous documentaries, television news programmes and mini-series and made-for-television films about the attacks – such as *9/11* (James Hanlon et al., 2002) or *National Geographic: Inside 9/11* (2005) – and later the feature films: *World Trade Center* (Oliver Stone, 2006) and *United 93*. There were the 'Epics': films such as the *Harry Potter* series (2001, 2002, 2005, etc.) and *The Lord of the Rings* series (2001, 2002, 2003), *King Arthur* (Antoine Fuqua, 2004), *Alexander* (Oliver Stone, 2004), *300* (Zack Snyder, 2006), *Apocalypto* (Mel Gibson, 2006), *The New World* (Terence Malick, 2005) and *Troy* (Wolfgang Peterson, 2004). Such films proffered a retreat into fantasy. Their battles, sometimes 'morally complex clash[es] of civilizations', have long passed, yet are revitalised for their escapism, family entertainment or clear-cut justification of bloodshed.[15] There were also the 'war on terror' films. These included *The Kingdom* (Peter Berg, 2007), *Rendition* (Gavin Hood, 2007), *Lions for Lambs* (Robert Redford, 2007), *Vantage Point* (Pete Travis, 2008), *In the Valley of Ellah* (Paul Haggis, 2007) and *Redacted* (Brian de Palma, 2007). Associated with this group is what Martin Barker calls the 'Toxic Genre' because of their failure at the box office. 'Between 2005 and 2008, at least 23 such fiction films emerged from in and around Hollywood'.[16] Finally, there were the 'Conflict and Complicity' films: those involved with a contemplative reappraisal of personal agency and guilt, and specifically around the issue of self-sacrifice. It is to this group, and its ethical import, that this chapter turns.

From Complacency to Culpability: Self-sacrifice and Post-9/11 Film

The new frontline of the cinematic imagining of war is not our focus here as we explore Hollywood's take on self-endangerment after the events of 11 September. The 'war on terror' film and its 'toxic genre', the Iraq war movie, provide a standard by which the films under discussion deviate in a number of key ways. Such war films' revenge fantasies or 'workings through', as well as the numerous other sites of 9/11's cultural impact, have provided a rich hub for public and academic debate already.[17] Our attention fixes instead upon an alternative set of examples, that I have called the conflict and complicity film. This set shares ground with the weighty issues characterising those existing debates, such as the moral or political justification of bloodshed, the processing of trauma, the narrativising of personal and national risk and such narratives' construction of social or even global obligation. It also shares a critical frame. Post-9/11 film culture can be approached from a range of angles: in terms of

American exceptionalism and anti-Americanism, geopolitics and United States foreign policy, millennial anxieties and postmodern excess. Perhaps the most popular approach has been in terms of the developing discourses on cultural memory and national trauma. These angles have populated work within the humanities in the last ten to fifteen years, that is, both pre- and post-9/11, and the question of a continuum of issues should not be overlooked.[18] While all these angles offer persuasive explanation for the more jagged preoccupations of contemporary Western film culture, especially as it bridges the new century or alters after 9/11, the angle I wish to distinguish and will come to prioritise is the turn to ethics in cultural theory during the same period. This ethical approach is a recurring focus in this book, but it emerges slowly here within our interest in the conscience-raising cinema after the 11 September events. The frontline of the cinematic imagining of war here, then, is rendered internal and the 'I' of the subtitle of this book's triumvirate moves, self-consciously, from previous chapters' interest in film's favourite subjects to an interior reckoning with one's own agency, not least when things look grim.

Hence we turn to the staging of conflict and, most importantly here, self-sacrifice in some of Western cinema's recent, critical and/or financial, successes in order to address film's role in enacting and interpreting not 'war', nor even trauma, but the processing of agency, of personal implication, of conscience, in relation to atrocity in the wake of 9/11. The films I dwell on here are *Blood Diamond* (Edward Zwick, 2006), *Children of Men* (Alfonso Cuarón, 2006), *The Constant Gardener* (Fernando Meirelles, 2005) and *Hotel Rwanda* (Terry George, 2004). These films have striking commonalities in their pivotal focus on complicity, accountability and self-sacrifice. They share key characteristics, which I'll outline below, that commend them for comparison. Many of these characteristics unite a much larger group of films produced in the same period and reflect, therefore, a more pervasive preoccupation with questions of sacrifice and/or responsibility. The larger group, which I can only point to here, includes: *Babel* (Alejandro González Iñárritu, 2006); *The Last King of Scotland* (Kevin MacDonald, 2006); *War of the Worlds* (Steven Spielberg, 2005); *The Three Burials of Melquidas Estrada* (Tommy Lee Jones, 2005); *Dogville* and *Manderlay* (Lars Von Trier, 2003 and 2005); *Catch a Fire* (Phillip Noyce 2006); *Country of My Skull* (John Boorman, 2004) and *Red Dust* (Tom Hooper. 2004).

Though the critical questions of sacrifice and responsibility are distilled in the four examples I am focusing on, they are not the most obvious examples of post-9/11 film. They are not, in other words, the rescheduled, the re-enactments or the 'war on terror' films which 'claimed a base in the real events and circumstances of the war' or in the push to patriotism surrounding them.[19] My four, instead, operate at a distance from 9/11 but there are compelling reasons for looking at them. Most prominent is the belief common within cultural studies that culture's most telling responses to events are often not writ large, or written even in the centre of culture, or in the immediate aftermath of an event. Frequently, instead, such responses occur in more muted forms, or unexpected genres, or on the outskirts of the mainstream.[20] As Thomas Doherty suggested in 2002: 'the first true wave of post-9/11 films will be one step removed, wrapped in disguise, erased from the skyline, revealing themselves as 'about' 9/11 only decades later'.[21] It is still early days, according to Doherty's wisdom, but I'm suggesting that we can discern a post-9/11 filmic unconscious or how film might be speaking to a post-9/11 sociocultural condition. My objective in this chapter is not to distinguish a 'true' wave, or the impostors, or to see 9/11 everywhere. Instead, I want to suggest how film shows the psychosocial security of the Western self to have shifted in the wake of 9/11 and how there is something politically and pedagogically productive about reading the current climate in these terms and, what is more, of seeing cinematic self risk as historically contingent as well as psychically purposeful. If the Iraq war films could be seen as toxic, my post-9/11 conflict and complicity films are ultimately palatable and even salubrious.

   Blood Diamond, *Children of Men*, *The Constant Gardener* and *Hotel Rwanda* are not traditional war films even though they all contain events of, or associated with, war, and the iconography of the war film genre. I am calling this group conflict and complicity films instead because their emphasis rests upon the dynamics between competing factions and factors, and upon the question of responsibility within them. This group has several key characteristics. First, each contains acts of militarised or militia violence, has military hardware on display, and includes the requisite spectacles of war: explosions, combat, refugees etc. Even those that are science fiction, like *Children of Men*, and *War of the Worlds* from the larger group – and *District 9* (Neill Blomkamp, 2009) from later years – repeat these generic tropes.

   Second, the group does not make explicit reference to 9/11. Some of the films enjoy a littering of indexical references to the 2001 events. The terrorist explosion that starts *Children of Men*, for example, is set clearly within the iconographic urban centre, in this case London. It comes from nowhere and causes devastation to the very workaday functioning of the big city at the beginning of an average day. Not only is St Paul's Cathedral centralised within the setting up of this sequence but, when the bomb explodes, the red double-decker bus also in the frame cannot help but reference the 7 July London bombings too. An explosion initiates a number of the 'war on terror' films, like *The Kingdom*, *Rendition*, and *Vantage Point*.[22] But these make explicit, even overdetermined, reference to 9/11 or the war on terror. Alternatively, an anti-war theme, expressed through hippy, peace activist, Jasper (Michael Caine) in *Children of Men* and by the outspoken Tessa (Rachel Weisz) in *The Constant Gardener* also references the post-9/11, war in Iraq, period. In the latter, our introduction to Tessa comes with her asking Justin (Ralph Fiennes), who is giving a talk on foreign policy, 'whose map is Britain using when it completely ignores the United Nations and decides to invade Iraq?' In this way, the specific sociohistorical setting for film production, rather than events themselves, are linked to 9/11. *War of the Worlds* holds a number of one-liners that firmly relocates its original tale to post-9/11 United States. Indeed its director, Steven Spielberg, freely made the connection, saying that his version 'shadows 9.11'.[23]

In their more abstract connections to the terrorist events, the films could also be seen as autoimmunitary. They seem to be about the condition, or concept, whereby the body, physical or national, is destroying itself. Each stages this kind of internal destruction or self-attack. In *Blood Diamond*, *Hotel Rwanda*, and *Children of Men*, this is conjured in the implosiveness or self-detonation of civil war and revolution and, in the last film, in the terminal stakes of infertility as well. In *The Constant Gardener*, as well as the damage promised by corrupt leadership, the drugs being trialled are neither curative nor prophylactic but can, instead, be fatal.

Third, the films are indexical, too, rather than gratuitous, in their representations of atrocity. They favour the act of witnessing and responding to violence over its graphicness: banal horror over blood and guts. Though less true of the blockbuster, *Blood Diamond*, even there the violence is shot and framed in such a way as to try to render it necessary, as a reflection of the more ethical intent of its protagonists and director.[24] The model of screening violence in these films, I'm suggesting, therefore, is not spectacle based so much as ethics based. This is emotive and empathic fare, with the emphasis upon encountering the suffering of others, and the individual's implication in it, rather than the generic use of foregrounding and heightening the damage done. *Children of Men*, the most critically praised of the group, and rightly so, has been seen to background violence. For Slavoj Žižek its being 'anamorphic' makes it more meaningful,[25] though Shohini Chaudhuri finds that it is the dynamic between the foregrounding and backgrounding of violence that gives the film its subversive (and postcolonial) edge.[26]

The four films are not generically or easily violent films, and they trade in the insinuation of the bystander, whether on screen or in the audience, in the violence shown. This violence is of the horrific, disturbing, variety. Of course, one must ask, what makes it so, what minimises its gratuitousness, what makes it disturb? *Blood Diamond* opens with extremely emotive and graphic sequences that move from one family's intimate exchanges, often as straight-on medium or close-up shots, to fast-moving camera action placing the viewer in the midst of unconscionable acts of violence, here the gunning down of this family's fellow villagers. *The Constant Gardener* is more understated – we won't see violence straight on – but no less palatable in its opening-shot tactics, especially cumulatively. Its first ten minutes glimpse a couple's goodbye and the canted angle of an overturned jeep, before dwelling on their romantic intimacy and then the husband's shaky point of view of the charred and bloody feet of his wife's body.

Similarly, *Hotel Rwanda* provides several powerful sequences that are horrific, not through sfx-enhanced spectacle, but in the banal horror of what has occurred. The perfect example of this is provided when Paul (Don Cheadle) comes to realise that the bumpy road he has just had trouble traversing is barely passable because it is covered with hundreds of dead bodies. The experience comes before the vision: the horror is removed from the spectacle and firmly attached to knowledge of it instead. The unpalatability is also conjured and underscored through consciously indexing other atrocities: the holocaust in *Hotel Rwanda*, where Paul performs a 'Schindler'-like saving of his charges, and in *Children of Men*, which also invokes 9/11. In the latter, the visual and ethnic links between its detention camps and those of Nazi Germany are reiterated by the playing of the Libertines track, 'Arbeit Macht Frei' which were the words inscribed above the entrance of Auschwitz.

Fourth, the films are not about North America or North Americans. Only two within the larger group have North American directors – the others are British or South American – but all represented large-scale investments by American production and distribution companies. They are all very much products of the contemporary Hollywood industry with these companies being joined by smaller, independent or European, production interests.[27] All the films draw on a set of international locations and creative talent, behind and in front of the cameras. Symptomatic of the globalisation of mainstream English-language film and industrial trends, this 'transnational aesthetic', if you like, speaks, perhaps overoptimistically, to a more 'non-unilateral' or decentralised turn within Hollywood film, post-9/11.[28]

Fifth, where heroism and valour have been seen to characterise film and television after 9/11, my four films all contain reluctant heroes.[29] Their self-risking acts on behalf of others operate in stark opposition to their professions: as diplomat in *The Constant Gardener* and mercenary in *Blood Diamond*. This is somewhat typical of the war genre and of the recruitment drive of the military – the idea that anyone can become a hero. Yet these films are not promoting the military (unlike the films made as a result of its 'cuddling' with Hollywood post-9/11).[30] In fact, Western forces are depicted as pretty despicable here. In *The Constant Gardener*, for example, (mass) murderous corruption is located at the heart of the establishment. In *Hotel Rwanda* the United Nations chief hangs his head in shame when he admits that they (the United Nations and/as the West) will do nothing to help the Tutsis. But, of course, while soldiers in war films are shown as 'everyman', as ordinary grunts, they have become professionals. In contrast, our heroes here are unexpected; they 'rise' to the occasion. This sets them apart, too, from the heroes of 1990s cinema. Its disaster movies, according to Despina Kakoudaki, depended on 'the professional who performed well' but also, interestingly, on 'evacuat[ing] the didactic narrative of human responsibility': in the 1990s, in other words, such heroes were not ethically engaged.[31] They were, however, similarly reflective of United States cultural politics and the 'citizen–subject's worth', and I shall return to this point later.[32]

Sixth, and most importantly, here, all the films possess, the larger group included, an emphasis on complicity. In their grand spectacles of conflict or suffering, they represent a significant and telling break with contemporary Hollywood's imagining of war. The films emphasise the implication of those looking on: while they stage the large-scale struggles between competing factions they consistently favour protagonists' internal battles, waged primarily between a distance from and complicity in others' suffering or wrongdoing. In these films, then, characters' personal responsibility wins out, finally, over other, more selfish, goals. Self-sacrificing figures frequent American film history but, here, reluctant heroes become martyrs, never simply for the nation, nor for the ones they love, nor for their beliefs alone, but through a far more complicated, and live, interconnection of them all. This quasi-call to arms, realised in these films as some kind of social activism, must be scrutinised, however, and will be below, for its capacity to assuage rather than engage the same urges, or at least sympathies, in the Western audience. And this is really what I am after in this discussion: the sense in which, and extent to which, these films offer a complicated vision of individual agency and ethical obligation in the post-9/11 era, rather than more simple statements on moral and national duty and the by now familiar or even requisite intertwining of them.[33]

Blood Diamond, *Children of Men*, *The Constant Gardener* and *Hotel Rwanda* are neither strictly North American nor about North America, nor are they simply about war or 9/11. What they have in common is that, against a backdrop of warfare, terrorism or civil unrest, they pit the individual against the horrors of history and, in so doing, engage that individual, and with him, for in all cases it is a male protagonist, the spectator, in a moral bind that demands an ethical rethink. Each film's male protagonist journeys – and there is an element of road movie existentialism at play, too – from a position of complacency to culpability to sacrifice. Not to be confused with the shift from innocence to guilt, these reluctant heroes accept their fates selflessly having increasingly, and in some cases belatedly, assumed a role of personal obligation and duty. And their decisions are not always easy or unmuddied by economic or other interests of the self, the nation, or the West. In this way, they appear far more realistic. These men then progress from being indifferent, resigned or complicit to intervening actively, for the good of others rather than the self, in the events going on around them. These films, and the characters at their heart, are all about the individuals confronted with the unconscionable, and risking their lives as a consequence. Theirs is an honourable self-endangerment or sacrifice for they are not obliged out of duty or law, or so at least it seems.

In *Blood Diamond*, Leonardo de Caprio is Danny Archer, a white southern African ex-mercenary soldier and now diamond smuggler in Sierra Leone during its civil war, who sacrifices himself finally to save local fisherman, Salomon (Djimon Hounsou), and his son. In *Children of Men*, Clive Owen plays Theo Faron, a morose ex-activist living in a childless dystopia, who gives his life to deliver a woman and her newborn baby to safety. In *The Constant Gardener*, Ralph Fiennes is gentlemanly diplomat, Justin Quayle, who, after his activist wife is murdered in Kenya, finishes off her investigation into the corruption of the big pharmaceutical companies and the government officials who collude with them. In *Hotel Rwanda*, Don Cheadle plays Paul Rusesabagina who, caught up in the ethnic cleansing in Rwanda, provides a safe haven for Tutsis and saved over twelve hundred lives.

In each of these films, the male protagonist initially and explicitly resists involvement in any kind of social activism but then becomes embroiled in the events surrounding him and responds to what is demanded of him. The men's growing or eventual action is the learning curve of the film which sees them make the final, ultimate, moral decision and/or sacrifice. Justin in *The Constant Gardener* provides the perfect example of this narrative arc. At the start of the film, he is the softly spoken, astonishingly peaceable, even passive, diplomat. When driving Tessa, his wife, away

Figure 3.1 Looking on in *Hotel Rwanda*.

from hospital after she has had a miscarriage, Tessa wants to stop to give a family walking the 40 miles home, a lift. Justin says: 'We can't involve ourselves in their lives, Tessa,' and states that 'we can't help everybody'. To this Tessa replies 'but we can help these three people right now'. At the end of the film, Justin will occupy precisely this position in reverse. As he flees a village under attack, he tries to rescue a local child by bringing it on to the safety of a departing Red Cross plane. He is told by the pilot to leave the child, however, for they can't help everyone. To this Justin replies that they 'can help this child right now'. Thus, the film sets diplomacy against direct action, and it is direct action, this 'involving ourselves' as ethical imperative, that comes out on top.

Something similar happens in *Hotel Rwanda*. In an early scene, Paul, a man with some standing among those of authority in Kigali, is asked by his wife, Tatiana (Sophie Okonedo), to intervene as they watch their neighbours being brutally arrested from their garden gate.

Paul replies that he can do nothing for he is saving up the favours that he is owed for when his own family is in need. There will be further occasions shortly afterwards where Paul similarly looks the other way but then a reversal happens again. Paul stops turning away and starts to act, to provide a sanctuary for the Tutsis. He not only intervenes on behalf of many others but comes to force others to do the same, summoning them into a similar state of response. The far more simplistic *Blood Diamond* – and it is the most strictly Hollywood film of the group – provides another version of the same process. During Danny's final scene in which he sacrifices himself for the safety of Salomon and his son, he takes the red earth of Africa between his fingers and says that 'he is exactly where he should be'. His amoral self is corrected and largely, though not triumphantly, redeemed.

In all four films it is the men who make these adjustments, and follow these arcs, and women who point them down the right path. The gender dynamics are fairly staid here, and in the larger group. Indeed, only in Lars Von Trier's films (*Dogville* and *Manderlay*) are women central to the ethical journeys undertaken, though these are far from linear or limited in his films or exceptional in his *oeuvre*. The centrality of the male experience does, however, reinforce their symbolic or synecdochical role: contributing to the grand proportions, and epicness, of these narratives.

According to Cynthia Weber, in her 2006 book *Imagining America at War*, the resounding theme of some of the films emerging in the immediate aftermath of 9/11 was what it meant to be a moral American. Weber writes that, during this period, 'who Americans were as citizens and what America was as a national and international space was not only in flux (which it always is) but in crisis', and this crisis 'led to a national debate . . . and the terms of this debate were primarily moral'.[34] Similarly, Guy Westwell, in his 2006 study of war cinema, distinguishes morality as the 'most significant component part of the contemporary cultural imagination of war'.[35] Crucially, he locates it within both a history of the genre and the important political and psychological work that such a genre affords and reflects, so that one can see how 'all recent foreign policy commitments have been phrased in these moral (that is, humanitarian) terms'.[36] And this is an important point: how the popularisation of morality (in cinema) dovetails with a professionalisation of 'morality' by the state. This morality, I would add, is often, though egregiously, called ethics. They are not to be confused, however, for there are important differences between them. As traced in the introduction, where both terms seem to describe the difference between right and wrong, with ethics these are reflected upon whereas with morality they are prescribed.

Films such as *Blood Diamond*, *Children of Men*, *The Constant Gardener* and *Hotel Rwanda* clearly convey war and conflict as 'a crucible of moral action' as Westwell says of the genre.[37] Scepticism about this moral emphasis is instructive on a number of counts, however. As Westwell also notes:

The problem with seeing and thinking about war in this way is that it blocks properly historical understanding of American strategy or political purpose, an

understanding that can only come from an appreciation of the complex, self-inter-
ested, often economic, motivations influencing America's [but not only America's]
entry into wars past and present.[38]

It is to this kind of understanding that this chapter is directed: to the self-
interest beneath the purported selflessness and to a fuller reckoning with
personal and national motivation within its socioeconomic surrounds.
This requires an unpicking of what appears uncomplicated and absolute
in post-9/11 films, as well as a historicisation of the issues and anxieties
they betray as attending pre- and post-9/11 Western culture. This sense
of a continuum of issues centres, most notably, on the fear of terrorism
and fundamentalism in the 1990s, which had already had an impact upon
American life, in terms of the massive increase in the purchase of home
security systems, and upon Hollywood narratives, such as in blockbuster
fodder like Zwick's *The Siege* (1998).[39] At the same time, our four films can
be contextualised within millennial cinema's apocalyptic predilections, its
shifts in the construction of masculinity and the 'salvific potential' associated with the disaster movie.[40] And they also operate within a longer span
of conflict and complicity films, such as *Under Fire* (Roger Spottiswoode,
1983) and *Salvador* (Oliver Stone, 1986).[41]

What is so striking about my group of conflict and complicity films is
how they centre on the self-endangerment of the male protagonist and,
in most cases, end with his death. Only Paul in *Hotel Rwanda* survives,
and against the odds. This personal, and unexpected, sacrifice is a rare
image for mainstream film which frequently glorifies the male hero for
his self-risking behaviour but rarely has him die, as we saw in Chapter 1,
especially for anything less than saving the planet. This was certainly true
of the spate of disaster-oriented films which appeared in the late 1990s and
which, like the proliferation of blockbuster horror and neo-noir during the
same period, are commonly attributed to technological developments and
pre-millennial anxieties or 'apocalyptic dread'.[42] It is easy to see how the
men's sacrifices in my group of films take on grand or epic proportions.
'Humanity' seems at stake, even in a small way, in all of them, though
the slippage between humanity and the humanitarian, between universal
concerns and Western intervention or benevolence, is duly noted and will
be explored later. *Hotel Rwanda*, for example, is on one level about Paul
'being a good man': the film will start with him asking his wife if he is one.
The high stakes are most in evidence, however, in *Children of Men* which
revs up the messianic gestures of its hero's sacrifice by having him give
his life to save the world's last baby, and with it the future of humankind.
And just in case we haven't caught the full, Judaeo-Christian, weight of

Figure 3.2 There will be a Tomorrow after all in *Children of Men*.

his actions in the final shots of the film, once Theo has slumped dead after rowing the woman and child to seeming safety, the boat to rescue them arrives and it is called *Tomorrow*.

But, even in *Blood Diamond*, there appears ultimately to be something unconditional about Danny's actions. His self-sacrifice is neither glorified nor ostentatious, as was the case in such disaster movies as *Armageddon* (Michael Bay, 1998) or *Independence Day* (Roland Emmerich, 1996), and as is typical of Zwick's work.[43] In the case of *The Constant Gardener* alone, Justin *chooses* to die and avoidably so. As with the others, the tragedy of his circumstances does not offset, but rather highlights, the tragedy in the bigger picture (of multinational companies exploiting Africa, of the West's reluctance and the United Nations's failure to help, or most crassly put, of the 'other' hating world). What is more, the self-endangering little men in these films (Paul is a hotel manager, Theo a pen-pusher, Justin, by and large, a gardener) resonate within a vein of Western representation in the 1990s. A new version of masculinity surfaced during this period, as softer, more vulnerable but alluring for it and capable of heroism, as was discussed in Chapter 1.[44]

According to Weber, morality characterised Hollywood films that came out immediately after 9/11, as American cinema popularised moral contemplation and action. *Blood Diamond*, *Children of Men*, *The Constant Gardener* and *Hotel Rwanda* contemplate something similar but they stage this contemplation in far more politically graphic and transnationally aware terms. They also clearly align moral action with its contemporary bedfellow: humanitarian action. On the website for *Blood Diamond* there is a link to Amnesty International's actions against diamond wars.[45] The United Nations and Médecins sans Frontières are in evidence in *Hotel Rwanda*, the United Nations and the Red Cross in *The Constant Gardener*. Scepticism about this moral and humanitarian emphasis, as stated earlier, is advisable, for a moral emphasis does not just simplify things for a 'line of least resistance' audience. Here, it specifically operates to smooth the manipulation of a guilty public by a government on a mission. There is, in other words, a lot invested in the declaration of morality and the collective absolution that it heralds. This political appropriation of morality or moralism is especially troubling. Henry Giroux, for example, warned of the 'moral absolutes' of the Bush administration and its policies that worked to 'exile politics' so that 'the strongest appeals to civic discourse are focused primarily on military defense, civil order, and domestic security'.[46] *Blood Diamond*, *Children of Men*, *The Constant Gardener* and *Hotel Rwanda* seem, from what I've suggested thus far, to resist this kind of blatant merging of moral and national imperatives to focus, instead, on ethical decisions and acts that are personal but not domesticated.

Oliver Stone's *World Trade Center* and Paul Greengrass's *United 93*, the first major feature films to re-enact the horrors of 9/11, were criticised, not least by Žižek, for a similar rejection of political and historical situatedness; for implying that they could for him have taken place anywhere and at anytime.[47] Yet, these two films have been distinguished for their therapeutic role in terms of memory and mourning for a nation in grief: for their importance as testimonials in dealing with national trauma. This raises the important issue of the potential conflict between this notion of healing and the notion of culpability. In other words, the cure or redemption inherent in the healing-testimony-trauma approach (and in the recovery momentum of mainstream film more broadly) compromises the self-reflection and self-renunciation inherent in the ethical approach. The tension between these two, between the self-centring of trauma, and the other-centring of ethics, underpins this book. Here, the confrontation with the horror of death, or tragedy, is not to be at the expense of our implication in it or of our, as Levinasian ethicists might put it, endless obligation to the other. What I mean by this is connected precisely to the recent cultural turn to ethics, often underwritten by the work of Emmanuel Levinas. Levinas's Kantian stance stressed the individual's responsibility as grounded in the intersubjective encounter and predicated on potential violence. Establishing ethics as personal responsibility emerging in that encounter between self and other, Levinas argued that it is only through this face-to-face meeting, and through a response to the other's difference, that we gain our sense of self.[48] Our response to the other (and specifically to his or her vulnerability) is as an obligation arising from the other's difference or alterity.[49] Crucially, such an obligation 'is not a matter of morality – of empathy or sympathy or reciprocity – but arises from our most primary, and unavoidable, implication in the other's potential death: the murderous impulse that frames self-interest'.[50]

This ethical dynamic or consciousness, of how my existence compromises someone else's, is perfectly staged in the conflict and complicity films. Paul, for example, looks on at his neighbours' arrest: Justin could 'help these three people right now'. This is true also of the larger group of films noted above: in fact, it underpins the entire narrative of *Last King of Scotland* as James McAvoy's Dr Garrigan comes to realise the good and ill of his actions and comes to act on others' behalf. For Levinas, the individual's responsibility for the other's well-being – the ethical interconnection between all people – is the most important and most primary of principles. It is this ethical interconnection, as an unavoidable obligation, that is expressed in these films which all trace the individual's intersubjective encounter with the other who summons them into a position of responsibility. The men can do nothing but oblige finally.

The journey from complacency to culpability is a not unfamiliar narrative passage in adventure, if not action, film where an unexpected hero is caught up in events and must act. What these conflict and complicity films provide is a more complicated and ethical version of the same journey for a post-9/11 mainstream audience. And, in being ethical, they are unavoidably political. Where moralism evacuates the political, ethics, as the obligation of the self to the (vulnerable) other, places it centre stage. This journey from complacency to culpability is also, of course, the story of the United States's role in 9/11 according to the American left. And the American left were much admonished for holding the United States accountable, and much criticised for not being appropriately patriotic. Judith Butler, writing in response to 9/11, pointed out that it was 'first world complacency' that was shattered by the 11 September events, but went on to ask whether 'we now seek to restore it as a way of healing from this wound?'[51] Complacency, personal, national and occidental, is tied to the logic of trauma and cure, of the working through of the recovery momentum of mainstream narrative. So tight is the knot that Carol Becker suggests that '[w]here there was complacency there is now trauma'.[52] These films seem to proffer an alternative narrative of traumatic events via the individual's implication in them. Complacency is shattered and replaced with complicity and, consequently, sacrifice which seals the transition with no return. Complacency is also evacuated, or so it seems. What is in it for the spectator, as for the protagonist, is the ethical realisation of doing the right thing.

In the final part of this chapter, I reconsider the conflict and complicity film through an intense focus on *Hotel Rwanda* as the perfect, and perfectly cinematic, dramatisation of the ethical charge I've suggested above, but one that can be seen to be exiling something else. George's film emphasises, often through framing and camera movement, the complicity inherent in regarding the suffering of others. It ties the spectator firmly into this emphasis and does so through an ethically entangled aesthetic. But, while this aesthetic would seem to support arguments for a new and even radical personal and global consciousness in the wake of 9/11, it is revealed, ultimately, to be both troubled and troubling in its disavowal of racial consciousness.

Looking On and Looking the Other Way: *Hotel Rwanda* and the Racialised Ethics of Spectatorship

Turning to *Hotel Rwanda*, I want to look closely at a series of scenes that lies at the very heart of the film. These scenes occur after the United Nations has secured safe exit only for the Westerners trapped at the Mille Collines, and Paul has told his wife the news and declared to her his own stupidity in thinking that everyone would be rescued. In pouring rain, the Westerners leave the hotel and board the bus: white and black filter out into those saved and those who are consigned to stay and, in all likelihood, die. Just under halfway through the film, these scenes mark a pivotal point in what is unfolding in terms of both the film's narrative and the wider narrative that the film represents. At the most basic level, the scenes literalise the West's abandonment of the Rwandans, which is the dramatic and moral centre of the film. They also evidence a crucial shift in terms of Paul's raised consciousness and his relationship to the events going on around him. Paul has stopped 'by-standing', he has stopped looking on as he did when his neighbours were arrested, and has become an agent of his own and, to an extent, his fellow Rwandans' volition. Finally, and connected to this, Paul, here, stops being the primary coordinate in the ethicisation of looking on. What I mean by this is that the individual's relationship to the suffering of others, which is the primary conceit of *Hotel Rwanda*, shifts in these scenes to be made explicitly not just about him, or even about the West, but about the Western spectator himself or herself.

In these highly emotive scenes, the horror of the 'selection lines' – of the filtering out of black and white, of those to be saved and those not to be saved – is heightened as a group of women, nuns and children run towards

Figure 3.3 Looking on, again, in *Hotel Rwanda*.

the bus. The frame becomes overcrowded: white fingers are prised from black children's arms; black and white are disentangled and pulled off in different directions. Paul moves through the Rwandans telling them: 'go inside the hotel. We will take care of you.' With all appropriately relocated, and the colour line fixed, the camera tracks slowly from left to right along the bus showing the white Westerners looking out. It is neither weeping nuns nor peaceworkers we see, nor the one black Westerner among the exodus, but the nameless white characters who first left the hotel and now sit staring at the scene.

One clasps a dog, another is taking a picture. Others have fists or fingers on their faces as if they are putting some additional barrier between themselves and 'our' vision of them: as if the glass, the bus, their guaranteed safety, and the relentless rain were not shielding enough. The Westerners take their seats, in their 'darkened auditorium', like an audience, like *the* audience: the West watching such atrocities from their position of both safety and very visible disquiet. This visibility is vital here, for it marks the West as moved by what is wrong with the picture, as both self-conscious and as having a conscience even as they are powerless to do anything about it. What is also being underscored, of course, is the West as white, a conflation-come-elision so pervasive in Hollywood yet so sustaining of racist paradigms: what is wrong with the bigger picture very much endures.

Only the picture taker faces the camera directly: the people on the bus, the Western audience, gaze off-screen back to the hotel, and to the Rwandans. Where the white Westerners resist 'to-be-looked-at-ness' utterly – obscured, pensive, looking elsewhere – the Rwandans, in total contrast, gather under the awning, the perfect spectacle.[53] Framed by the white pillars, huddled and sheltering from the 'elements', the full force of their status as spectacle to the Westerners within and beyond the film expands exponentially, for it is this image that becomes the movie's advertising shot: soliciting attention and patronage.

Hotel Rwanda and, more specifically, Paul Rusesabagina provide a clear and intense version of the summoning into action and dramatisation of the response to others' suffering integral to Levinasian ethical criticism, as outlined above.[54] While *Hotel Rwanda*, like *The Constant Gardener* and *Blood Diamond* especially, *can* be interpreted in this way, there is a major problem with this reading. After all, where Paul is summoned to act, the West is rendered impotent. The racist history that is being traced perpetuates more than it undoes the racist practices the film means to condemn. It is important to note, however, that this racist history is not only the legacy of a colonial past and geopolitical 'present' for Rwanda but also the legacy of slavery, of race crimes, within the United States itself that is always at stake in its cinematic unconscious as I will elucidate in Chapter 5. *Hotel Rwanda*, rife with racial stereotype but, more than this, with a US/Eurocentric perspective, naturalises white Western concerns while pretending otherwise. It uses Rwandans' stories and suffering to privilege those of the West (on- and off-screen).[55] That these post-9/11 films situate white self-consciousness in Africa – or, in the case of *Children of Men*, in the dark continent of a dystopian future – means that the pretence, and its recuperation of a horrific imperial past, should be all the more transparent. *Hotel Rwanda*'s ethical dynamics, then, are utterly racialised: though noteworthy in their emphasis upon implication and obligation, one must ask what this emphasis serves?

Hotel Rwanda repeats the racist clichés associated with Hollywood's depiction of Africa and Africans on film.[56] Most prominent is the savagery of the African in contrast to the European's civility and civilising affect. The Belgian-owned Mille Colline is a sanctuary of calm efficiency in contrast to the barbaric and bloody mayhem beyond its gates. It is more than striking, however, how orderly, smooth and 'clean' the hotel-come-refugee camp remains. Indeed, as Madelaine Hron suggests, such characteristics firmly align the film with the Holocaust's version of genocide – a highly Eurocentric imaginary – rather than the Rwandan experience that was markedly different in look and actualisation.[57] The 'selection line', too, recalls similar processes within Nazi concentration camps, especially as envisaged by Hollywood. That Rusesabagina was likened to Oskar Schindler and *Hotel Rwanda* to *Schindler's List* (Steven Spielberg, 1993), confirms George's aim to make the film 'comprehensible and tolerable to Western viewers' and his success in achieving this.[58] These scenes' neat choreography of the unconscionable, however, in contrast to the brutal tribalism outside, manages to privilege Western history and Western stereotype while simultaneously erasing African history and black specificity.

The only specific reference in these film moments to the horror on Kigali's streets is when a Rwandan woman pleads with Jack (Joaquin Phoenix), the American photographer, not to leave her: 'They'll chop me' she says. Emotivity, brewing through Jack's disquiet cum shame, is tied firmly to the prism of white experience in these sequences. Crucially, this prism keeps the postcolonial dynamic in play. The shot-reverse-shot of Jack and the woman's exchange shows her upset and his flustered discomfort. He tries frantically to get money out and give it to her but she refuses. He pulls Paul over: 'If there's anything she wants . . . anything.' Paul simply says, 'This is not necessary' as Jack, repeats 'Anything' while extricating himself.

Another key trope within Hollywood's representation of Africa is its dehistoricisation: a mythic, one-dimensional Africa provides a mere backdrop for the Western narrative.[59] *Hotel Rwanda* does acknowledge this myth but it also preserves it. Paul says to his wife just prior to these scenes, 'I have no history. I have no memory' – but this sits within the confession to Tatiana of his flaws: 'They told me I was one of them, and . . . I swallowed all of it.' His confession operates as a classic tale of the awakening of the 'house negro' – one strongly associated with the United States – and leads straight on from Paul's exchange with the UN's Colonel Oliver (Nick Nolte). Oliver, telling him of the West's abandonment, states: 'You're dirt. We think you're dirt . . . You're not even a nigger . . . you're an African.' From dirt/African to house negro to Sonderkommando (as he smoothes the segregation of the selection line) the terms of Paul's relentless subordination change little vis-à-vis the master, that is, the US/Eurocentric, narrative. While Tatiana will tell her husband, 'I know who you are,' the film itself denies such surety.

Hotel Rwanda's relationship to cliché and myth is, then, more complicated than it seems. While wanting and seeming to step away from them, they remain entrenched. As a result, viewers, as Mohamed Adhikari suggests, '[fall] back on shop-worn, racist conventions of Western attitudes toward Africa. Indeed, the film inadvertently reinforces such mystification.'[60] But does 'inadvertent' cover it? I would suggest that what the film is doing is better understood as disavowal: as a wilful, though unconscious, repression of the obvious to obscure, and hence reinforce, that which is too difficult to admit. What is disavowed in *Hotel Rwanda* are the enduring racist practices of the white West which depends on the ongoing mystification and subordination of 'others' for its status as civilised and self-perception as progressive and, especially for the United States, as exceptional. This enduring racism is bolstered precisely through its supposed rejection, and epitomised by the act of self-sacrifice, which typifies the nobility and the ultimate sovereignty of the individual involved. This double play, this balancing act, pervades these film moments.

The shot of the first flow of Westerners from the hotel, flanked by Belgian soldiers on either side, is accompanied by a radio report from 'News service Africa' declaring that the 'US and British representatives on the Security Council will lobby for the removal of all UN peacekeepers from Rwanda'. The matter-of-fact voice-over immediately historicises the scene's events, underscoring their facticity and with it their inevitability. The camera is static and the whites walk towards it and then away towards the bus, with umbrella-toting or case-carrying hotel porters running alongside. All perform their roles unquestionably. Objectivity and historical veracity are stressed: indeed, there is a glaring absence of point-of-view shots throughout these sequences. Instead, a combination of the unavoidable and the tragic presides through a determinedly disinterested narration. The whites can do nothing but follow instructions; the Rwandans can do nothing but smooth the whites' exodus: to serve, to save, to salve. The camera records these truisms impartially. This is a faux disinterest, however: not only does the film's affective register feed Western sentiment but the subject–object power dynamics of 'looking on' are classically, and racially, constructed. In case the bias isn't clear, when the film cuts next to the interior, the shot is of a desk just inside the hotel and a seated soldier checking the papers of the exiting Westerners. The slight low angle puts the camera, and the spectator with it, at seat, that is, soldier level, aligning 'us' firmly with them.

Regarding the suffering of the black other has been a longstanding preoccupation of American culture. While its revival in contemporary Hollywood aims to expose racism as 'hateful', the real goal of films like *Hotel Rwanda* – or *The Green Mile* (Frank Darabont, 1999), or *Monster's Ball* (Marc Forster, 2001) which I shall address in the next part – is to redeem and reinvent the ethically enlightened but impotent whites. This is 'what is in it' for the spectator. And this redemption, and ethical reinvention, is premised precisely upon black suffering or 'blackpain' as Debra Walker King calls it.[61] This is true of all these conflict and complicity films that have 'blackpain' as the backdrop to their ethical engagement. It is most excessively and incontrovertibly dramatised in *Blood Diamond*, 'the classic African saga' with its 'breathtaking backdrop of white redemption',[62] which while 'presumably opposed to Western exploitation of Africa exhibits a heartbeat only when slaughtering its anonymous, dark-skinned extras'.[63] It is most revised, and potentially undermined, in *Children of Men* which widens its net beyond black and white, to interweave, dystopically, xenophobia and racism past and future in order to critique, rather than reinforce, the 'neo-imperial politics of the present'.[64] Cuarón's film cannot, according to Kirk Boyle, be reduced to Theo's redemption, for it 'harnesses the political potentials of anamorphosis [to] ironize the consumerism of late capitalism',[65] and, one might add, its social politics. That said, it still depends upon the martyred white male and an 'excessively fertile black woman' and therefore, as Zahid Chaudhary adds, cannot 'escape the gendered and racial inscriptions that haunt the discourse on immigration and race'.[66] It also, of course, despite its radicalism, ends with the image of the usual suspects, that is white men, still steering Tomorrow.

The Constant Gardener operates somewhere between these two. Garnering praise and awards, despite its familiarly redemptive trajectory, it was found by some to be quite subversive.[67] Roger Ebert, for example, considered it uniquely 'cynical about international politics and commerce'.[68] But, as Michael Atkinson wrote of it in the *Village Voice*, dissing 'decentred' Hollywood as well as the film, Mereilles, its middle-class Brazilian director, is 'just as dedicated to pounding home a lurid idea of dangerous African otherness as any commercial Brit filmmaker'.[69] Libby Saxton clarifies the implications: 'The film's adherence to the perspectival and generic conventions of dominant Western cinemas thus reveals its ostensible ethical commitment to dispensing justice and restoring equality to be merely white conscience salving.'[70] More than mere recovery or redemption, or recovery as redemption, what we have in these films is the absolutory momentum of mainstream cinema.

But there is even more to it than this. As Heike Härting argues, these spectacles of black suffering 'legitimize the perceived need for economic and institutional aid while producing and reifying the inhabitants of [Africa] . . . as dependent nonsubjects'.[71] In other words, regarding the suffering of the black other works to license and extol the West's ongoing intervention in the global south and in other 'needy' nations, in terms that uphold imperialist dynamics, albeit that the nature of intervention has changed. Western armies are replaced with peaceforces and aid organisations and activists but the structures of power and patronage remain the same. The UN's Colonel Oliver is a focal point in the scenes from *Hotel Rwanda*. Immobile, silent, shifting uneasily, he becomes metonymic of the West's or rather the United States's paternalism-in-perpetuity: American actor, Nolte, plays the Canadian colonel, and his presence cannot help but reference his earlier leading role in the urtext of the white-conscience film, Spottiswoode's *Under Fire* (1983).[72]

Returning to our ethical approach, where Paul is summoned to act, the West is summoned only to feel. Its necessitated action shifts elsewhere. The swell of feeling, then, is not meant only to absolve the audience, collectively and ritualistically as Franco Moretti might have it,[73] but, as responsibility displaced and deferred, to foment and reinforce support for Western governments' humanitarian 'interests': to summon and legitimise their acts. What's in it for the spectator cannot be removed from what's in it for the West, and for the ongoing dynamics of neo-imperial geopolitics. Though *Hotel Rwanda*, unlike all other conflict and complicity films committed to ethical reflection, does not have a white or Western protagonist, it still centralises the white/Western experience, perspective and priorities.

The psychosocial reward of these films seems clear: to free the Western protagonist and, thus, spectator from their complacent pasts. In the years after 9/11, with the United States's trauma of the 'double suicide' (of its complicity in what happened) most effervescent or 'acted out' – from their streets' vast flags and their screens' epic battles to the razor-sharp critiques of a 'mutinous' left – this past was caught up with and this psychosocial reassurance most needed. It is little surprise then that this kind of pseudo-ethical consciousness would emerge. It is 'pseudo' for, while it claims to be about an obligation to the other, it betrays ultimately (if not throughout) an obligation to the self, and the self as standing in, as always, for the state. It betrays, as Leslie Wade puts it, the 'rationalist egoism of Western thinking . . . which understands the world (and others) only through modes of self-identification and a logic of the Same'.[74] It is neither arbitrary nor irregular nor simply reflective of the importance of 'stars' that in *Blood Diamond* and, even more importantly, *Hotel Rwanda* the African heroes are played by American actors. Don Cheadle's role, and the general familiarity of the film narrative, made the American audience aware finally of the Rwandan genocide, long after another African American celebrity had helped keep it from them: the all-action cop chase of O. J Simpson along the Los Angeles highways filled the news channels in place of the events in Rwanda in June 1994.[75]

The cost of the redemption and absolution promised by the conflict and complicity film is not only the cowering or culling of 'others' but also, inextricably linked to it, the sacrifice of the protagonist. This sacrifice is, as sacrifices always are, substitutional. It takes the place of, it saves, something of even greater value. The sacrifice is, in this way, 'not vengeful but somehow or other propitiatory', 'not reparative but prophylactic, preventive'.[76] It is, in other words, an exchange or compensation shrewdly made or, as Adorno and Horkheimer would call it in their history of humanity, the cunning of sacrifice: '[t]he faculty by which the self survives adventures, throwing itself away in order to preserve itself, is cunning'.[77] This sacrifice is, therefore and yet again, timeless. Despite the currency of these films, and the necessity of sociohistorical contextualisation, we are still returned to something seemingly eternal in mainstream film's flirtation with death.[78]

The moral worth that the heroes of *Hotel Rwanda*, *The Constant Gardener*, *Blood Diamond*, and *Children of Men* symbolise through their sacrifice stands in for the moral worth of the Western audience after 9/11. But this is only one part of a double sacrifice which it depends upon for its potency. The cowering and culling of those 'others' in these films represent deaths that, as David Slocum put it, 'are consistently sacrificial – that is, serving as an underlying modality or logic through which violence occurs, narrative is comprehended, and the values of the larger society are affirmed'.[79] Though here they are seen on screen and become a basic tenet of Wade's 'rationalist egoism of western thinking' and of Slocum's (or the last chapter's) logic of mainstream film, mostly these deaths are invisible. Indeed, they comprise a much larger mortal economy: that of Western 'society', which cinema 'merely' reinforces. For, as Derrida recounted, this '"society" puts to death or . . . allows to die of hunger and disease tens of millions of children . . . without any moral or legal tribunal ever being considered competent to judge such a sacrifice, the sacrifice of others to avoid being sacrificed oneself'.[80] What is more, as he continues, 'the smooth functioning of [society's] moral discourse and good conscience presupposes the permanent operation of this sacrifice'. The pseudo-ethics of these films are integral to this smooth functioning post-9/11. The adjustment that is made is in the double sacrifice and its seeming reform of the presupposition of that permanent operation but the result, or resulting hope, remains the same. *Hotel Rwanda*, *The Constant Gardener*, *Blood Diamond*, and *Children of Men*, face up or 'fess up' to the sacrifice of 'millions', to the deaths of these distant others. Each depicts the huddling, silenced, crowd and infers the epidemic and/or genocidal proportions of what is taking place, and each man's ethical journey develops alongside this depiction. But the hero also sacrifices himself. Indeed, his sacrifice eclipses their sacrifice. Their oft-unseen and assumed substitution for our survival is overwhelmed by (the cunning of) self-protection. That which is most lauded – and we are so used to the extraordinariness, invincibility and metonymy of the Hollywood hero, to those 'favourite subjects' of Chapter 1 – now 'throws itself away in order to preserve itself', to project and protect the moral worth and infinite justice of the West.[81]

With the events of 11 September, sacrifice, or honourable suicide or self-risk, gained new currency in Western culture. The violent relationality of geopolitics – how my well-being comes at the expense of yours in international, as well as interpersonal, terms – was brought home, literally, with the terrorist attacks on New York City. The pseudo-ethics of these post-9/11 films reflect this even as they reveal the enduring logic of mainstream cinema. 9/11's double suicide becomes the double sacrifice of the conflict and complicity movie: the United States's autoimmunity, how it 'worked to destroy its own protection',[82] is treated, vaccinated against even, in these films by the absolution and self-preservation underpinning self-sacrifice.

The characteristics of the small and larger group of conflict and complicity films endure to become an abiding, albeit often watered-down, preoccupation of contemporary cinema. We might identify this as a theme of certain directors who reached even greater prominence during this period: in particular, Lars Von Trier and Michael Haneke who have been much discussed for their ethical film-making.[83] We might also attach it to Bollywood blockbusters, especially those targeting the diasporic Indian community and crossover international audience, that blended escapist and family entertainment imperatives with grittier and relatively ethical post-9/11 concerns. Such films included *I am Khan* (Karan Johar, 2010) – a kind of *Forest Gump* (Robert Zemeckis, 1994) meets *Spartacus* (Stanley Kubrick, 1960) – and *New York* (Kabir Khan, 2009).

In the years since this particular period in American and film history, pseudo-ethical engagement has become almost de rigueur in Hollywood's spectacular or epic genres, and in those of other cinemas too. Now the brooding heroes of the action film actually (like Jason Bourne and Batman) or virtually (like Cobb in Christopher Nolan's 2010 film *Inception*) shuffle off their mortal coils wracked with responsibility for the ill they've caused or lives they've cost and confident in the greater good their deaths will bring. The enduring lure of the apocalypse in our globally warmed, resource-depleted, millennially challenged, post-9/11 world, sees its latterly little men, like Wikus (Sharlto Copley) in *District 9* (Neill Blomkamp, 2009), grow large with the weight of right action. In this Australian film, as in the three Christopher Nolan-directed Batman movies (*Batman Begins* 2005, *The Knight* 2008, *The Dark Knight Rises* 2012), there is a pronounced reckoning with both complicity and race or class consciousness.[84] In all these cases, the nobility of the hero, reluctant or otherwise, and the stakes of the self-sacrificial act, are spotlit far more than consciousness is raised. Redemption and absolution, local and universal, remain Western and white. Racially conscious ethical engagement outside Hollywood is not so different. Explicitly post- or anti-colonial fare – films as diverse as *White Material* (Claire Denis, France, 2009), *Even the Rain* (Iciar Bollain,

Spain, 2010) and *Tabu* (Miguel Gomes, Mexico, 2012) – provides far more knowing and complex negotiations of power and privilege and yet still focalise the white/European–colonial experience and reduce indigenous characters to a silent or stoic, but certainly superficial, presence.

Writing a month after the 9/11 events, B. Ruby Rich speculated on the terrorist attacks' impact on cinema.[85] She anticipated the emphasis on escapism, and on the revision of the action film, and we've noted all these above. She feared an embrace of paranoia but also hoped for 'dramatic visions of coexistence, humanity and peace . . . films that can project hope and internationalism onto the screen, and fast'.[86] The epic proportions of the conflict and complicity films, their worldly sights, might gesture towards such utopian possibility but their negotiation of the racial and colonial unconscious of Western culture is ultimately fretful and defensive. Rather than evade and move on from the mortal economies of mainstream cinema, these films return the spectator to the needs of the self and of the West's 'good conscience'. The pseudo-ethics of the powerful dramas of elsewhere discussed in this chapter afford this psychosocial, but highly political, manoeuvre. But what happens to the ideology, iconography and I of these mortal economies when we come face to face with death? In the next part, we will consider just that.

Part II

During – Depicting Death

CHAPTER 4

The Cinematic Language of Dying

Where the Lumière brothers' *Train Pulling into a Station* opened the first part of the book, this one begins with reference to another early film, indeed, that which appears to be cinema's first snuff film: Thomas Edison's *Electrocuting an Elephant* of 1903. Topsy, an unruly resident of Coney Island's Lunar Park, was to be put down for bad behaviour. Edison, keen to display the dangers of his competitor's rival alternating current (AC), stepped in to test said current on the elephant. A shackled Topsy is connected up, the switch is pulled and, in a matter of seconds, the hulking figure falls to the ground. Topsy topples: the alternating current is deadly indeed. The execution is declared in its title, and the film's content is 'purely' a taking of life. From the first, dying is rendered by film a spectacle, a cinematic spectacle, to behold. The matter-of-factness of Topsy's demise, the pain-free finality (and punitive purpose) of it merges, somehow, with the grandeur of the display. This merging or combination – of the details and duties of dying, and its entertainment value – will resonate in the chapters to follow as we explore mainstream cinema's representations of the final act and their far from simple or singular import.

In this second part of the book, then, we turn from the anticipation of death towards its experience, from its proximity to its presence, and, most importantly, to its impact upon the body. The focus falls upon a broad range of filmic depictions of terminal illness and injury from *Dark Victory* (Edmund Goulding, 1939) to *The Death of Mr Lazarescu* (Cristi Puiu, 2005), from Topsy to *Monster's Ball* (Marc Forster, 2001), and from 'fiction' to documentary 'fictionalisation'. Underpinning the interests of this part is the issue, arising from Elaine Scarry's work, of the unshareability and inexpressibility of dying in culture: how the host of problems surrounding dying, and these will get named as the discussions develop, results in the closed circuit of its contorted and exploited presence.[1] Though Scarry's eye was fixed on pain, the salience of her terms alters little for the analysis of cultural manifestations of dying. The centrality of these connected aspects, of 'inexpressibility' and 'unshareability' holds true for dying in cinema even as they are revised by the specifications, and ideological overtime, of the medium. The centrality and revision of dying's inexpressibility and unshareability in film, then, shape this section which will reveal the highly contingent conditions, the deathly and even lively capabilities, of the medium itself. In this fourth chapter, we shall unearth a cinematic language of dying and, in so doing, scrutinise the various registers and test the perimeters of its expressibility within the mainstream. In Chapter 5, our emphasis falls on the matter-of-factness or prescriptiveness of this language: the punitive and political grammar underpinning it. When we recall that Topsy was also the name of a key character in Harriet Beecher Stowe's anti-racist novel, *Uncle Tom's Cabin*, and that Edison produced its first screen adaptation in 1903, as well, we get a fuller sense of the cultural resonances of the spectacle of dying. In Chapter 6, the question of its very watchability, or shareability, will be confronted.

In *The Body in Pain*, Scarry famously writes of how deficient language, and with it the history of literature, are in terms of articulating pain. Noting the rarity of its expression, she declared how 'consistently art confers visibility on other forms of distress'.[2] Upon entering culture, dying, like pain, is subject to displacement. The general and local, social and semiotic, obstacles to its expression, force it to be translated into or on to other sites that come to carry its presence instead. For Scarry, this displacement appears to take place through two main routes. Where language faltered, pain could be conveyed firstly through emotional rather than physical suffering and secondly via the weapons or wounds of its causation.[3] The cultural manifestations of dying are characterised by a similar gap: the dying individual recedes as the emphasis falls instead on either the distress of others or the more material cause of death (however, symbolically laden, here). What is more, it is 'not just that pain can be apprehended in the image of the weapon (or wound) but that it almost cannot be apprehended without it'.[4] The necessity of this move away from the interiority of the body, from embodiment, will be shown to characterise mainstream cinema too, where dying, like pain, is displaced from corporeal to psychological suffering, from experience to inference, and from physical event to dramatic scene.

There could be no simpler example of just this kind of scenario or slippage – or more obvious primal scene of the displacement of dying in cinema – than one of Disney's classic animations. In *Bambi* (James Algar et al., 1942) a little deer's mother, suddenly alert to the presence of hunters, flees with her son, telling him to run and to keep running. Bambi is perennially cited as the most moving death scene in film – at least since I started asking this question of students – yet we don't see Bambi's mother die or her dead body after the fact. We hear only a gun shot and later a breathless Bambi turning around and saying 'we made it, we made it mother, we . . . Mother . . . Mother?' The mother's death is signified by both Bambi's anguish and the noise of the weapon, and the snowy setting enhances all. Here, the language of displacement privileges feelings, especially loss, over other faculties, and the accoutrement of dying's *mise en scène* over exanimation itself. Something similar happens in *Terms of Endearment* (James L. Brooks, 1983) where, in place of the agony and immobility of death, we see Aurora Greenway (Shirley MacLaine) jogging around the nurses' station waxing hysterical about her dying daughter's need for pain relief.

Dying in mainstream cinema is also to be understood as subject to distortion. Ned Schultz and Lisa Huet have summarised its misrepresentation in Hollywood thus: 'death is distorted into a sensational stream of violent attacks by males, with fear, injury, further aggression, and the absence of normal grief reactions as the most common responses'.[5] This sensational stream or 'surplus of spectacle', as John Tercier put it, perverts the 'truth' of dying in the gross imbalance it symbolises but the far less frequent depiction of terminal illness distorts dying, too, in its prodigious inaccuracies.[6] According to Fran McInerney, fidelity to bodily symptom falls very short of fact, and '[n]either violent death nor the sentimental departures [of Hollywood film] . . . reflect the more mundane dying that most in the developed West ultimately experience'.[7] Similarly, Talha Burki asks of Hollywood's patients: 'what cancer is it they're suffering from?'[8] Mainstream cinema could also be seen to stray from, rather than distort, Elisabeth Kübler-Ross's 'stages of grief' from her groundbreaking book *On Death and Dying*.[9] Though initially describing the process of loss, this broadened to include all kinds of personal catastrophe, including the onset of disease, and came to dominate medical, and popular, understandings of terminal illness.

The journey Kübler-Ross tracked, from denial to acceptance, has some confluence with the trajectories traced below. By and large, however, the cinematic language of dying answers much more to the call of Hollywood than to the crude common sense of her model. That said, unlike all the other fictional narratives scrutinised in this study, the discrepant representation of death and dying in the terminal illness film can perform a useful social function. It can facilitate, rather than exacerbate, grief, distract from, rather than intensify, 'real-life' sorrows. In this chapter, as throughout,

I concentrate upon the gaps between a 'truth' of death and its cinematic representation. These gaps premise the 'necropolitical grammar of dying' that forms the subject matter of Chapter 5. They also testify to an investment in human invulnerability and disconnectedness so fundamental to our emerging ethics of watching death. But they are relatively innocuous when considered in isolation. In contrast, the psychosocial 'benefits' of the representation of death described in the rest of this study are far more destructive.

The twisting of terminal illness for the purpose of sensationalism or sentimentality on-screen will preoccupy us here but it is important to add the place of symbolism within it. The distortion and displacement of dying are joined, or enhanced, by its figurative role. In her seminal analysis of the cultural and ideological role of illness, Susan Sontag distinguished its multiple uses 'as a figure of metaphor'.[10] While this has proved a rich source for ongoing ideological analyses of its cultural life, not least in the AIDS era and not least in this book, it is worth noting the potential positivity of metaphor. This is especially relevant given the prominence of art therapies during this same period, particularly within palliative or bereavement care, and of the potential therapeutics of film.[11] Lucy Bending, responding to Scarry rather than Sontag, suggests the productivity rather than diminishment of the figurative: '[t]he proliferation of metaphor is not a "sign of pain's triumph" but instead is a mode of coming to terms with the nature of [dying], a way of explaining and of understanding, both in personal terms, and for others'.[12] In what follows, cinema's fantastical treatment of terminal illness will not preclude a hierarchisation, and thus distinction, of metaphor's, and film's, potential value.

This chapter, then, aims to distinguish and evaluate a cinematic language of dying through surveying a selection (and not an exhaustive list) of the principle mainstream films. Rather than defining its deficiency within culture, à la Scarry, mainstream cinema will be found to provide a rich language. Though rife with displacement and distortion and conservatism, this cinematic language does nevertheless communicate dying. It is even capable, especially as we move away from mainstream American cinema, of doing this without prohibiting the truths of the body or of the mundane, and of expressing something beyond the self. Film's potential for a more 'extra-sensorial' expression will be taken up further in Chapter 6 but, for now, let's turn to the 'truth' of dying according to the terminal illness film.

In Morte Veritas: the Lexicon of Dying in the Mainstream Terminal Illness Film

Know how sublime a thing it is
To suffer and be strong

Henry Wadsworth Longfellow

Edmund Goulding's *Dark Victory* (1939) is, arguably, the touchstone of the terminal illness film. Although unusual in actually showing the protagonist's final moments and her being alone, it nevertheless encapsulates some of the key elements in Hollywood's depiction of dying.[13] Indeed, an analysis of its final scenes furnishes us with all the codes – aural, visual, cinematic, and thematic – through which mainstream film conveys this subject. It is the aim of this chapter to distinguish these codes through the idiomatic practices of seminal mainstream films and through contrast to more independent, or non-Hollywood, works.

Judy (Bette Davis), a socialite reformed through an inoperable brain tumour and the love of a good doctor, realises the end is nigh when blindness, which she knows foreshadows death, strikes. Pretending all is well, she 'sees' her husband off to the city.[14] She and her best friend Anne (Geraldine Fitzgerald) continue gardening and say goodbye, for she will send her away too. Before doing so, Judy instructs Anne to look after both her plants and her husband and thereby passes the mantle of responsibility for their future nurturing to her. As Anne runs off, the sound and then sight of children emerge in the background into which she runs, lending Anne's assumption of responsibility its full procreative promise.

Judy meanwhile heads inside and climbs the stairs to her room as if ascending to heaven. Celestial music marks out this slow ascent, and the preceding self-sacrifice, as martyrdom. The nobility and beauty of this pain-free passing clearly distort the reality of physical decline from a brain tumour to emphasise other things but the metaphors shored up in these scenes are common to nearly all terminal illness films, if not to most heroic demises. The primary one is announced in the film's title and cemented in Judy's valiant departure: the triumph within tragedy.

This is not just the stuff of the woman's film, or melodrama more broadly, but characteristic of personal narratives of illness too. According to Jackie Stacey, such narratives are invariably triumphant.[15] Characterising all of them is an air of heroism regardless of prognosis. As Stacey puts it: 'there is always room for heroism in tragedy and many such stories . . . document the triumphs along the way, even in the event of death'.[16] What is more, she notes, grave illness also affords the opportunity 'to find oneself'.[17] This is certainly true of Judy who accepts her fate and blossoms into better ways

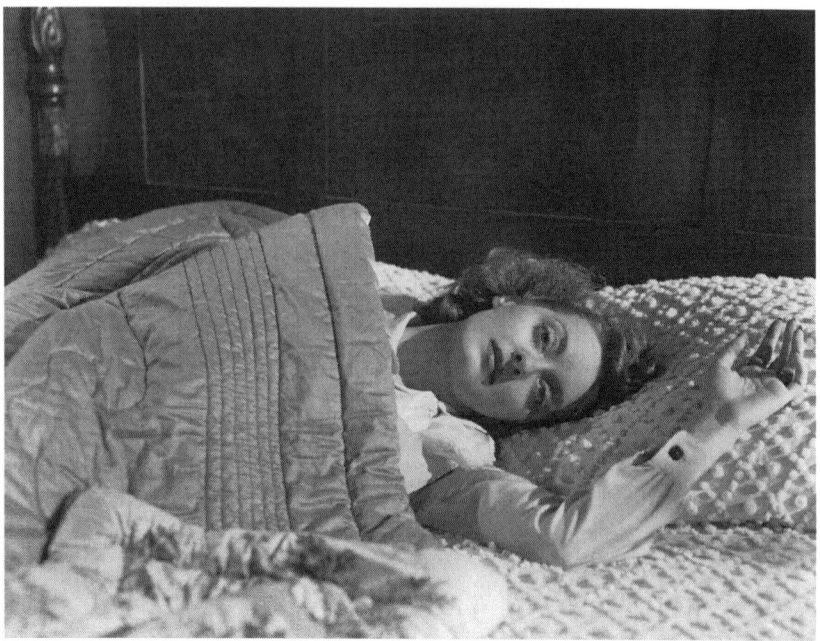

Figure 4.1 *Dark Victory*: the triumph within tragedy.

through her decline. Twice in this swan song she'll declare to Anne how happy she is. Frivolity has been replaced with forbearance, lackadaisicality with love. That growing self-knowledge and joy parallel her assumption of a corrected femininity – her good wifeliness – is worth noting even if it is not our concern here. Instead, the redemptive trajectory, chiming as it does with both the recovery and absolutory momenta of Part I, bestows on the dying mastery and rectitude. This is the 'good death' according to Hollywood: one's house in order, one's fate embraced, and the future, and a reproductive one at that, secured as others' inheritance.

A lexicon for cinematic dying begins to emerge: self-sacrifice, saintliness, triumph, self-discovery, painlessness, stoicism, futurism, beauty, and the good death. All these are present in mainstream tales of dying, though a hierarchy will become apparent with triumph and futurism at its peak and to which the others build. *Dark Victory* establishes this lexicon in a variety of ways, through, that is, film's different 'linguistic' registers: through Judy's words and deeds, through the music, set and lighting, and of course through Davis's acting tour de force. The star might have 'liked her big scenes not to be underscored', but Max Steinham's accompaniment to her last climb provided the necessary deific and emotive emphasis, and impaired the actress's efficacy not at all.[18] This is melodrama par excellence in its music and drama combo but there are other textual strategies involved in the acceptance and control of fate that come to communicate Judy's victorious end. Editing and camera movement, for example, contribute to the language of dying through embedding the assumption of control in technique. According to Deborah Holdstein, the scenes of Judy's illness and dying are tight, still compositions; they are shot quite differently from the dynamism of the libertarian pictured at the start of the film. 'Such "flatness"', Holdstein argues, 'underscores Traherne's immutable place within cinematic (and societal) convention, especially in contrast to earlier high-key, sun-drenched sequences of free, spirited motion (Judy at parties, Judy on horseback, etc.).'[19]

In another key terminal illness film, *Love Story* (Arthur Hiller, 1970), the move towards death is embedded in other technical strategies too. The spirited motion and passion of the young lovers are echoed in the extensive use of on-location shooting. The clichéd presence of snowy scenes throughout is more than mere euphemism for death, however: it initiates the association of Jennifer (Ali McGraw) especially with vigour and purity which reach their apotheosis as she approaches death. The excessive beauty and innocence of her lying in the hospital bed are conjured not only in her angelic figuring – all in white, telling Ollie (Ryan O'Neil) that 'it doesn't hurt' and he shouldn't blame himself – but through her more 'spiritual' illness. As Susan Sontag put it: Jennifer 'dies of leukemia – the "white" or TB-like form of the disease, for which no mutilating surgery can be proposed – not of stomach or breast cancer'.[20] Leukaemia is a less abject 'more romantic disease which cuts off young life'.[21] This privileging of youth and beauty (and associated disdain of the aging) perseveres in films even about the frailties of the old. *Iris* (Richard Eyre, 2001), *The Notebook* (Nick Cassavetes, 2004), *Evening* (Lajos Koltai, 2007) and *The Iron Lady* (Phyllida Lloyd, 2011), for example, all provide extended flashbacks centring on their protagonists' attractive younger selves.

The use of pronounced editing techniques to symbolise, and milk, death's realisation has stood the test of time: the death-defying freeze-frame from *Butch Cassidy and the Sundance Kid* (George Roy Hill, 1969) to *Thelma and Louise* (Ridley Scott, 1991); the orgasmic slow motion from *Bonnie and Clyde* (Arthur Penn, 1967) to *Set It Off* (F. Gary Gray, 1996); the necromantic long take from *Dark Victory* to *The House of Mirth* (Terence Davies, 2000). In the terminal illness film, editing also has a part to play in the gradual move towards death, especially as the drama unfolds within the straightforward 'before and after prognosis' structure as found in *Dark Victory*. The newly enlightened imminently dead are established thus in part through the contrast of technique between their vibrant devil-may-care ways at the start of such films and their increasing pensiveness as it progresses. This is especially evident in those films that also use sport to embellish the shift. Horse riding highlights Judy's physical vitality in the first section and her later inactivity. It is, however, in the highly successful made-for-television movie *Brian's Song* (Buzz Kulik, 1971), as well as in the more recent *All Things Fall Apart* (Mario Van Peebles, 2011) that the camera most vividly captures this vitality.[22] Both films include extended sequences of American football. In the former, original footage of the Chicago Bears players, upon whom the film is based, lends veracity to Pic's (James Caan) vital signs. In *All Things Fall Apart* Van Peebles has the camera on the field close to the action and thus matches the athleticism of the players with that of the filming.

When the bed-ridden hospitalised men fill and hold the frame, the contrast couldn't be more striking. While Pic is a sweatier stiller version of himself, African American Dion's (50 cent) transformation in *All Things Fall Apart* is more extensive. Character and camera movement are finally calmed but, more than this, Dion's beefed-up, clothes-clad and dreadlocked appearance has been exchanged for a bald, near-naked, semi-emaciated state. White boxer shorts and bed sheets here initiate the kind of canonisation process we can expect from the genre and which sees his slow, and temporary, recovery seasoned with self-improvement. Dion's 'good death', as the culmination of this process, is achieved through his choice to die in his own way and to spare his family and friends his suffering. He throws what is ostensibly a farewell party and, in the large, white, gold-hued marquee filled with white evening-dressed guests, he nudges his nearest and dearest further along better paths. Selfless now, he has mended his ways and his relationships. The excessive inspirational and aspirational iconography of this scene – race and class marked as it is – sees Dion bring his parents back together and 'make good' with his brother and coach. With everything sorted, he steps outside. He smiles at his mother, wells up at the moon and starts his final, fatal sprint across the football field for, as he's been told, he'll not survive such exertion. The frame freezes with his arm raised triumphantly above his head, and then fades, typically, to white.

The indomitable, nay maverick, spirit of the American male lurks within these images, too, as do their racial implications. Though the sociocultural coordinates of cinematic dying will be pursued in the next chapter, their iconographic and technical dimensions are relevant here. *Brian's Song* ends with Pic's death fast approaching and the final close-up on his face cutting to the scene of him and Gale (Billy Dee Williams) racing through the park. The flashback freezes, and the film ends, on his exhilaration and athleticism.[23] In John Gray's less lauded 2001 remake, this recuperative manoeuvre is even more explicit. Lying on his deathbed, Gray's Pic (Sean Maher) opens his eyes and the frame becomes superimposed with his healthy self, sprinting on the football field. The dying image of this Pic is slowly overwhelmed and obscured by the timeless victory of the all-American football star. Something similar occurs in *Life as a House* (Irwin Winkler, 2001). Through cancer and with not long to live, George (Kevin Kline) finally tunnels quirky non-conformity into realisable dream: he spends his last months building a house, and rebuilding his bonds, with his formerly estranged family. As well as celebrating the singularity of the American male, the free spirit of the Californian and the frontier forging of the westward-ho are piled on for good measure. Sontag's claim that the 'romantic treatment of death asserts that people were made singular, made more interesting, by their illnesses' finds its natural home in Hollywood.[24]

Films actually showing the moment of death are rare. These exceptional cases are precisely that: departures from the norm that aggrandise the extraordinariness of the protagonist. Their deathbeds defy everydayness or secularisation, instilling and distilling holier themes instead. There is nothing banal about Dion, or Dion's death, of course, but, in comparison to Judy's, it is definitely down to earth. The Mexican–Spanish co-production *Biutiful* (Alejandro González Iñárritu, 2010) provides a much harsher 'everyday' than *All Things Fall Apart* or, in fact, any other terminal illness movie. Its main character, Uxbal (Javier Bardem), navigates the rough realities of poverty-line life in Barcelona, has a troubled ex-partner, two kids, blood-filled urine and waning strength. There is nought beautiful, clear or clean about his last days and moments, bar his love for, and relationships with, his children, and yet we get to share them. We are permitted this it would seem, because this everyman is not so everyman-ly at all. Uxbal has 'a gift', and a religious one at that: he can commune with the dead. He is exceptional and his death is not the end. In fact, the existence of the afterlife is made even more evident when we see a second him, healthy and seated and waiting, presumably to escort him to a better place, across the room from his fading body.

Though it is not a terminal illness film, it is worth mentioning *Imitation of Life* (Douglas Sirk, 1959), for it ends with the fully witnessed deceasing of an exceptional character and one that reiterates the previous points. When African American Annie (Juanita Moore) dies, the sacred and instructive weight of her deathbed is even more explicit than in *Dark Victory*. Her priest is at hand and she speaks of her hopes for heaven. When she dies the scene dissolves into the next one: the church service and Mahalia Jackson singing. Death exposes the seamlessness between earthly goodness and religious eternity. Integral to Anne's saintliness is her capacity to redeem not herself through death – she is in no need of redemption, 'you've been so good' Lora (Lana Turner) splutters – but others, in particular white Lora but also her passing-as-white daughter Sarah Jane (Susan Kohner). So powerful is her goodness, so epitomised by her dying is it, that it causes others to discover themselves too. There is an all too familiar racial politics to this flawless servitude, to how '[u]seful people tend to become useful to all those with whom they come in contact', as Michele Wallace put it, and this will be thoroughly examined in the next chapter.[25] Here, the general point is significant, nevertheless: dying allows the stricken individuals to discover themselves and, crucially, it allows others to do so too.

In place of the moment of death, then, for the more earthly types, film employs other tropes. The flashback, 'real' or reimagined, and freeze-frame are frequently used, sealing the protagonists in their moments of triumph. Common, too, is the 'vacated space'. Seemingly less fetishistic, it doesn't, after all, furnish such a blatant or literal covering up of the brutal truth but is euphemistic all the same. The now empty hospital bed in *Life as a House* declares George deceased, as does the now empty wheelchair in *Boys on the Side* (Herbert Ross, 1995). At stake in the protagonists' departures is the cementing of triumph and/or futurism, and often triumph as futurism. Indeed, when the protagonist is childless, this benevolent or reproductive gesturing is all the more pronounced.

Boys on the Side (Herbert Ross, 1995) tells of the unlikely friendship between Robin (Mary-Louise Parker) and Jane (Whoopi Goldberg) who end up setting up home together when the HIV-positive Robin (Mary Louise Parker) succumbs to AIDS. Wheelchair bound, increasingly frail, but back from hospital, a final party is thrown at the house. Jane sings to Robin 'Anything you want you got it' as the camera moves around the room showing the gathered friends and family. As the song enters the instrumental section, the light dims and the camera moves on again from a mid-shot of Jane to retrace the path around the room, only this time all the seats are empty. The camera comes to settle finally on the vacated wheelchair, and absence proves terminal indeed.

Boys on the Side endeavoured to break with convention and depicted the previously ignored image of a woman with AIDS. It established an alternative family unit with a queer bond between straight Robin and lesbian Jane at its centre, and their unruly surrogate offspring, Holly (Drew Barrimore), at its side. Its ultimate message is far from radical, however, not least in its erasure of the realities of HIV/AIDS and its desexualising of Jane. For Kathleen Waites 'the risky elements that it presents with one hand are quickly removed from sight by the other'.[26] At the heart of the supposedly alternative family/death scene is the young heterosexual couple with new child. As Waites notes:

> Shot-reverse-shots of the HIV/AIDS woman juxtaposed with the young family and hope of the future reinforce the primacy of the family and Robin's own redemption, secured by her part in recreating the perfect family that she herself could not attain. Although she is sentenced to die for her errant sex with the promiscuous bartender, she has been restored to her sanctioned role as nicegirl/virtuous mother figure. A final close-up of Robin surrounded by Jane and Holly and cradling the newborn in this sequence does little to recuperate the regressive meanings of the film text.[27]

Following the close-up on Robin's empty wheelchair, Jane vacates the building. We watch her walk to the door to be greeted by Holly. Just in case we missed the full futurist promise that this film has reached towards, however coyly, when Holly nags Jane about various things, she replies with the film's final words: 'ok Mom'.

Beaches (Garry Marshall, 1988) is also about the intense but complicated friendship between two very different women: Hillary (Barbara Hershey) and C.C. (Bette Midler). Hillary's terminal illness takes up only the last third of this film but allows them to work through all their difficulties. Her death distils not only the sublimity of love but also all the conventional signifiers of cinematic dying. The last scene of Hillary alive has her seated on the deck of her beach house with C.C. The euphemism of the setting sun confirms her approaching night, as does her semi-concealed, soon-to-be-absent, state: we see only the back of Hillary's head in these shots. The film then cuts to her funeral. Bridging these scenes, non-diegetically, is Midler's track 'Wind beneath my wings', with the lyrics 'Did you ever know that you're my hero?' playing as C.C. sits down next to Hillary, smiling at her and then off towards the darkening vibrant sky. The combination of darkness and victory couldn't be more vividly sounded. That the recuperative arc of the film is realised, finally, through C.C.'s assumption of motherhood – Hillary's will asks that C.C. look after her daughter, Victoria (Grace Johnston) – can come as no surprise in this film which is, as Robert Ebert put it, 'completely constructed out of other movies – out of cliches [*sic*] and archetypes that were old before most of the cast members were born'.[28]

Closure echoes Hillary and C.C.'s first meeting: C.C. singing the same song, 'that's the story of love', on stage, then recounting the story of that childhood encounter to Victoria who waits for her in the wings. The new family unit is firmly installed but only in sync with the perseverance of the idealised past.[29] As the two wander off, a voice-over of the young Hillary and C.C.'s parting promise to each other to stay friends is heard. The film ends with a montage of photo-booth snaps of the little girls, the last one held briefly as the final image.

Where the final freeze-frame of children in *Beaches* emphasises its story of love, the same in *Philadelphia* (Jonathan Demme, 1993) serves a very different purpose. Though Andy (Tom Hanks) is vindicated and celebrated by the time of his death from AIDS at the film's end, *Philadelphia*, the first mainstream representation of this particular terminal illness, uses children more cynically. At the memorial party for Andy, closing the film, the excess of babies present provides a striking overstatement of the perseverance of the American domestic, though not as Andy's inheritance but deliberately outside it. If that isn't enough to recover him into the grand narrative of regular life, albeit as the worthy uncle, then its closing image must complete the job. The scene settles on a home video of a pre-school Andy and family, and the gay man is recuperated as innocent child, with final frame frozen briefly for reiteration. The lasting triumph of this dying man is realised not through his success in court but can come only after his death and through the restoration of a pre-adult – that is an unsexed – innocence. This is the only terminal illness film that feels the need to do this.[30]

Stepmom's (Chris Columbus, 1998) closing scenes up the ante on the triumphant futurism of the freeze-frame. The last ten minutes are dedicated to cancer sufferer Jackie Harrison (Susan Sarandon) saying goodbye to her kids through giving them their Christmas presents. Jackie has finally bonded with her ex-husband's young wife, Isabel (Julia Roberts), and smoothed her children's transition into life in this new family and without her.[31] These scenes culminate in photographer Isabel snapping the children and parents. Jackie then suggests they have a photo of 'all the family'. Isabel sets the timer and sits down beside Jackie whose hand she clasps when it promptly makes its way around her shoulder. This black-and-white picture furnishes the film with its closing image of the new family in sync, again, with a preserved past: a pseudo freeze-frame cum immortalising snapshot in which the surmounting of past difficulties is more than sealed, it is captured for posterity.

Jackie's dying has proved edifying to all – each character has reconciled himself or herself to life's problems and each other and moved on – and such edification is intimately tied to family. Crucially, cancer serves not only as catalyst for this process but as its cement. More than mere metaphor, illness is the nuts and bolts of human adjustment; it provides the opportunity not only as Stacey had it, to discover oneself, but to better oneself too. The child-focused future that Jackie bequeaths sends all characters on a journey and concretises their arrival. A kind of living will,

Jackie's legacy, like those of the dying protagonists before her, must be initiated before death. The seeds must be sown in the diegesis. But the concretisation of triumph comes through the welding of past and future epitomised by the use photographs in the film. As well as that final snapshot, other pictures perform a similar role.[32] Jackie gives her magic-mad young son a cape and her tween-age daughter a quilt embroidered with photographs of mother and child. Where the cape conjures the death-defying feats of the imagination, the quilt keeps tradition warm for coming life. History and dream, having and not having, loss and its assuaging, are made material here.

Such death-defying gestures, such attempts to preserve the past to protect against grief, are understandable and technology-enabled responses to dying, and especially to those anxieties surrounding legacy intensified by having children. *Stepmom* is far from being the only film to use such gestures to create a quasi-afterlife as prophylactic against finitude and loss. Both *My Life* (Bruce Joel Rubin, 1993) and *My Life without Me* (Isabel Coixet, 2003) take this further. In each, the parent diagnosed with a terminal illness prepares for their offspring's future. In the former, Bob (Michael Keaton) makes a film to teach his new son all about his dad and to guide him through his young life. His filming takes on metaphorical proportions. The more he films and speaks the more he examines his subject, himself. Though commending film-making as therapy, self-centredness rather than self-sacrifice characterises *My Life*. Indeed, it could not be more preservationist, or conservative, in its use of the medium. What is being preserved is the centrality of the white middle-class American male: his needs ultimately rather than his son's. Despite being diagnosed with a few months to live at the start of the film, Bob doesn't begin to look ill until its last twenty minutes. Where *My Life* points towards preservation, *My Life without Me* is, as its title suggests, less self-indulgent or self-centred and accepts its own limitations with the humility so lacking in the former. Ann (Sara Polley) makes a list of the things she wants to do before she dies which includes making cassette tapes for the birthdays of both her daughters until they are eighteen. Her path is familiarly and abidingly melodramatic in its emphasis on maternal self-sacrifice, and some have criticised Coixet for this.[33] This Spanish–Canadian co-production, however, contrasts with the Hollywood model too. Opening with a long take of Ann standing alone in the rain flexing her toes into wet grass, the film combines the mundane realities of its working-class hero with a quirky and even haptic sensibility.

My Life's highly clichéd and faux futurist path of triumph is strewn with fades to black and white and an assortment of other sentimental journeys.

'Starburst' scenes, where the frame fills with radiating light, accompany Bob's Chinese healings which, in the end, achieve more spiritually than physically. Though the film, as Robert Clark points out, 'corresponds temporally to public debate and initiatives in public policy concerning alternative therapies', these merely provide an alternative setting for the narrative of triumph and nod to God.[34] Bob is cured of his anger, though not his cancer, and the emphasis of victory despite prognosis is clear. These scenes reach their apotheosis upon his death. Bob's eventual and swift physical decline, which sees a hospital bed and palliative care nurse installed in his house, culminates in a final exhalation following his wife's kiss. The close-up of his head fades to a gold-tinted white, a searing or burning disappearance, a 'melting into the sun' perhaps.[35] We then see Bob on a roller coaster – the same one he'd hated as a kid and returned to during his 'treatment' – conquering his fears, embracing the ascent.

Though these films incorporate self-reflexive techniques – the machinery of their own production – they are not *critically* metacinematic. Their intertextuality is not in the service of self-consciousness but its effacement. Rather than drawing our attention to the fabrication or contrivance of feeling in film, such devices enhance it. Much like the musical, such self-reflexivity fortifies the genre's aggrandising of emotion and spectacle. Jane Feuer made this perfectly clear in her seminal discussion of the classical musical's 'myth of spontaneity' which worked to naturalise artificiality.[36] The self-reflexive devices in the terminal illness genre aggrandise film itself, defying death by giving the protagonist an afterlife. The photographs, cassette tapes, or films, provide an alternative legacy and one that is grounded in the wonder of the media of verisimilitudinal record. *My Life* with its celebration and centring of the white American male also celebrates and centres his favourite medium: film.

These self-reflexive devices, which forestall loss and defy death, cover over the brutal truth of death, of absence, with something else, with some kind of presence. In place of Bob, of Jackie, of Ann, and so on, are the records they made of themselves. Their absence is recuperated as presence and, as Laura Tanner suggests of such images of the deceased, as a 'sustained fantasy presence of the lost subject naturalized in an embodied form'.[37] This naturalisation depends upon an ersatz embodiment, which displaces the abject truth of death – the great unseen and unknown – yet again. And it also keeps the deceased on the side of the living forever. Though they have crossed over from dying into death, this fantasy presence seals them on the side of life, freezing them for immortal contemplation.

Such self-reflexive devices, like the self-reflections inherent in decline, crystallise the dying individuals' journey of acceptance, and, therefore, their 'good death'. According to Mary Bradbury's ethnographic study, there are three types of 'good death' invoked in contemporary dying: the sacred, the medical and the natural.[38] Each represents a decent departure in terms of a particular emphasis, be it religious or therapeutic or neither: stripped, that is, of the influence of the other two. Bradbury points out how these are not discrete terms: the sacred, the medical and the natural are not mutually exclusive. Each will be involved in the decisions of dying but in different proportions. Clearly, as the films discussed here have shown, Hollywood turns these three to its own ends. Though it becomes increasingly secularised, the 'good death' remains sacrosanct in cinema. The deathbed scene might be the pinnacle of the sacred death in real life[39] but only in *Dark Victory*, *Brian's Song* and *My Life* can it hold this value. In the other films, as I argued above, the sacred journeys of the dying individuals are more diffuse or encapsulated in other or final gestures, though their sum is the same.

In all the films there is a distinct absence of medical involvement or intervention. Even the ones that take place in a hospital, use hospital equipment, or show a degree of disability (such as *My Life*, *Brian's Song*, *Life as a House*, *My Sister's Keeper* [Nick Cassavetes, 2009], *Boys on the Side*), sideline palliative care. And dying remains relatively pain-free. Instead emotional pain is emphasised, and worked with and through. All the characters achieve a good death and, if not a good one, then a better one than could have been envisaged when first they were diagnosed. This achievement comes with acceptance and preparation: Bob in *My Life* is told to 'get your house in order', George, in *Life as a House*, does this literally. This certainly parallels Kübler-Ross's final stage of grieving and, in fact, *My Life* follows these most religiously but is fairly unusual in this. Indeed, and as I've argued above, mainstream film's trajectory and lexicon for describing dying stay far truer to the practices of Hollywood than to the actual experience of dying.

Hollywood's language of dying, then, is multilingual. It articulates disease and decline through a gamut of textual strategies, and it does so idiomatically as metaphor progresses, aptly of course, towards dead metaphor. It has a limited lexicon, with triumph and futurism as its principle terms. Such triumph involves at least self-discovery and, at most, the bettering of others as well as the self. And it speaks in tongues: even when God or saintliness isn't involved, a spiritual dimension describes the character's changed ways. It is also a fetishistic or prophylactic language. Where, according to Tanner, '[t]he terminally ill body . . . threaten[s] to unveil without fetishistic mediation the viewing subject's vulnerability',[40] dying here covers over the truth of death, of human vulnerability, with overvalued alternatives: with various forms of fantasy and that pervasive promise for the future. In all these cases, and through all these distortions and displacements, death makes good. Despite the comfort of this for the bereaved, or for those seeking only escapism in cinema, the cinematic language of dying according to Hollywood is, then, a conservative one. It is inherently, and paradoxically, preservationist: making dying not an embrace of the end but of new beginnings.

In looking beyond Hollywood we find fictional feature length film for a mass audience dealing with dying differently. Of course, living, beyond Hollywood, is dealt with differently too. In the rest of this chapter, I want to consider the language of dying in some other terminal illness films, some that are far removed from the examples above and some that aren't. These work contrary to the Hollywood model and, as such, illuminate it, and its implications, further. They will also, however, sketch an alternate set of coordinates for the cultural articulation of dying. At its core will be a different sense of the body, one that includes vulnerability and challenges, if only by reworking, some of the fantasies promulgated elsewhere. The question of human vulnerability, and mainstream documentary's capacity to confront rather than conceal it, will be taken up again in Chapter 6. Here, however, more embodied accounts of dying, and the inclusivity that might come with them, are to be revealed in even the feature film.

Beyond Hollywood: Human Fallibility and Bodily Failure

Anand Tucker, director of the 1998 British film *Hilary and Jackie*, knows that the language of dying, like that of film itself, does not reside in words or images alone. What is more, dying is not all the body does that is remarkable or allegorical in this film. The true-story-based tale of Jacqueline du Pré's triumph as cellist and decline from multiple sclerosis depends upon a strikingly different iconography and narrative arc than the formulaic treatment of terminal illness by Hollywood. Dying is not glorious here, music is. Jackie (Emily Watson) is rendered neither noble nor wise, neither disciplined nor loving, through illness. Her diagnosis and decline lack instruction and redemption: no state of grace, or betterment, is to be attained by the deceased-in-waiting or her loved ones. Indeed, Jackie remains a pretty unpleasant character throughout. She is extraordinary, and leaves a legacy, not as a result of her disease but despite it. Like Pic in *Brian's Song*, the other 'real' and celebrated figure of these stories, du Pré has nothing to prove or to recover, and no future to insure, through death. Yet, as will be shown, some familiar elements frequent this otherwise radical shift. Sustaining some of Hollywood's idioms of dying while casting off the rest, *Hilary and Jackie* proffers an alternative vision and version of both the body in decline and the body in relation to its environment. Rather than the romanticised distortions and distances which mark out Hollywood's treatment, this film's communication of the body in its skin and also in situ, embodied and part of the natural world, provides a more realistic, raw and perhaps honest portrayal not only of death's approach but of life lived.

When first diagnosed, Jackie jokes: 'I've got a fatal illness, but you mustn't worry as I've got it very mildly.' This is less irreverence or a denial of mortality, à la Kübler-Ross's stages, than knowingness about both. Such flouting of romanticised dying, of the unsaid or the unsanitary, characterises and distinguishes the film. Where the gaining of control through the acceptance of prognosis marked other protagonists' journeys, control is precisely what Jackie loses as the illness progresses. From numb fingertips to bedriddenness, via wet seats and wheelchairs, multiple sclerosis charts a course from loss of sensation to loss of control of the body entirely. Inexpressibility is key here – Jacqueline literally loses her power to communicate, through music initially and finally through words – but it does not result in silence, far from it. Inexpressibility, then, is not about dying denying language and convention but about the physical difficulty of communicating and the different modes of communication that tell, or write, the body's secrets.[41]

Unlike so many other films, *Hilary and Jackie* does not 'ignore the lengthy periods of disability that typically characterize such dying'.[42] Where those films might be seen as sustaining disability as 'the ubiquitous unspoken topic in contemporary culture', Tucker's, in contrast, reckons with it to some extent even as it leaves pain unremarked upon still.[43] Their protagonists, in their distorted representations of disease, accomplish implausible feats, even new forms of communication, as they approach death. Robin will sing to Jane in her final scene in *Boys on the Side*; Bob near his will mount stairs for a cot-side monologue in *My Life. My Sister's Keeper*, with its teenaged bald, pale, protagonist and her accompanying oxygen canisters, emphasises bodily change, frailty, and medicalisation but the film 'succumbs, in the end, to creepy and unconvincing redemptive impulses'.[44] *Hilary and Jackie*, however, tries to stay true to the failing body. Its early and last manifestations are profoundly physical. First there is the problem sounding notes; finally Jackie cannot speak. Yet the film keeps allowing her to communicate, albeit that the language becomes more and more non-verbal. In this way, *Hilary and Jackie* defies the disembodiment of pain and illness found in those more saintly and saccharine stories. Dying remains fairly pain-free – where medical practitioners once considered MS a 'painless disease', this is no longer the case, with 50 per cent of cases now presenting pain[45] – or rather pain remains unspeakable and mired in obstacles: in a final scene, Jackie's husband Danny (James Frain) declares 'I don't understand what she wants. I think she's in some sort of pain.' Emotional pain is evident throughout but not at the expense of the body entirely.

Discussing cancer Susan Sontag suggested that the disease which 'can strike [or impact] anywhere, is a disease of the body. Far from revealing anything spiritual, it reveals that the body is, all too woefully, just the body.'[46] Where other seemingly (or artificially) localised illnesses afford a claim, at least in art, to the sacred, that which indiscriminately ravages all parts of the body, like multiple sclerosis, resists such romanticism. This is certainly true of *Hilary and Jackie* which defies the salvation and disembodiment of those films discussed above.[47] In being of the body rather than the soul, it is no surprise, then, that it would tell of the retention, rather than redemption, of flaws.[48] The relationship between the sisters, Hilary (Rachel Griffiths) and Jackie, remains turbulent but intense until the end. No apology comes forth from Jackie for her self-obsessions or mistreatment of her sister but there is, in her final moments, a reunification and a surrender to love. Bettering neither character, it does nevertheless provide a calming resolution.

Though the film seems anti-spiritual – one of Jackie's last acts of sentience has her raspberrying at a rabbi – there is an extrasensory dimension to it. I mean various things by this. Firstly, *Hilary and Jackie* provides a more embodied and expansive sensory experience. It breaks down the barriers and binaries that keep the dying at a distance and its lexicon constrained, and it does so beyond the privileging of either vision or sound, or even of the haptic. Secondly, the bond between the sisters, so fundamental to the tale, takes place on, and is expressed through, uncommon, unconventional and even supernatural registers. Thirdly, the film's alternative language of dying grounds illness in the body but not at the cost of metaphor. It is figurative, and aestheticised, still.

Music is key to the extrasensorial experience of the film, not least in its sublimity, in the aura of Jackie's exceptional talent. As well as providing a primary mode of communication, it underpins the film's alternate expression of kinship. It is expressed from the first as familial and intimate: it is one of the ways in which bonds are formed. Our introduction to the sisters as children sees them rising from bed to play a piece of music just composed for them by their mother. Where young Jackie once played with Hilary, adult Jackie then plays with Danny. Bonds are musically wrought and, in true Oedipal fashion, they move from out of the home to the husband. That they turn back to the home – Hilary enables Jackie to have an affair with her husband – implies Jackie's arrested development, how she is stuck in childlike dependency because of her illness, her genius but also her character.

Hilary and Jackie is a film full of music. Though it regularly provides an important non-diegetic layer of signification, of emotional expressiveness, or contextual cue in cinema, here it works somewhat differently. As Claudia Gorbman notes, '[m]usic diegeticized as the product of a character can serve double duty in a film score', reiterating the depth and passion of the musician-characters.[49] Here, however, it is not Jackie's soul or personality that is intensified by her playing but something more body bound.[50] Music doesn't operate as device or as a symptom in this film either. For Geoffrey Nowell-Smith, in his discussion of melodrama, music represents an outpouring where otherwise there is constraint; a return, of sorts, of what is repressed so that a film 'somatises its own unaccommodated excesses'.[51] Here, music does not act out what was held back. The film accommodates the excesses, the taboo and inexpressibility, of dying and, in fact, of living. Music is not a displacement of meaning but holds, retains, and enriches it. It is not a soundtrack to the body's mysteries but to its revelations.

In *Hilary and Jackie*, then, music, musicality and the body converge. It is through Jackie's musicality that her illness is first evident. More than this, there is a graphic connection between the sweeps and expressiveness of her cello playing and the physical expression of her disease. Consolidating, and perhaps romanticising, Jacqueline's status as natural genius, as force of nature, other graphic echoes and editing techniques in the film expand the field of signification, or simile, beyond the customary realms in a similarly embodied *and* metaphysical way. This is most evident in the film's closing scenes when Jackie is in the final stages of decline.

The parallel Tucker strikes between an impending storm and Jackie's approaching death accentuates rather than euphemises dying, and gives the body, and the havoc of dying, their due. Following a shot of Jackie weeping as she listens to Elgar's Cello Concerto in E Minor, her most famous recording, the film cuts to rather lengthy 'live' footage of Michael Fish delivering the BBC weather forecast for that day. Informing us that a woman has rung to say there is a hurricane on the way, Fish remarks 'Don't worry, there isn't…but the weather will become very windy'. The film announces the arrival of the end in a strangely comforting, matter-of-fact, and even typically British, way.[52] The devastation to come, though ominous, is not, let us remember, the hand of God.

In the next shot, a blustery scene in the country has Hilary and Kiffer (David Morrissey) swiftly bringing things inside their home. This is followed by a low-angle shot of Margot Fonteyn's flat in London, where Jackie has been living, and leaves swirling in the wind. Inside, Danny holds and secures Jackie's arms which circle wildly like those leaves in the brewing storm. She is breathing heavily and shaking. Her previous tempestuousness has reached its climax. She is the hurricane.

The rabbi attempts some comforting words to soothe her: 'there is someone who hears your thoughts. Do not worry. God hears them all . . . he can hear every thought.' Jackie rejects these and wails. We're a long way from the sacred deathbed here. The sound of Jackie's wail merges with that of the wind which bridges into the next scene back in the countryside. The camera twists, rotating tornado-like, towards Hilary's house and bursts through the front door. Hilary starts suddenly awake. The wind and wailing then recede. God failed to reach Jackie but Hilary can hear her thoughts. Hilary heads with her brother, Piers (Rupert Penry-Jones), to London. Jackie is soothed finally only when Hilary relieves Danny and takes her sister in her arms. Only at this moment is the storm abated and Jackie still: only through the restitution of the sisters' love.

That this restitution takes place through the ancient composition of mother and child and, even more evocatively, of the *Pieta* – 'the quintessential image-frame of death and the maternal' – is telling.[53] It comes, too, on the coat-tails of the most vivid construction of the tempestuousness of woman: Jackie is aligned so fully with nature that she becomes meteorological. The film, and its language of dying, are not without their maternal or their martyrs it seems, nor the classical iconography of femininity or mythical death that has been so central to the Western imaginary, as we saw in Chapter 2. What is so striking, of course, in this film is that none of these figures is attached to the usual suspects. Jackie is neither Judy nor Lily (of *Dark Victory* or *The House of Mirth*), neither Jesus nor Mary. It is Hilary who has allowed her sister such enormous liberties and still gives, unconditionally, in this their final scene.[54] It is she who is the adult, and parent, and Jackie who is once again, or still, the child. Far from the futurism of dying elsewhere, this finale, instead, looks back. Indeed, the film's closing fantasy will return the sisters to girls upon a beach, the image that started it. Here, however, Hilary cradles her sister and tries to feed her and then tells her a story. When the storm is over, so is she. Her death is even announced on the radio after the report on storm damage.

Figure 4.2 Hilary and Jackie's *Pieta*.

The cinematic language of dying in this musical film goes a cappella. Discarding the backing track of triumph or betterment, this is 'playing the body' as it were – as a cappella but also as *l'écriture féminine*'s distinctly embodied and oppositional language. In its cinematographic tour de force, the sequences explored above break down the usual barriers of space, time, and taboo. More than the 'haptic' of film, where 'all senses work together in the embodied experience of cinema', the urgency of the extrasensory in this film includes or requires the out-of-body experience too.[55] According to Tanner, '[t]he diseased body frequently refuses to maintain the distance that marks separation between subjects; when the body is overwhelmed by illness, it begins to swell, ooze, sweat, and bleed until it intrudes upon public space'.[56] Jackie sweats. She wets herself. Her illness intrudes in the most public places, disrupting her performances. This kind of intrusion, this breaching of borders, which reveals them, of course, as permeable, characterises the film in other ways too. It is there, particularly, in the graphic echoes and meteorological *mise en scène* and metaphor discussed above which lend the film another layer of permeability, or porosity, as sound, shot and image, bridge from one scene to the next, bleeding through the cuts.

Hilary and Jackie expands upon, and even parodies, the more conventional and conservative depictions of dying already explored. Its extrasensory language of dying (and living) is distinctly embodied and connected to the vitality of being, and of film-making. Yet it is grounded in, but not constrained by, the body. It is figurative and metaphysical too. As such, though, it cannot help but further rarefy its subjects. Dying here remains

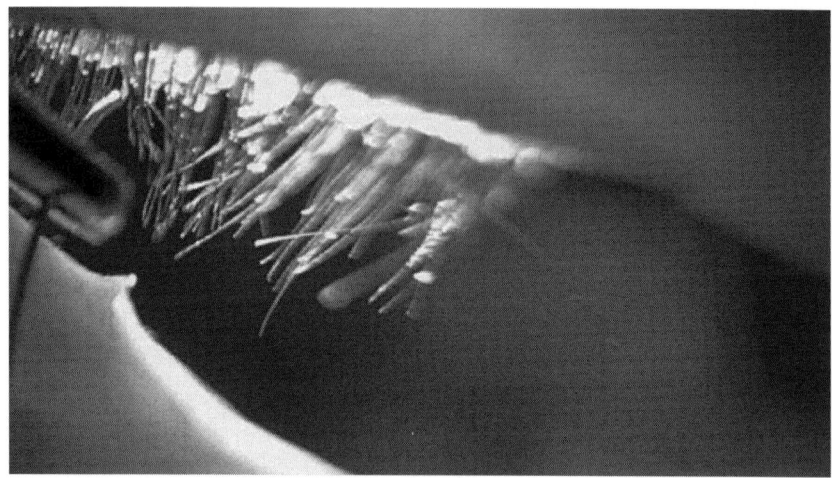

Figure 4.3 The Embodied POV or ultimate 'iris-out'.

indistinguishable from extraordinariness, from du Pré's exceptional talent and audacious character and the privilege, especially in terms of class, which funds them. At the end of what will be her last concert, Jackie can't get up. Danny, once the audience has left, will carry her, and the problem this represents – the intrusion of illness into the public sphere – dissolves as does the image of the pair moving off the stage.

The exceptionalism that is attached to dying, that most pronounced and enduring of distinctions, perseveres in other otherwise realistic accounts of terminality. Julian Schnabel's true-story-based film, *The Diving Bell and the Butterfly* (2007), for example, provides a remarkable account of the editor of *Elle* magazine Jean-Dominique Bauby's (Mathieu Amalric) experience of 'locked-in syndrome', his near complete paralysis. Fusing cinematographic gusto, bravura performance, and embodied narration, the film disrupts those barriers mentioned above, too, and yet still sustains other myths about dying. Its opening scenes perform a powerful feat of 'embodied' film-making. When Bauby awakes from his stroke-induced coma, point-of-view shots of hands massaging his limbs reveal his slowly sharpening sight. The later sewing shut of his right eye provides an extraordinarily literal iris-out.

The film embarks through the eye of its dying individual, just as the memoir upon which it was based came from that same source: the paralysed Jean-Do's dictation via blinks of its lid. In this way, the entire film narrative is the expression of the inexpressible. Not only does the film tell of the triumph of communication, and over inexpressibility, but also the life lived, endured and ended is once again framed by the formidable feats of its talented protagonist (and film-maker).

Though the HBO (Home Box Office) film for television, *Wit* (Mike Nichols, 2001), also rarefies its subject, it does so to redress, and negotiate, the very problem of the exceptionalism attending the cultural interpretation of mortality. The film centres upon self-assured professor of English, Vivian Bearing (Emma Thompson), who undergoes aggressive and excessive chemotherapy for her advanced cancer. The film follows her full medical treatment and its bodily impact. Personal accomplishment, *Wit* tells us, counts for nothing in the end. It is no amulet against affliction (though its cultural preconditions – quality of life, access to healthcare – should not to be forgotten). Beyond a provisional appreciation of the value of research, the brutal truth of her pain and degeneration, and the coldness of the clinicians who treat her, prove for Professor Bearing, a great leveller. Alongside the gentle critique of the ceremonies of self – humbling the scholar from curmudgeonly aesthete to warmth-seeking patient – there stands a much coarser indictment of the medical care of the dying. It is perhaps no surprise that *Wit* is the only film to be deemed instructive for medical students.[57] While Hollywood's good deaths 'serve the purpose of the legitimization of medical authority', *Wit*'s quite clear depiction of the opposite performs a powerful disclaimer.[58] Not only is Vivian's physical suffering, seclusion and fear emphasised but, when her DNR (do not resuscitate) order is disregarded by the young doctor, even her final 'peace' is violated.

Dying in *Wit* is characterised by none of Hollywood's saccharine and melodramatic tendencies. The film depicts severe pain. The cancer, and its treatment, involve hair loss, vomiting, tears, drugs and degradation. Triumph and calm appear ridiculous in the 'real' face of death. Vivian's direct address throughout operates as a knowing commentary on Hollywood's tendencies. Self-reflexivity here is thoroughly critical of a range of 'media': the Hollywood film (and its distortion of dying); the fictions or techniques of the self (Vivian's confidence in her own significance); the discourse of doctors'/bedside care (the deficient medical language of dying). Ultimately, the film disputes the repressive responses to mortality within society, within the hospital and within the self. In its place, it instates dying as not only an event of the body but a stage, or process, of life. Vivian's imagined or remembered lesson with her academic adviser, E. M Ashford (Eileen Atkins), punctuates the film, and pivots upon the critical analysis of a John Donne poem. Ashford's preferred reading provides a powerful statement on how dying 'should' be understood and on the lesson of Vivian's experience, for her and for the audience. She says:

Very simple: with the original punctuation restored, death is no longer something to act out on a stage with exclamation marks. It is a comma. A pause . . . Life, death, soul, god, past, present, Not insuperable barriers. Not semi-colons. Just a comma . . . It's not wit, it's the truth.

The metaphysical poem, poet, pursuit, merge with the physicality of life's stages, of dying. There is no God or divinity, or metaphor, here, just human fallibility and bodily failure. Rather than being or remaining estranged from death, punctuation is restored. It is a punctuation of life, not its own separate language. Indeed, despite its expectorations, the film's flow of words, rather than senses, expresses dying. Vivian's realisation of this truer meter, of emphasis in its right place, comes via a maternal moment, yet again. As Vivian nears her end, Ashford reads her favourite children's story to her. Real or imagined, this scene is restorative, and regressive, and backs away from triumph and futurism in ways not dissimilar to *Hilary and Jackie*. Lacking, indeed deconstructing, the exclamation marks of more fantastical renditions, dying in *Wit* is not idealised, sentimentalised or venerating.

Another film that starts, as *Wit* does, with its solitary protagonist receiving the prognosis that he hasn't long to live is *Ikiru* (Akira Kurosawa, 1952). But unassuming and long-serving public servant Kanji Watanabe (Takashi Shimura) couldn't be further from Bearing's bumptiousness, or from the environment in which she ends her days. Having spent thirty years pen-pushing in a bureaucracy-beset office, Watanabe dedicates his final weeks to living fully (and *Ikiru* means 'to live') which for him is realised by getting a children's playground built. As in *Last Holiday* and *Life as a House*, his death sentence is liberating: it enables the dying individual to re-evaluate his life and strive to take pleasure and pride in things before it is too late. Unlike these two Hollywood films, and all the others' resolved storylines, *Ikiru* decentres its protagonist at the same time as venerating him.

Veneration is attached to Watanabe's actions and not to his self: neither he nor anyone he knows is bettered through his dying. In fact, at his wake, those gathered argue even about his selfless accomplishment. Proclaiming him saintly, their drunken reappraisal is untrustworthy and, while they vow to echo his example, their betterment through his death is short-lived. Only one man, it seems, will keep the faith. Though one man, as we've seen (and as we'll see again in Chapter 7), is all it need take. In this way, it is typical of Kurosawa's emphasis on 'enlightenment rather than catharsis'.[59] Likewise, the futuristic promise of the playground, the generic emphasis on happy but backgrounded children that frame this tale, as they did *Dark Victory*, are characterised by an unconditional and selfless, rather than sentimental and dynastic, gift. The children are not his own or even known to him. The film appears to share the mainstream language of dying in moving towards the futuristically marked triumph of its protagonist. And it expounds the value of life, and a spiritualised value at that, through dying. But this triumph and future and movement are undercut by various methods of decentring Watanabe's experience.

His death is announced early and occurs part way through. He becomes a quiet spectral presence, encapsulated by his photograph above the 'altar' at his wake, as attention shifts to others' piecing together their own experiences as they compile his. The film operates outside linear time with the events occurring in flashback. The omniscient voice-over, which introduces the protagonist at the start, tells us he will die and follows the course of events. Distracting from emotional pain or loss, the death has already happened. As in *Wit*, death is restored to its place as stage in the individual's life but, unlike *Wit*, this depends upon a deprivileging of the dying individual.

Our final example, the Romanian film, *The Death of Mr Lazarescu/ Moartea domnului Lazarescu* (Cristi Puiu, 2005), stands apart from all the films already mentioned. Its cinematic language of dying provides a radical shift from the Hollywood model and from its residue or resonance in the three alternatives just discussed. *The Death* doesn't so much invert the lexicon of cinematic dying – to journey away from triumph and futurism, like *Hilary and Jackie* and *Wit*, or towards but amending them, like *Ikiru* – as negate it. Indeed, the film dismisses, rather than rescripts, metaphorical and allegorical gestures altogether. Banality replaces extraordinariness: embodiment and porosity come not with the glory of genius but the insignificance of self. Banality is key, in fact, in the final undoing of the exceptionalism of dying that *Hilary and Jackie* and even *Ikiru* cannot help but propagate. And while *Wit* would come to render the self insignificant, it did so through sustaining its centrality. But death, too, is decentred in Puiu's film. It isn't just a stage but a sideshow in life's passage, and one lacking exclamation marks. So comfortable with death is Puiu's film, and so contrary to the 'Life' terms and resurrectional investments of Hollywood, that it announces this in its title. Where other films, from *Dark Victory* and *Ikiru* to *Stepmom* and *All Things Fall Apart*, headed their heroes for heaven or at least saintliness, or secured some other sort of afterlife, this film keeps it contrary. Not even Lazarus can rise here.

Puiu's film tells of the decline and death of a man aged as much by non-event and neglect as passing years. The long day's night of his demise is marked by the mundane: tea and cats and mobile phones, the minutiae of everyday life. The confined quarters of his flat are exchanged for those of the ambulance and then various hospital rooms. Slow, cluttered, gossipy, this is relentlessly banal but 'absolutely real' stuff.[60] Though a major car crash has occurred – spectacular fodder for other films – it serves only as a strain on resources here, causing our two protagonists, Mr Lazarescu (Ioan Fiscuteanu) and the paramedic Mioara (Luminita Gheorghiu), to drive from one hospital to another in search of treatment. Mr Lazarescu becomes steadily less lucid, more ill, and increasingly peripheral. Though ever present, he fades into the background. We do not even see the moment of his death: neither his life nor his death is grandstanded. Though it is announced in the title, we won't witness it: the screen fades to black after he's been prepared for surgery. This surgery is serious but likely to be successful. But the problem with his liver is not curable and he will most certainly die, just not on screen. The film resists the money shot of the moment of death (or of enlightenment) and trades the spectacle of emergency rooms for the monotony of referral. Dying is embodied but without any fanfare. Like *Hilary and Jackie*, *The Death* ignores the redemptive, godly, or generative promise of terminal illness. Unlike Tucker's film, however, the dying individual is sidelined rather than privileged. Even the gaze, which fixed upon him immediately, becomes ever more untethered in its attentions. Various vignettes, of other characters' conversations or small talk, fill the narrative. Increasingly backgrounded, his focalisation, and our identification with him, are undermined.

Our introduction to Mr Lazarescu is to a man in pain. If the film succeeds in expressing pain more honestly than others, it does so by revealing not simply the doubt or difficulty that operates in its apprehension but the intervention of other doubts and difficulties, other obstacles to its apprehension and recognition. Though Scarry draws attention to the problem of communicating pain, to the gap between its experience and its reception, Puiu's film clouds the certainty of having it and of treating it.[61] The simple ways, and advancing mumbles, of Mr Lazarescu combine with the mixed reactions and competencies of the various medical professionals he encounters to ensure the absence of surety entirely. There is to be no sovereignty in this film, no confident soul or seat of knowledge. Favoured instead is the material reality of managing doubt and limited resources within a highly flawed health care system as per 'real' life.

Most importantly, Mr Lazarescu is a long way from the middle-class figures in the affluent and high-tech milieux of mainstream Western terminal illness films, or the emboldened bureaucrat on a mission in *Ikiru*. Middle-aged, in poor shape and partial to drink, he has only cats for company, a wife who has died, an acrimonious relationship with his sister, and a daughter who has deserted him for Canada. He couldn't be more different from Bob, George, and Judy, or Jackie, or Vivian or even Uxbal. And the care he receives is perfunctory and professional at best; partial, cold and negligent at worst. Mr Lazarescu doesn't even get a deathbed: the stretcher he has been lying and dying on for the majority of the film is taken away and replaced with a wheeled stretcher. The film is free of all niceties, of the figurative, of filmic flourish or classical allusion. Bar the titular joke, *The Death* undercuts, rather than embellishes, a language of dying. It seems, if only unavoidably, political in this too. The film was taken as a critique of Romanian health care but, more than this, where culture 'rarely take[s] up disability as an experience of social and political dimensions' Puiu involves this broader context.[62]

The dying body in Puiu's film is not held at a distance: except for the film's first and last scenes, Mr Lazarescu is never alone or segregated. And it intrudes, indeed, on the public sphere. In contrast to the limitedly leaking body of du Pré, or the quarantines of *Wit* or *Ikiru*, Mr Lazarescu's odour pervades the film. At its start the smell of his flat, and of his drinking, are noted; finally, it is his soiling himself. Characters refer to the smell and, though various nurses will lift up his covers and look, he is not cleaned up until the very end of the film. When Jackie wets herself unwittingly in the dressing room, she is alone. The fluid is clear and the dress, though soiled, is immediately disposed of. There is no stain or scent and no witness to this most intimate 'indiscretion'. In Mr Lazarescu's case such extrasensorial seepage, like dying itself, is shared, social and standard fare.[63] Vivian's dying in *Wit* is depicted similarly as an exchange of sorts between her and her carer(s) within the hospital, as something happening for all of them.[64] Her enduring isolation, however, will overwhelm any sense of this more social understanding of death: it punctuates her paragraph of life rather than the public sphere. But, in *The Death*, dying is a socialised or communitarian occurrence. Its potential as such will preoccupy this book's last two chapters.

Tanner claims that representations of the dying body 'uncover both the uncomfortable fact of impending death and the seemingly absolute boundaries between health and illness erected by our culture, boundaries which implicitly disavow the shared vulnerability of embodiment'.[65] The barriers between the ill or dying body and the world are fiercely and figuratively erected in mainstream cinema, as we saw in our opening survey of terminal illness films. In these less formulaic examples – and there are many others from outside, and occasionally inside, Hollywood, like *Third Star* (Hattie Dalton, 2010) or *All That Jazz* (Bob Fosse, 1979) or *Amour* (Michael Haneke, 2012) – a different balance is struck between dying and its metaphors, and for different creative or discursive reasons. Only in *The Death* are these barriers missing and the cinematic language of dying rescripted entirely.[66] A firewall of sorts, those barriers keep out the threatening knowledge of our own mortality, that this fate of bodily decline awaits us too. They displace and distort dying to comfort and distract us instead. Puiu's film alone allows the full sense, or stench, of the banality of bodily decline to be shared and, crucially, within a fiction film for the relatively 'mass' audience of its, albeit limited, international exhibition. Devoid of sentimentality, spirituality, or any of the ceremonies of the self so fundamental to narrative cinema, it conjures that 'more mundane dying' so thoroughly occluded elsewhere.[67]

CHAPTER 5

Grammar Lessons:
Dying and Difference

In the broadest terms, how a character dies in mainstream film – by whose hand or what logic, whether as murderer or victim, with a good or bad death – is influenced, if not determined, by the gender, sexuality or race of this character, to name the usual suspects on the list of personal specifications. From gunshot or on a hospital trolley, at speed or prolonged, with dignity or decrepitude, cinematic dying is shaped by the 'social' make-up of the woman or man in question. By social I mean those recognisable visual, physical or cultural markers that distinguish one person from another. Genre is crucial but not crucial enough: though it determines the function and frequency, if not method, of death in film – the blood fest spurring our main man on to greater heroism in the war film or the 'monster' on to crueller carnage in horror – identity is a stronger force. So, for example, in Hollywood, in a serial killer film, the murderer is among the gathered crowd but will *not* be the black character, and only white people, it seems, and rarely men or the working, or non-working, poor, succumb to terminal illnesses.[1] Though genre, or subgenre, will be spoken of, most of what follows lies outside, or beyond, its mode of classification. The relationship between dying and difference is pre- rather than post- genre, for the scaffolding it stems from came long before the moving image though it would find a natural home there.[2]

In this chapter I shall map the simple, even crass, relationship between dying and sociocultural difference in mainstream cinema. Filling in the gaps of the preceding chapter's conclusions, unfolding their full logic, the ideological weight of the good death will be revealed. But the main concern of this chapter is bad death, that is, death that is bad, and bad in two key ways: firstly, as dying characterised by passivity or prematurity, by the inversion of all those aspirational threads to terminal illness outlined in the last chapter, especially the inevitably holy trinity of triumph, betterment and futurism; secondly, and most importantly, as making good death bad, as pulling back the curtain and revealing this death's divinity as rotten all along. Good death goes bad in this way because embedded in its politics are all kinds of socioeconomic and historical criteria and disavowals but, more than this, a grammar of dying preceding and predetermining it.

The impact that difference or identity has on death in film has been felt already and throughout this book. Nationality (Americanness), gender (femininity) and coloniality (subalternism) have either infused or framed the arguments in Part I. In the last chapter, politics, though kept at bay, was a palpable presence all the same. Indeed, it proved impossible to ignore the doctrinal charge of the social coordinates of the cinematic language of dying reiterated, as they were, to the point of persuasion, or rather fluency. Inherent, then, in that filmic lexicon, in the self-discoveries and triumphs that characterised dying, is a *right* path; one wedded to identity and ridden with ideological assumptions about correctitude and the morality of mortality. As Robert McRuer puts it: 'The representation of the [bodily] process of breakdown or incapacity is fraught with political and ideological significance.'[3]

A basic, and pedagogically useful, way of approaching the relationship between dying and ideology in film would be to consider the following simple questions and the patterns they reveal. Who dies? Who suffers or survives? Who recovers? Who saves? Who kills? Who watches? What belief systems are being challenged, confirmed or reinforced through the image or narrative of dying, and what audience is it targeting? These questions will be addressed, at least broadly, in what follows but, rather than trace only a crude tale of how, say, messy or meaningless death punishes evil and pain-free expiration rewards nobility, of how good girls go to heaven and bad girls go everywhere else in Hollywood, I want instead to chart a more complex, more intersectional course. Such a course tracks the (codependent) exchanges between the purity *and* punitivity, the absolution *and* violence, that characterise representations of dying in mainstream film but also between the structural and aesthetic, or the sexual and racial, dimensions of cinema's natural or unnatural deaths. It criss-crosses, in other words, both thematic and methodological approaches to this subject and, in so doing, I hope, provides something more critically accented, thereby giving the complexity of life, and death, in film its due. Let's return briefly to the terminal illness film before opening out the discussion beyond this genre.

The Holy Trinity: Triumph, Betterment, Futurism (a.k.a. Whiteness, Rightness and Compulsory Heteronormativity)

Inherent in the holy trinity of triumph, betterment, and futurism, the key elements in the lexicon of cinematic dying, is identity. Revisiting the terminal illness film now, I want to reveal how sociocultural coordinates are reinforced and promulgated within its idealisations. I shall then expand this discussion into mainstream film more broadly.

The cinematic language of dying is clearly gendered, and biased with it. When Judy, in *Dark Victory*, threw off more selfish ways, her prize was a husband and fulfilment or, rather, a husband as fulfilment.[4] Her route to triumph mirrored that of the Freudian assumption of a correct and mature femininity, one not centred on the self (masturbatory, clitorally inclined) but on the male partner (marital, penetrative and procreative if only *in potentia*). The presence or promise of children underwrites this correct, or corrected, femininity in the terminal illness film and, as in the maternal melodrama, the woman's glory is accentuated through sacrifice.[5] Judy, Hillary (*Beaches*), Jackie (*Stepmom*), and Ann (*My Life without Me*) were all rendered or confirmed as good by relinquishing, and passing on, maternality to another woman. In this way, the maternal as coterminous with femininity, and the interchangeability of women, are reiterated. When we look to terminally ill men in mainstream film – of whom there are far fewer examples – the story is very different. Bob in *My Life* does the opposite of relinquishing his parental hold: he clings to it fiercely, remaining 'alive' in it even after death. His glory is tied up with the maintenance of his position as the father even beyond the grave. So singular is man, is the father, so extreme, it seems, is the unease attending his biological guarantee and legacy, that he must survive even the greatest breach. *My Life* is, of course, very much of its time and reflects the growing anxiety about absent fathers in 1990s American society. This was, after all, a period of significant change in the cultural discussion of fatherhood and family owing to, among other things, the dramatic increase in divorce rates since the mid-1980s.[6] Elsewhere in the terminal illness film, the topic of fatherhood is simply avoided: dying men don't have children yet (*All Things Fall Apart*) or they remain off-screen (*Brian's Song*).[7] Children are not, in other words, intimately linked to character formation or our judgement of the men in these films. Masculinity or worth is neither proven nor epitomised through parenting. *Life is a House* stands apart here, drawing its power from its precise opposition to this norm: both father and son are redeemed through its alternative vision of kinship.[8]

There is more to it than this. In the case of *All Things Fall Apart*, the black male protagonist doesn't even have a relationship. His attainment of 'sainthood' requires him to relinquish all romantic bonds and become desexualised. Dion (50 cent) casts off his macho virility en route to salvation. As with Jane (Whoopi Goldberg) in *Boys on the Side*, this neutering of a central black character appears obligatory to terminal illness films. Something similar happens in *The Bucket List* (Rob Reiner, 2007) which I explore at length below. Again, though Carter (Morgan Freeman) has adult children and a loving wife of twenty-eight years, the image of a sexually active *and* saintly black man cannot be accommodated. Jack Nicolson's character, Edward, has a female prostitute try to seduce him but there is no swaying the sage-like Carter. What is more, Carter's relapse occurs when he has reconciled with his family and is just on the verge of having sex with his wife: she emerges from the bathroom having slipped into something more comfortable and he has fallen to the floor.

The terms of triumph are not only gendered but racialised. Dion's decline and departure are so sanitised, his triumph so bleached. Mario Van Peebles's reference points here come not from black-authored tales of black heroism drawn from African American traditions in literature and painting and even film, but from white and female melodramatic history.[9] Dion's embrace of death bears no correlation to the slave who preferred to die or to chose suicide over bondage, as we saw in Chapter 2, or to the 'vernacular cultural history' or 'discourse of black spirituality' that for Paul Gilroy memorialised the slaves' experience (and as an alternative eschatological frame to modernity).[10] In addition, according to Hollywood, African American women do not suffer from terminal illness. Neither, it should be mentioned, do they, or African American men, treat it. Where, as Robert Clark suggests, *Stepmom* is the only cancer film with a black (woman) oncologist, Queen Latifah's small role as a palliative-care nurse in *My Life* speaks more to the 'mammy' convention than anything else.[11] Similarly, where *Last Holiday* (Wayne Wang, 2006) finally shows a black woman with a terminal illness – Queen Latifah as Georgia – remarkably, her diagnosis turns out to have been an error. This fake dying film repeats the genre's codes nevertheless. Georgia realises her dreams through her prognosis but, like Annie in *Imitation of Life* before her and Carter just after, she has already lived a life of hard graft and selflessness. It is, instead, all those around the terminally ill black character who are bettered and redeemed through her influence and, more precisely, through her endless sacrifice. Interestingly, though Georgia is characterised as both passionate and sexualised, and *Last Holiday* is a romantic comedy, she remains chaste and her man mostly absent throughout. Sensual delight and carnal pleasure are indulged in the movie but through food and cooking, more than innuendo, and explicitly not through sex.[12]

Where the saintliness of the dying black character requires desexualisation, the white characters' diagnosis can incorporate romance. Indeed, their romantic attachment usually works to foment their beauty or allure, self-acceptance and enhanced worth. This is not the same as the 'pulling through pity' principle employed in *50/50* (Jonathan Levine, 2011) where Adam (Joseph Gordon-Levitt) is convinced by his best friend that he can get the girls by dropping his having cancer into conversation. Rather, Judy in *Dark Victory*, Robin in *Boys*, Anne in *My Life Without Me* and George in *Life is a House* will have a partner post-prognosis whether or not their lover knows of their illness. Key here is heterosexuality, however. When the terminally ill character is gay – and there was a slew of films about AIDS in the 1990s, especially – passion is untenable. Indeed, mainstream cinema's relationship to gay men dying of AIDS has been one of acceptance and redemption via various forms of sanitisation. This was best illustrated in *Philadelphia*'s humanising of the homosexual and AIDS but foretold in films such as *Longtime Companion* (Norman René, 1989) and *Peter's Friends* (Kenneth Branagh, 1992), all of which occluded sexualised displays of gay intimacy. In contrast, the emerging New Queer Cinema of the early 1990s and such films as *The Living End* (Gregg Araki, 1992), *Zero Patience* (John Greyson, 1993) and *Swoon* (Tom Kalin, 1992) kept passion centre-frame as they defiantly entangled homosexual desire and death. Helmed by gay and lesbian directors, such authorial identity, however, is no guarantee of radicalism here or elsewhere, or of normativity in any or every form.[13]

The terms of triumph and betterment in the terminal illness film are also, then, heteronormative. Returning to our straight white woman swooning into sainthood, it must be remembered that the premise or promise of children inherent in her journey not only shores up her worth as martyr/mater but also instates a compulsory normativity. The futurism of the terminal illness film is a reproductive futurism in which, as Lee Edelman argues, 'the Child [is] the emblem of futurity's unquestioned value'.[14] This is normativity rather than heteronormativity or heterosexuality because the emphasis upon children as our future, upon their redemptive power, is not simply a straight thing or bound to personal procreation. Reproductive futurism is enlisted for gay characters or settings, too, at least in mainstream film. This is epitomised by the ending of *Philadelphia*, as I mentioned in the last chapter, which rescues Andy fully through its emphasis upon children but underlies other liberalist visions that bring gay parenting into the frame, such as *The Object of My Affection*

(Nicholas Hytner, 1998) and *The Next Best Thing* (John Schlesinger, 2000).[15]

The humanisation, rather than glorification, characterising gay characters' dying in these 1990s mainstream terminal illness films squares with the tolerance project and 'AIDS activism-lite' of post-Reagan America but also with gay accession to various rights following their entry into the grand narratives of modernity post-Stonewall: love, death, marriage, family.[16] This humanisation, however, involves the depiction of suffering as physically and medically wrought in a manner uncommon to the largely pain-free declines elsewhere. Andy Beckett's (Tom Hanks) progressing frailty in *Philadelphia*, his breathing difficulties and diminishing faculties, contrast sharply with the extraordinary capacity, vitality even, of his straight counterparts' demise. This is not just a question of the distortion of illness for the fictions of film – as Talha Burki asks of *The Bucket List* in the *Lancet Oncology*: 'what cancer is it they're suffering from?'[17] – but of the identity-determined relationship of suffering and frailty to redemption and salvation. This relationship is prestructured, dependent on a grammar of dying moulded by race but also sexuality, and I'll return to this below. It also should be noted, though I can't pursue this here, that it speaks to a longer cultural history of pain: its secularised, then medicalised, trajectory since the eighteenth century. Signifying punishment or later reward, and then the efficacy of medicine itself, pain, as Steven Bruhm clarifies, 'can never be understood outside its culture' or, as K. D. Craig suggests, as totally outside '[e]thnocultural differences'.[18]

The mapping of identity-inflected worth on to dying operates far beyond the terminal illness film. In the basic universe of mainstream cinema bad characters die. But bad is, of course, a loaded term. Women who, for example, are sexually assertive, unduly powerful or independent, get their comeuppance and lavishly so in, say, film noir or classic horror films. The femme fatale of the 1940s and 1950s, in films like *Double Indemnity* (Billy Wilder, 1944), *The Killers* (Robert Siodmak, 1946) or *Out of the Past* (Jacques Tournier, 1947), fell victim to her own ambitions and phallic appropriation. In more contemporary versions of the 'genre' – the erotic thriller of the home entertainment era – this conclusion was not always guaranteed. In *Basic Instinct* (Paul Verhoeven, 1992), *The Last Seduction* (John Dahl, 1994) and *Bound* (Andy and Gary Wachowski, 1996), say, a new breed of femme fatale could get away with it. The appeal of the threat that she represented to the viewers, now at full titillating tilt, outshone the need to punish her. The privatisation of the pleasures offered by the video cassette recorder expanded the caveats of the moral universe and made this open ending more than OK.

Women who 'actually' kill in mainstream cinema, rather, that is, than being prime suspects or grooming men to murder for them, are always pathologised as perverse. Indeed, the evil of woman is invariably sexualised: the noir world merges female sexuality with fatal consequence. Where their very irresistibility caused the poor fools who loved them to do the deed, in the later films, sex itself could kill. Sharon Stone's Catherine Trammell in *Basic Instinct* stabs her lover during 'love-making': sleeping with Madonna is so overexciting in *Body of Evidence* (Uli Edel, 1992) that Rebecca Carlson's lover has a fatal heart attack. Even when women kill dutifully, for just cause or altruism, they remain sexualised in their goodness. There's no more perfect symbol of this than the hypersexualised Lara Croft but there are other examples.[19]

Perversity has an overdetermined relationship to murder in mainstream film. There is a direct link between excessive or inappropriate sexualisation and murder and death. That *Basic Instinct*'s Catherine is bisexual and *Body of Evidence*'s Rebecca is into sadomasochism should come as no surprise. Where the former is recuperable (through heterosexual coupling) and Catherine survives, the latter isn't. When we turn to homosexuality itself, there was no reprieve, not least historically. Screenwriter Arthur Laurents, speaking of classical Hollywood, put it thus: 'If you're a woman who commits adultery you're only put out in the storm. If you're a woman who has another woman, you better go hang yourself. It's a question of degree. And certainly if you're gay, you have to do real penance – die.'[20]

Homosexuality was punished repeatedly and lavishly by Hollywood. Time and time again the gay or lesbian character gets killed off by the film's conclusion, either murdered or subject to some freak and nasty accident. Vito Russo's 'necrology' at the back of his American history of gay film makes this case well, of the inevitable demise of the gay character.[21] Suicide often serves as the necessary penalty for deviance. As distinguished in Chapter 2, this kind of dishonourable suicide is a popular trope of punitive cinema, and a result of cowardice and admission of wrongdoing, laden with a broader ideology of punishment. When Martha (Shirley MacLaine) hangs herself at the end of *The Children's Hour* (William Wyler, 1961) it is the inevitable product of her admission of guilt, of her confession of lesbian tendencies. We don't see her take her own life nor do we see her dead body. In fact, her body remains 'moving': Karen (Audrey Hepburn) breaks down upon finding it but, more than this, the shadow, which is all we are shown, sways. This fosters a certain ambiguity surrounding her guilt. It is also indicative of the shifts within American society in the late 1950s and 1960s to think of homosexuality as a source of pity rather than simply punishment, and of the relaxation of the production code which allowed homosexuality to enter cinema, albeit in whispers. At the same time, the pretty young Hollywood actress is a far cry from Rod Steiger's violently repressed character who commits suicide in *The Sergeant* (John Flynn, 1968).

Homosexuality remained shorthand for villainy. Its binding to criminality and to death underpinned the depiction of murderers too. Even in the post-Stonewall love-in of the 1970s, perversity met excessive punishment. Lacking any ambiguity in terms of its castigation of evil, the 'transvestite' criminal in *Freebie and the Bean* (Richard Rush, 1974) gets what 'he' has coming in an overwhelming recovery of order. Detective Freebie (James Caan) in pursuit is doubly disarmed both by having to enter the Ladies and having lost his gun by the high-kick of the stiletto-wielding transvestite (Christopher Morley). 'The transvestite', as he was billed in the cast list, has the upper hand and makes light work of repeatedly kicking the hero to the ground until knocked off balance. Freebie regains his gun and shoots, and shoots and shoots. The repeated shots kill the transvestite swiftly but keep reanimating his body: an antigravitational frenzy of the visible, an orgasmic dance of death as not only punishment but also entertainment. The ease, and relish, with which Hollywood equated homosexuality with criminality and murder is, by now, well known.[22] From the 'child' killers of Hitchcock's *Rope* (1948) to the serial killer of *Cruising* (William Friedkin, 1980) to the lesbian-couples-who-kill of the mid-1990s, the sexually perverse character makes the ideal and even photogenic psychopath.[23]

When we turn to race, things are familiar but different. The criminalisation of ethnic or national otherness in Hollywood cinema has been well stated and historically and ahistorically contextualised. Disney's duplicitous 'orientals', for example, or 1980s, and only 1980s, action cinema's predilection for Russian baddies join with the Arab villains of *True Lies* (James Cameron, 1994) or *The Siege* (Edward Zwick, 1998), who disappear post-9/11, in one span of this criminalisation.[24] In terms of African American imagery, there is something more complicated going on. In many ways, Hollywood, or better still 'white Hollywood' – where its assumed racial consciousness does not go without saying – has spent the last century trying to cast off its racist history and its primal scene of Gus's death in *Birth of a Nation* (D. W. Griffith, 1915).[25] For Clyde Taylor, this film and its interpretation entrenched 'the passive racism of film studies'.[26] Racial stereotype is rife in the depiction of African Americans in Hollywood, albeit precisely not as murderers.[27] Indeed, there is a dearth of imagery of black murderers until we get to Blaxploitation and then the so-called new black wave of the 1990s where we find a more stereotypical embrace of crime and homicide.

There is, then, a particular relationship between dying and African American identity in Hollywood. This can be understood in three interrelated ways: through stereotype; through violent reality; and through symbolism. The first two ways have been much discussed within film studies, and I don't want to add to this discussion here. Stereotypes abound that connect and constrain African Americans to various (less) threatening states of inferiority. But, in the black-authored hood film of the 1990s, a 'truth' of black death, of the life expectancy and perils facing African American youth in inner-city 'ghettos', was confronted. In response to these hood films, and their success, bell hooks declared that 'sorrowful black death is not a hot ticket'.[28] She was responding to the glamorisation of violence in these films and to the racial politics of melodrama more broadly but pointing, ultimately, to the lack of tears and time given to black characters' deaths even by African American film-makers. This sense of the cheapness, or 'dead meat', of black life will resonate in what follows.[29] There are occasions, however, and an increasing number, where the tragedy of black death and dying appears to be reckoned with, to be given its due. It is here that the symbolism of African American death and dying is most explicit but also that it becomes very much a hot ticket. It is to the 'popularity' and symbolism of black dying that I now turn, and to two films that represent what could be seen as high points in Hollywood's anti-racism.

The Grammar of Dying I:
White Redemption and Black Death

While firmly located in the tradition of Hollywood's terminal illness genre, Rob Reiner's *The Bucket List* (2007) seems to break with it in one striking way: the character who dies is neither young nor beautiful nor white. As will become clear below, however, this film remains characterised by white triumph and (normative) futurism. More than this, and despite its comedic commitments, I'll argue that it offers a profound statement on the intertwining of Hollywood, American culture and racial politics, one that is both rooted in and potentised by death.

The film combines many of the existing tropes of the terminal illness film in a seemingly unusual set-up. Two men, advanced in years, are diagnosed with potentially terminal cancer. One is white, the other black, and they meet in the room they share in hospital, a hospital that the white man owns. Reminding us that the terminal illness film is frequently a buddy film and that the buddy film is a form of romance (*Beaches, Hilary and Jackie, Boys on the Side*), and often an interracial one, *Bucket List* follows the developing relationship between Edward (Jack Nicolson) and Carter (Morgan Freeman). Both men find themselves, though to different extents, through their illnesses and especially through their bond. What is more, as in *Last Holiday*, *My life without Me*, and even *Ikuru*, dying affords working-class, and in many ways previously constrained, protagonists the opportunity and drive to do something important in what's left of their lives. Here, the 'bucket list' is a list of things to achieve or dreams to realise before death, before 'kicking the bucket'.[30] Funded by Edward's millions, the two men work their way through a list of adventures and experiences from skydiving to visiting the pyramids. Where Edward's financial benevolence will serve Carter well, it is the latter's spiritual benevolence that will save Edward.

Carter will learn from his experiences and be restored to his role as good husband and father. He'll feel alive again, albeit briefly, and reconcile himself to his dreams, his choices and, ultimately, his death. As with other dearly departing African American characters, however, namely Annie in *Imitation of Life* and Georgia in *Last Holiday*, Carter does not need to be saved through dying, he is already a good egg, ever enhanced through contrast to Edward's decadence. Instead, it is Edward who truly discovers and betters himself through his friend's dying. Carter sets a less selfish example for Edward and pushes him to reconnect with his daughter. Ultimately, the black man's suffering and death save the white man, not just from his sins but also from the clutches of death itself. Edward survives against the odds of his illness, though not against that of his race or class, and lives many years more.

White redemption through black suffering and death is an old but oft-unspoken story and one that has a particular relationship to visual culture in the United States. Crudely put, there are two sides to it. On one side is the annihilatory ousting of black 'evil' in racist culture epitomised by Griffith's *Birth of a Nation* (1915) and the 'traffic in lynching photographs that [ran] parallel to the history of American photography's democratization at the turn of the nineteenth century'.[31] In these, the white race is saved through destroying the black threat. This 'side' extends to the ongoing stereotyping, narrative containment or simple making invisible of African Americans, as well as of other others. On the alternate side, is the anti-racist outcry at, and use of, such images to garner support for, say, anti-lynching, social reform, and civil rights movements. In these cases, activist whites were freed from the crimes of bigotry through a different kind of witnessing of these spectacles.[32] This side or form of redemption extends to the anti- or post-racist representation of African Americans in contemporary Hollywood as enablers of white fulfilment or salvation.

Bucket List reveals, and even revels in, this latter category. Where Robert Ebert's review of the film was conscious of its racial politics, it was alive only to some of it: 'I'm thinking, just once, couldn't a movie open with the voiceover telling us what a great guy the Morgan Freeman character is?' instead of 'extolling the saintly virtues of a white person who deserves our reverence'.[33] *Bucket List* binds it, metatextually and cinephilically, to American history. *Bucket List*'s repetition of cultural mores about race, however, is very telling not only of its centrality to Hollywood narratives but also of the place of film in this per se.

Carter's is an earthly goodness – we'll first meet him, oily fingered and overalled, under the bonnet of a car – yet his spiritual proportions are both inevitable and pre-existing. The saintliness of his demise is imbued with the familiarly holy rhetoric of the terminal illness film but triumph, betterment, and futurism are not for him. When Carter dies at the end of the film, his voice-over kicks in and confirms both his death and his goodly/godly self through this symptom of an afterlife. But this voice-over honours the virtue of Edward and reveals Carter's sole, indeed soul, purpose as redeeming his white friend. Though the voice-over will bridge the array of final scenes, including Edward's eulogy at Carter's funeral, the image is subordinated to the pre-eminence, the other-worldly authority, of the voice from beyond the grave, a voice so resonant with deific import that Edward's is a mere point of plot. More cynically put, Edward's praising of Carter most effectively heaps praise on himself. As Carter is minimised, removed from real life, Edward is maximised. More than this, that the voice-over repeats precisely the voice-over accompanying the opening scenes, Freeman/Carter's supernatural and redemptive role must be seen as predetermining the film. It is not that that opening voice is now revealed as owned by Carter – it was always recognisable as Freeman – but that it is revealed as having been dead or magical all along. In this way, white redemption was always already guaranteed by black death.

Various writers have identified the noble or 'magical negro' as a stock character within 'progressive anti-racist' contemporary cinema from *Ghost* (Jerry Zucker, 1990) to the *Green Mile* (Frank Darabont, 1999).[34] Such a character, as Michael Hughey has more recently summarised, is often

> a lower class, uneducated black person who posseses [*sic*] supernatural or magical powers. These powers are used to save and transform disheveled, uncultured, lost, or broken whites (almost exclusively white men) into competent, successful, and content people within the context of the American myth of redemption and salvation.[35]

The recent international hit, *Intouchables* (Oliver Nakache and Eric Toledano, 2011), repeats this very formula.[36] Though in Carter's 'earthliness', *Bucket List* is somewhat different from the films Hughey looks at (which include Morgan Freeman's star turn as God in *Bruce Almighty* and *Evan Almighty*) it is similarly characterised by 'colour-blindness'. For like them, Reiner's film poses as post-racist, as beyond such debates or concerns, and like them and '[n]ot ironically, this form of color-blind racism still transmits the ideology of white supremacy and normativity, but in a subtle, symbolic, and polite way'.[37] In *Bucket List* this transmission, this faux and normativised colour-blindness, is especially potent through precisely its cinephilic and deathly coordinates.

Cerise Glenn and Landra Cunningham in their discussion of the trend of 'magical negro' films, distinguished between those where benefits were felt by the black as well as the white character and those where they weren't; where the utter imbalance in rewards is self-evident.[38] *Green Mile* epitomises this latter scenario yet *Bucket List*, I would suggest, is not so far away. Not only because it offers such a clear case of the 'Master's House' – *Green Mile*'s state penitentiary is replaced by Edward's ownership of the hospital in *Bucket List* – but also because of the film's deathly coordinates. (Indeed, one could think of *Bucket List* as *Green Mile* meets *Grumpy Old Men* [Donald Petrie, 1993].) The stakes are the same: dead man walking is replaced with dead–already man dying. The 'magical negro' film is not just about stereotype and the history of racism but about the deathly dynamic between race and representation as played out by Hollywood.[39] This couldn't be clearer in *Bucket List* in which the terminal illness formula lends itself to this far more common story.

Bucket List, then, like so many other films, makes clear a prestructure, or ontology, of dying which needs the black man to die to save the white man. This is not the salving of the white man's conscience, the redemption of the Western spectator as we saw in Chapter 3 – the more 'advanced', internationalised and post-9/11 version of the 'anti-racist' narrative – but, in some ways, its back story, something more integral, more primary, to American history, and to cinema itself.

Bucket List is not metacinematic; it does not reveal the technology of its own manufacture or constructedness of experience, as *My Life* does. It is, however, beset with a cinematic, or rather cinephilic, self-consciousness. Its inter- and paratextual allusions to Hollywood work similarly to aggrandise the medium and naturalise its fictions as truth. It does this in a number of ways. First, it does this through its use of the stars Morgan Freeman and Jack Nicholson. Both play to type, their personas in full flourish: Nicholson as devilish white, Anglo-Saxon, Protestant (WASP) playboy,

Freeman as African American sage. In the familiarity of their roles, and of the actors themselves, old pleasures are guaranteed and renewed. Of course, these two star personas could easily be renamed: Freeman's as magical negro, and Nicholson's as the magical negro's new best friend, the 'bigot with a heart of gold' (BHG), as Christopher Farley calls him.[40] For Farley, the BHG 'offer[s] the possibility of grace to all the bigots in the audience'.[41] Secondly, a cinephilic referentiality is evident in Freeman/Carter's comments, the 'in-jokes' of the film. When he says to Edward that his younger self's bucket list included being the first black president and making a million dollars, we know both of these have been realised by Freeman through Hollywood. He played Tom Beck, the United States president in *Deep Impact* (Mimi Lederer, 1998) and is one of the highest-earning actors.[42] That Freeman's real son (Alfonso Freeman) takes the role of his son in the film furthers this self-consciousness.

In Xan Brooks's review of the film, she remarks how 'Freeman again finds himself installed as the sad-eyed emblem of American integrity' but it is the racial politics underwriting this American integrity that is key here, though the film works hard to hide this.[43] While Freeman's dulcet tones, which launch the film, are familiar and plug us into a metacinematic consciousness, there is more to this American integrity than meets the ear. Not only is Freeman/Carter always already dead at the start of the film but that we do not realise this until the words are repeated at the end underscores the sheer durability, or endless cycle, of black death-bound subjectivity. Carter's particular dead-already-ness feels a long way off from the subaltern/slave's of Chapter 2. Instead, it serves the wonder of cinema itself: its capacious immortality or the supernaturalism of manipulated time. Indeed, the dead-already-ness of the voice-over merges with the grandeur of Hollywood. The film starts in the most cinematic and grandiose of contexts: opening on a soaring shot of the top of mountains and with the words, 'Edward Perriman Cole died in May, it was a Sunday afternoon and there wasn't a cloud in the sky'. We assume the voice is not that of the dead character or of someone who has died. The disembodied voice and sublime location give a God-like quality but also meld this to the deific proportions and properties of cinema. As well as the majesty of the spectacle, those mountains bear a graphic correlation to the 'Paramount pictures' icon – their opening studio credit – thereby weaving such wonder back into the industry itself.[44]

The film makes invisible racial difference even as it elaborates the initial conflict between the two men. Class and character mark the sharp divide between Edward and Carter. Yet, the terms of their conflict are ridden with exactly the racial consciousness that the film wants to ignore.

Edward's arrogant disregard for others has him regularly calling people by whatever name comes to mind. For Carter, and Carter alone, however, this is racialised: he is 'Duke'. He is 'Ray'. Though no demotion exactly, and Freeman might be up there with Ellington and Charles as African American greats, this does reiterate the commonly elided racism of this kind of slippage. And there is also 'Zombie Boy', Edward's first naming of Carter. A mild slap at Carter's more advanced state of illness and treatment perhaps (though it is only Edward we see with symptoms) but the dead-already slave 'boy' is far from 'lite' in this context. For all of Edward's sins – and they are laid out in the film for our perusal – racism is not meant to be one of them. Indeed, as Eduardo Bonilla-Silva puts it, colour-blindness, like its associated slippages, is 'a new racial ideology that has an arsenal of rhetorical tools to avoid the appearance of racism'.[45]

The reproductive futurism in the film is there as Carter's dying causes Edward to reconnect with his daughter and to meet his granddaughter: the generative promise fully evidenced by that last addition of an extra generation. More than this, the emphasis on white children at the expense of black lives, and especially black children's lives, illuminates the full power of the mammy stereotype which, as I'll argue below, is tied to the death, figurative and literal, of black children. In this way, we start to understand the broader ideological weight of reproductive futurism. Lauren Berlant gestures towards it in her remarks on the back cover of Edelman's book. She writes of how culture: 'uses the bribe of futurity to distract us from the ongoing work of social violence and death'.[46] Where Edelman does not reveal the racial coordinates of this, I want, in the next section, to identify and explore fully the dynamic between black death and the white future, between the bribe and its distractions.

The Grammar of Dying II:
Hollywood's Unconscious and Black Progenicide

The foregoing reading of *Bucket List* therefore establishes, one might say, the basic grammar of dying: how black dying and dead-already-ness fuel white redemption but, more than this, perhaps, how Hollywood cinema celebrates itself – its wares and progressiveness – through the repetition, but simultaneous repression, of this grammar. This grammar is most evident in 'progressive' films or, rather, it is in the quest for post-racism that the repetition of this structure, the transmission of racist rhetoric, is most insidious, or where, as Frank Wilderson puts it, the 'Settler/ Master's sinews are most resilient'.[47] There could be no greater claim for the supposed benignity of such post-racist projects, or for the frippery of repression, than that made by comedy.

There is, however, another forum for the grammar lesson. In addition to the faux colour-blindness of (Northern) comedies, like *Ghost*, *Bruce Almighty* and *Evan Almighty*, *Bucket List* and so on, there is the faux equilibrating of Southern dramas like *Green Mile* or *Monster's Ball* or more recently *The Help*.[48] Where the first set assumes a post-racist world, while revealing its implausibility, the second confronts and 'cures' racism head-on, ultimately rendering whites and blacks equal, but only superficially. The price and process are the same: the erasure of black life to guarantee white subjectivity and redemption. The script, however, is different: polite, light-hearted, post-racism is replaced with the explicit return of the repressed. Good death gives way to bad. Set in the South, the 'id of the United States', as Sharon Holland calls it, these dramas make race and racism highly visible in order to move beyond them but, in so doing, they locate the grammar of dying firmly in America's national and historical unconscious.[49] Indeed, they engage that unconscious *so as* to put it to rest, albeit that, as I'll demonstrate below, this involves a further repression.

Of course, and as critical race theorists argue, America's national and historical unconscious is always at stake in the representation of black suffering. For Debra Walker King, 'blackpain' – and so codependent are race and suffering in American culture that for her the words collide – always serves the larger, national, project, as 'a sign representing America's desire for a pain-free existence'.[50] Blackpain is precisely what guarantees white redemption, for it 'defines and cleanses the white nation' which weeps over the wounds of its African American compatriots, wounds which it recognises its responsibility for while consoling itself with one common humanity.[51] The explicitness of these wounds varies, as my two forums for the grammar lesson imply and the analgesics of the Northern comedies make evident. In contrast, the suppurating Southern dramas – with their far more vivid imprint of slavery – provide injuries in need of dressing, for there is, as Aimee Carillo Rowe demonstrates, a lot at stake:

> If the South may be redeemed – that is, distinguished from its white supremacist past – then so may the nation. The cultural work done in this contact zone serves the strategic function of claiming a place for this new white Southern man within multicultural nationalism. The South occupies a particular border zone, as the repository of racism within multicultural America, and as such serves as a productive site for the recuperation of a nation in crisis.[52]

In the *Green Mile*'s death row of the 1930s, the magical negro's function is explicit and overblown; the hulking stereotype, Coffey (Michael Clarke

Duncan), literally absorbs the white characters' pain. Debra King reminds us that 'the black man's magical talent – one he uses to free several white characters of pain, suffering, and disease – makes clear his usefulness to the nation-state'.[53] In more 'liberal' settings, of the 1960s for *The Help* (Tate Taylor, 2011) and 'now' for *Monster's Ball*, the grammar of black suffering, and its promotion of the new white Southerner, proves more complex. Its articulation in these cases negotiates the un/conscious realms in more nuanced ways. Neither magic nor stereotype need be quite so magnified in these films. The latter is certainly, and ceaselessly, present, with the mammy and Jezebel figures central, respectively, to each.[54] The magic, however, shifts in its emphasis from the supernatural antics of the African American character to the sheer wonder of the salvation s/he promises.[55] Though *Monster's Ball* and *The Help*, like *Bucket List*, show both black and white protagonists benefiting from their shared journeys, again and as I'll argue below, this alters the grammar not at all but instead reveals the full weight of its deathly coordinates.

In what follows I explore the erasure of black life within the national and historical un/conscious of *Monster's Ball* and the fallacious fresh start to which the film lays claim. This much-lauded Southern drama achieves its end and accolades via a violent and highly situated version of the grammar of dying. The white man is saved, from himself and his racist past, through a narrative abounding in bad death: state execution, suicide and progenicide, the death of a child. The film is besieged by the South's racial and slave history: in its words ('niggers used to know their place'), deeds (capital punishment/running black kids off white land with a shotgun) and images (the 'coffle' under Southern skies).[56] It will reject them all. Its protagonist, Hank Grotowski (Billy Bob Thornton), will eject his racist father from his home, change his ways and job and give himself over to his interracial relationship with Leticia (Halle Berry). Despite this personal redemption, the coffle of capital punishment remains, of course, not only because the correction system carries on without Hank but also because the iconography, as well as the less fetishised unconscious, of Southern and slave history endures. The film bespeaks a timelessness which its upending of expectations seeks to forestall. In other words, racism might seem to be rejected but the larger picture remains intact. In fact, even on the local level, I'll argue, the 'cure' of recalibration is false: Hank and Leticia's dynamic remains ridden with racialised imbalance. The film's post-racist pursuit of equivalence, its equilibrating, is to be revealed, then, as the ballast keeping the grammar in place. It is the wind beneath its wings rather than that which blows it away.

Still centralising, serving and salving white consciences, and correcting the historical record with compassion, *Monster's Ball*, my focus here, reveals this more advanced, but no less familiar, racial grammar of dying. This grammar is embedded in and fuelled by, but never neutralised through, the film's attempts to level its key characters' experiences: the equilibrating of the film. Equilibrating, as narrative strategy, provides my main discussion here but the film contends with its racist past, with repression and the unconscious, in other ways, which I shall also address. The (pseudo-) disinterest of the camera, for example, will be shown to undercut white authority. Obsessed with patterns, in terms of both narrative and style, I'll illustrate, too, how the film negotiates, consciously and less consciously, the imprint and echoes of the past in striving towards a post-racist future. Finally, tying my discussion back to the holy trinity of cinematic dying, I shall end this chapter by arguing that both the language and grammar of dying, in Hollywood film at least, depend not on the death of the black character alone but on the death of the black child and the future this child promises. In this way, the relationship between dying and difference is given its full progenicidal due.

Equilibration

In *Monster's Ball*, prison guards Hank and Sonny (Heath Ledger) Grotowski assist with the execution of Lawrence Musgrove (Sean Combs). Soon after, Sonny, Hank's son, commits suicide and Hank encounters Leticia (Halle Berry), Lawrence's estranged wife. They begin a relationship, following the death of Tyrell (Coronji Calhoun), Leticia and Lawrence's son, in a hit-and-run. When Leticia meets Buck (Peter Boyle), Hank's racist father, the relationship is tested. Having moved into Hank's house (once Buck has been moved out) Leticia discovers Lawrence's sketches of his prison officers and realises Hank's role in the execution. The film ends with Leticia accepting, choosing not to act on, this disturbing knowledge.

On the surface *Monster's Ball* rescues both its key characters from their difficulties and discontent: (Polish-American) 'white' Hank and (light-skinned/mixed race) 'black' Leticia. Their salvation stretches beyond race and racism and is epitomised by their relationship and the film's happy ending of them sitting together on the porch of their now shared home. Post-racism or colour-blindness doesn't kick-start redemption here but marks its endpoint. The redemptive trajectory depends, instead, on the growing equivalence of Hank and Leticia, and their common journey from entrapment to release and from misery to contentment. This, the film's equilibrating, operates on various levels. It is a journey to union underscored by related and repeated events. Where, at the film's start, Hank and Leticia are polarised, at its end they are side by side. Between, their stories, experiences and desires converge increasingly. They experience Musgrove's execution from opposing camps: Hank runs the procedure at the corrections facility; Leticia and Tyrell wait at home for a last phone call from Lawrence which Hank doesn't permit. They both punish their sons for their weaknesses but, where Hank admits to never loving Sonny, just prior to his suicide, Leticia's grief is palpable. Indeed, her narrative journey will involve an ever-quieter containing of her distress. The deaths of their children in different times and places, draw them together, until their convergence and coupling are complete.

Monster's Ball appears conscious of its racial baggage, specifically of the inevitable association of black subjectivity with pain and death. The execution of Lawrence Musgrove, which preoccupies the first forty minutes of the film, is characterised by ritual and foregone conclusion. 'Just press the button' are Lawrence's last words. Where he had 'gone got himself electrocuted', according to his wife, as if he's performed to spec, so too was overweight Tyrell's, their son's, death in a hit-and-run, somehow inescapable. 'I did not want my baby to be fat like that' Leticia says, 'cos I know, a black man in America, you can't be like that'. In both cases, and not least for Leticia, what happens to the black male was waiting to happen to him. Black subjectivity in *Monster's Ball* is familiarly, but also explicitly, death-bound. Despite this racial, or grammatical, consciousness, however, the film's equilibrating frames Hank with the foregone as well.

Hank's personal interaction with death ritual – in this case his son's burial – is also marked by matter-of-fact-ness. 'I just want to hear the earth hit the coffin' he says in a manner that betrays his coldness but cannot help but echo a resignation to the inevitable. The deaths of both Leticia's and Hank's sons equate their experiences but also produce repeated imagery. Hank will clean Sonny's blood from an armchair at home and Tyrell's from the back seat of his car. Blood is on his furniture, and on his hands, for both: directly, in the case of Sonny whom he bullied, and indirectly, the film suggests, for Tyrell. Yet, where Sonny's suicide couldn't be more domestic, surrounded by his only family and in his front room, Tyrell's couldn't be more public (bar a state execution perhaps). Knocked down on the street, he dies in a stranger's car. The tragic inevitability of Tyrell's death mirrors Sonny's repetition of his mother's fate, his inheritance. Sonny's death is characterised as his predetermined maternal legacy, however, his inexorable repetition of her weakness in committing suicide. His fate is rooted in kinship, personal circumstance and agency or choice, rather than in the natural order of things. The black male's weddedness to death, in contrast, relies upon a far more undifferentiated trope: a history, in particular, Southern slave history. Tyrell's streetside demise, like Lawrence's execution, cannot help but reference lynching, and the endurance and reinscription of the South's 'strange fruit'.[57] For all its pretensions, disruption of this old story seems almost no part of this 'progressive' film's aim.

The continuum of images of murdered, and especially Southern, black men has been well noted. Holland pointed to it thus: 'racial subjuga- tion goes hand in hand with capital punishment in the southern script . . . [It] carries a certain negative history that connects it, in the minds of death penalty abolitionists, to present practices.'[58] This continuum, this long history of racial subjugation's death-bound logic, and its nec- ropolitical place in culture, reached new heights with Hurricane Katrina, and its always-already 'death-world' of southern Louisiana.[59] Wilderson, drawing upon David Marriot's work, finds *Monster's Ball*'s 'lynching' to decompose and dehumanise the slave, yet simultaneously 'the capacity for composition and recomposition of White subjectivity is accomplished by the White body's insertion into, and exchange of, this "grotesque family album" of Black flesh'.[60] We're reminded of the refortification of white subjectivity through the erasure of black life but of other elements too. Firstly, not only do black lives operate as currency, within the (enduring) narrative of slavery, but black deaths as well. (This isn't the same as saying that blacks are always-already slaves/dead, but to see how dying and death function in a particular way even as they confirm the latter. This is, for these purposes, a crucial distinction.) Where lynching photographs circu- lated as both pro- and anti-racist spectacle, *Monster's Ball* speaks similarly to the white appetite for the black dead.[61] Secondly, as *Monster's Ball* and its 'grotesque family album' make most clear, it is the death of the black lineage, of futurity, that is fundamental here.

Monster's Ball in many ways *knows* this continuum, this prehistory or grammar, and aims to intervene into it, to opt out of the prestructuring of black death. The extent, or good intent, of this knowledge is, however, hard to discern as there is always a self-fulfilling edge to it. When we first meet father/grandfather Buck, the eldest now ex-death-row guard, he sits with his macabre scrapbook of executions. We are initiated into this 'grotesque family album' early. Hank passes him the newspaper that tells of Musgrove's fate, Buck cuts out the item and sticks it into the awaiting space. The inevitability of this act, of filling in the gap, completing the awaiting scaffold, does not distance us from the authority of death-bound logic but enforces its predetermination.

The film's equilibrating is grounded in the convergence and levelling of

Figure 5.1 View from the stoop within the title sequence.

Hank and Leticia's lives but it operates less thematically too. It is forged through their paralleled, then shared, experiences but also through a narration preoccupied with repetition, or echo, which instils pattern in order, I'd suggest, to afford its rupture. Not only are words, acts and imagery repeated, but particular styles of shot too. *Monster's Ball* is patterned in narrative, cinematic, and extratextual terms – on conscious and less conscious levels – so that patterns can be shown to be broken.

The film's title sequence shows Hank asleep in bed, a ceiling fan casting a steady and repeated shadow across the frame. The frame splits to reveal a mindscape, his dream perhaps, but also later scenes from the film. The closing image is even contained within it: the view from the porch to the gravestones and through a wagon wheel.

The iconography of the frontier and the homestead, within an American narrative of new beginnings, should not be lost on us but this presaging of the closing scene, though subliminal, recalls the similar strategy in *Bucket List*. Such repetition is, of course, a common narrative device but, here again, it works to foretell and privilege white characters' deaths.[62] We can't appreciate the full, obfuscating weight of this privileging until the end of either film but the cycle, or grammar, starts here. So, too, does the film's investment in blurring conscious and unconscious realms. *Monster's Ball*'s opening images, also, on closer, stilled scrutiny, locate the Grotowski headstones within a semi-made set (not unlike Buck's 'in-progress' scrapbook). As props rather than scene, signifiers rather than sentence, the full fiction, or the lure of fiction at least, is undone. This metacinematic moment, submerged though it is, refuses the authority of the artifice, the surrender to story, despite the seamlessness of what follows.

This betrayal of the bigger picture – of reality beyond the set – is indicative of what we might think of as the film's split or even double conscious-

Figure 5.2 View from the stoop in the closing scene.

ness which is far more apparent, more fully built, elsewhere. *Monster's Ball* always seems to be saying two things at once. It doesn't so much hold these things in tension but says one much louder: one is far more desirable to hear. These two things are best described as its racist and post-racist pretexts. Racism, repressed and otherwise, is reckoned with so that post-racism can be achieved. The film is split between proving and disproving the racial grammar of dying, between the inescapability of racist imbalance and its own equilibrating momentum. It reiterates the death–bound-ness of black subjectivity yet attempts to equalise its protagonists. Racism is revealed as grammatical, as prestructured, and yet overcome: it is insurmountable and yet it is surmounted. This is the 'impossible' project of *Monster's Ball*, and it succeeds in it, ostensibly and Oscar winningly, through the displacement and repression of its protagonists' enduring imbalance. The difficulties between Leticia and Hank are, ultimately, subsumed into the romance narrative. Leticia's final outcry is held back: she silences herself and represses her knowledge of Hank's part in her husband's death. The film is all about the return of the repressed and the return to repression. But the former belongs to the white characters and the latter is all Leticia's. The film starts with Hank dreaming and throwing up, and ends with Leticia's acquiescence. Where she wails and wants, Hank waits. She slaps her thigh laughing and he fidgets uncomfortably and confesses that he doesn't know what to do during their first evening together. Hank exhibits complexity, Leticia immediacy. Where James Berardinelli celebrated the film as 'anti-Hollywood' because it provided 'fully three-dimensional characters',[63] the gaps between the characters, his take and the truth of the film, couldn't be more pronounced.

The film repeats certain shots and, in so doing, grounds its aesthetic in pattern. Scenes are regularly shot from a variety of angles and often include obstructions to seeing. The camera is positioned behind curtains, bars, or windows; it moves from straight-on shots to high angles or cuts away to the distance. It pulls focus to reveal these obstructions, further undercutting the veracity and privilege of what is seen. The camera claims disinterest (which the narrative's patterns shore up, too, in emphasising style or surface). It seems, with its skilful use of screen space, to denounce and decentre the totalising vision of the gaze, the singularity or fixity of perspective. Where the frame may hold racist content, the film-making, even from the first, positions itself against its authority.

The scenes following the title sequence provide a useful example of this. The camera is outside Hank's bedroom window watching him sleep and then inside his room. It takes up a position in the empty hall of his house and, during a fairly long take, observes Hank cross from one room to another. The most interesting and contentious example of this is the film's first sex scene when Leticia, drunk with grief and whiskey, tells Hank she just wants him to make her 'feel good'. The scene interweaves entrapment and release, with subliminal shots of a hand reaching towards a caged bird intercutting the two having sex. Though hard to discern, except in slow motion and repeated viewing, it is Leticia doing the reaching and, presumably, releasing of the caged bird. While the director has suggested his allusion to Maya Angelou's autobiography, *I Know Why the Caged Bird Sings*, the far more resonant connection is to the caged Lawrence.[64] The intertext cannot be Angelou's when the internal and external references to black incarceration are so pervasive. Forster's good intentions are again overwhelmed by the bigger picture's bad faith or, as Melissa Anyiwo suggests: 'Forster is not the victim here; instead he is the unthinking liberal whose prejudices come from centuries of negative imagery internalized by the white male audience of which he is a part.'[65]

Lines, sentiments and actions are repeated in the film. Hank will tell Sonny he's weak like his mother; Buck will say the same to Hank when he resigns from his job. Patterns are revealed in past actions too: the suicide of the wife; the suicide of the son. The most obvious patterning and continuity come from the multiple generations of the Grotowski family who all hold the same job, prostitute, residence and resting place.[66] The film creates and favours these internal or local patterns in the hope of dislodging, or rather displacing, the larger structure. It shifts attention from black to white experience and, in so doing, emphasises the redemption of the latter. It also moves from the historical to the local, from pattern to contingent event, from things being beyond control, inevitable, to being mastered.

Hank is a creature of habit. His trips to the diner, with his favourite seat and same order of chocolate ice cream with a plastic spoon, cannot help but point both to obsessive compulsion and his taste for 'nigger juice' that his father will boast to Leticia must run in the family. When, in the final scene, Leticia shares the ice cream with Hank, progress would seem to have been made, and the racist allusions left behind, or her acquiescence takes on an even more troubling edge. As Wilderson makes clear, the chocolate ice cream is one of many symptoms of the consumptive and differently death-bound stakes of Hank and Leticia's always racialised dynamic. Like 'cunnilingus, sign-gazing, body gazing, strip-searching, head-shaving, electrocution', it is for him one of the film's repeated 'necrophilic acts', what we might think of as repeated spectacles of white appetite for black subjugation.[67] The sexual nature of this appetite is crystal clear in terms of Leticia, as it was in terms of lynching.

Hank's redemption doesn't simply depend upon the erasure of black lives but feeds off them. The film's equilibrating of Hank and Leticia masks this but it remains the case. And, while Leticia will ask Hank to 'make her feel good', the film is dedicated to making Hank (and the audience) feel good, to redeeming them. For Wilderson this is an inherently cannibalistic or vampiric dynamic, grounded in the revitalising of white subjectivity through draining black subjectivity. In contrast, though not in conflict, with this, Rowe speaks of such acts slightly differently. Her feminist reading emphasises the generative capacity of Leticia's flesh:

> Feeling the interior of her dark body (a feeling symbolized in the film through fucking and fellatio) becomes the vehicle for his rebirth. In this sense, the black female body is utilized for its reproductive purpose, in service of the master, in ways that reproduce and rewrite the material conditions of slavery.[68]

In this way, the vomiting of the opening scene foretells (re)birth as well as the return of the repressed. But, what is apposite in this is how it emphasises white rebirth through the black body. Redemption as white reproductive futurism to the exclusion of the black child. Reproductive futurism as *the* happy ending, melodrama's ultimate and only closure, depends on the displacement and erasure of not only black life but, specifically, of black progeny.

This echoful emphasis on legacy is attached to the white experience alone. In striking contrast, the Musgroves are firmly denied legacy, kinship and community. As Kwakiutl Dreher makes clear:

> When Tyrell dies, we would expect the teacher and students from his school to pay respects to their deceased classmate. But the movie grants no traditional venue for

mourning nor is Leticia's house an available space for people from any community to present condolences. There is no community in the film of which Leticia is a part.[69]

Sonny, however, has a funeral: emotionally impoverished though it is, it happens. And Sonny joins the other graves in the garden. Lawrence and Tyrell's dead bodies received and deserved, it seems, no such formality or ritual or acknowledgement.

The broader implications of all these manoeuvres are clear. As Rowe states: 'The redemption of the Southern white man, occasioned through his empathic and sexual connection with a black woman, is metonymic of a form of national redemption disarticulated from state redress – in this case, slave reparations'.[70] Hank's post-racist rebirth involves both relinquishment and making amends but these 'reparations' are kept highly personal: he'll give up his job, his dad, and carrying his shotgun, and he'll provide Leticia with a car, a home and even a business. We move from white redemption as compassion at blackpain to notional reparation for black suffering as neo-liberal action by the individual alone.

The narrative's strategies of equilibration aim to redeem Hank and equalise and, in fact, neutralise difference. As I've suggested, this equilibrating is successful only on a superficial level. The film's unconscious, as it were, makes the perseverance of racialised pattern inevitable. Wilderson speaks of something similar in suggesting that *Monster's Ball*'s 'narrative strategies . . . democratiz[e] the personal pronoun *we*'.[71] The film works to universalise the experience into 'we', to disavow and repress racism. Moreover, '[t]he inspiration of *we* . . . is a form of *suture*. It papers over any contemplation of violence as a structuring matrix – and weds us to the notion of violence as a contingent event'.[72] The shift from the historical to the personal, from state to intimate reparations reiterates this. The notion of the echo is also interesting in this regard. Edward Branigan notes how Jean-Pierre Oudart, in his seminal work on suture, 'uses the sonic metaphor "echo" fourteen times in his essay in order to focus, I believe, on this notion of absence in a single shot ("echo" suggests the intangible, invisible, and perhaps imaginary)'.[73] Suture is the mechanism whereby the spectator retains omnipotence, and echo the technique that keeps that omnipotence resonating.

The main characters' relationships to agency and to death, however, are very different. Where Hank redecorates, Leticia is evicted. Where Hank resigns, Leticia is sacked. Where Sonny commits suicide, Tyrell is (ostensibly) murdered. The porch that is sat upon, the ice cream shared, the patterns repeated are all Hank's.

Despite the levelling of the two characters implicit in the film's final

Figure 5.3 Side by side: a new beginning.

scene, racialised imbalance is sustained: it has been firmly removed from the centre of the frame but remains in its unconscious. Leticia's near-smiling silence, here, represents the ultimate acquiescence to the logic of white redemption, and the film's ultimate repression. This is an enforced acquiescence born of poverty and little choice. She acquiesces into the identity she is given: testimony to Hank's hailing of her and her hailed-ness. That the film ends with compliance and repression suggests that the terms of the 'id' endure. The terms of recovery are continued white ownership and black submission.

At the same time, the two characters' side-by-side-ness masks, or covers over, still-centred Hank, further fetishising interracial union. For Rowe, Hank and Leticia's union 'stand[s] in [metonymically] for color-blind race relations in the U.S., displacing the cultural work of racial healing from history and politics [and] placing it squarely within the realm of interpersonal contact'.[74] This manoeuvre from the state to the home, from racial to domestic politics, from drama to romance, from structure to effect, has been variously described. For Rowe it traces the shift from 'a productive to a narcissistic empathy. The former can provide a kind of racial healing, the latter is too individualistic and tied up in "the logics of liberal cultural pluralism"'.[75] For Wilderson, the shift operates from an 'analytic' to an 'empathetic' film aesthetic, and this is a similarly impoverished function for the film.[76] Empathy, which comes under further fire in the next chapter, is important here in generating necessary feelings and promoting humanity but it keeps things local, individual and contingent again rather than a product of institutions and history.

Finally, though this scene symbolises the (post-racial) 'new beginning' that the narrative has been working towards, it does so through enshrining the imprint of the past and its inheritance. Leticia looks out across the yard from the porch to the gravestones of the Grotowski family: not only is inheritance, and the film's echo-laden emphasis on legacy, the white man's but the haunting presence of history, and of death, remains.

White Futurity = Black Progenicide?

Monster's Ball is a grim film filled with death, the most horrendous deaths, and the whole gamut of them (execution, suicide, 'manslaughter'), and yet is a love story with a happy ending. The charge of this happy ending is the further or reiterated entrenchment of the race crimes of the United States. That this film is about the past, and so cemented in history, is evident not only in the time trap of the South but also because the future is denied: the two main characters lose their children. This does *not* level their experience but further clarifies the 'colour' of futurity. As Kwakiutl Dreher affirms: '*Monster's Ball* initiates a purposeful and egregious marginalization and annihilation. To clear the road for the White male to co-opt the loyalties of Black motherhood the Black child has to be extinguished from his mother's life.'[77]

This extinguishing of the black child is an uncommon symptom of the death-boundness of black identity in cinema. I do not mean that it is infrequent – it is, in fact, rife in figurative, if not literal, terms – but that it deserves singular note not least because it is so overlooked. As I've illustrated in this chapter, the refusal of black futurity is the flipside and fuel of white futurity in Hollywood. In *Bucket List* and *Monster's Ball*, the process of white redemption depends upon the literal or figurative death of black children and emphasis on white kinship and legacy. This dynamic is not restricted, however, to the terminal illness film or Southern melodrama. The erasure of black children underpins the impossibility of black motherhood (and black fatherhood) elsewhere. The 'mammy' is ubiquitous in the enduring visions of black women raising white children, rather than their own, or nurturing them to better lives, all the way from *Gone with the Wind* (Victor Fleming, 1939) to *Girl Interrupted* (James Mangold, 1999). This impossibility underpins the outstanding films – outstanding because of the sheer absence of black mothers elsewhere – of the two adaptations of Fannie Hurst's *Imitation of Life* (John M. Stahl, 1934 and Douglas Sirk, 1959).[78] In these, the saintly black housekeeper mothers both a white and her own child, yet her own child is, tellingly, 'mulatto' – 'concrete evidence of white exploitation' – and spurns her, resulting, it seems, in her death: an impossible family indeed.[79] In this seminal text, the black mother births, and rebirths, only 'white' characters yet again.

Black mothers have made more of an appearance in the last two decades'

films. The compulsory death of a black son, and concomitant pathologisation or demonisation of black mothers and failure of black paternity,
underpinned the black-authored hood film of the early 1990s and perse-
vered, at least figuratively, in its more revisionist fare such as *Set It Off*
(F. Gary Gray, 1996). This genre contrasts with all other films discussed
here, not just in terms of their literal white authorship but also in terms of
Hollywood's rhetorical whiteness too. Much like *Monster's Ball*, the hood
film suggests that 'Black women cannot raise healthy, strong, and self-
sufficient Black men, and that if no father is present, their sons will fail
in life and perhaps even end up dead.'[80] At the same time, black women
remain peripheral, invisible, here as they are in American society more
broadly and in public narratives of urban/gang culture which these films
'modelled'.[81] Though heroic black mothers appear in the same period's
sci-fi flicks, like *Strange Days* (Kathryn Bigelow, 1995), *Star Trek: First
Contact* (Jonathan Frakes, 1996) or *The Matrix* (Wachowski Bros, 1999),
they, too, have been identified ultimately as mammies to white maturation
despite their groundbreaking roles.[82]

It is in the most celebrated or vigorous post- or anti-racist narratives of
contemporary cinema that the dynamic between white futurity and black
progenicide is especially heightened or overdetermined but startlingly
clear nevertheless. In the potentially postcolonial *Children of Men*, West
African Kee is the only fertile woman on Earth. Though stereotypically
carnal, this black mother holds the promise of reproductive generation for
the entire planet. She is, as I argued in Chapter 3, still framed via a whit-
ened tomorrow, not least in terms of the redemption of white hero, Theo,
whose son's name her baby gains. A far more pat post-apocalyptic film
repeats this pronounced 'moving on from' the West's racist history via its
formative state, the transatlantic slave trade. In *2012* (Roland Emmerich,
2009) Africa, the only land above the water, becomes the site for the new
tomorrow where the multiracial populations of the 'Arks' that escaped the
flood will go forth and multiply. It is perhaps little surprise that science
fiction as a concept should prove most actively progressive, with all the
caveats that this term has been shown to entail.[83] Back with the Southern
melodrama, nothing much has changed. Regardless of the emotive and
corrective efforts of the recent award-winning film, *The Help*, black progenicide, the compulsory erasure of the black child, lies again and as ever
beneath white salvation.

The road to equivalence, to post-racism, isn't peppered with potholes
but impossibility. It is a cul-de-sac posturing as a motorway, littered
with the bodies of mammies' and magical negroes' dead children. These
children are literally dead, as in *Monster's Ball* and *The Help*, and/or

figuratively dead as in every film – and the list is long – in which black characters nurture white children (or the childlike) at the expense of having, or being with, their own.

Debra King has contended that 'when the representation of the black body is too closely tied to a history of terror, suffering, torture, and national woundedness, it cannot break free'.[84] I've argued here that the representation of the black body is always too closely tied to this history, even when blackpain is repressed or displaced or soothed on-screen. Extending Wilderson's tighter focus, I've suggested that one doesn't have to look only to melodramas of race, but to comedies and beyond, to unearth this logic. While he argued, and so persuasively, for how white identity 'exists ontologically as a position of life in relation to the Black or Slave position, [as] one of death',[85] I've wanted, through examining dying, death-bounded-ness *and* futurity in mainstream film, to tease out yet further complexities of this dynamic and the grammar it determines.

In this chapter we have seen how the cinematic language of death and dying is gendered, racialised, normative. The identity-determined relationship of suffering and frailty to redemption and salvation is pre-structured. It is, in other words, dependent on a grammar of dying that precedes and predetermines it. The racial coordinates of this grammar prove the richest dialect in Hollywood: the most unconsciously unalterable despite seemingly dramatic shifts in social history. The mortal economies of Part I, then, combine here with the ideological grammar of dying, especially the death-boundness of black characters, to cohere the necropolitics of mainstream film. In the next chapter we shall consider how the medium might resist.

CHAPTER 6

Watching Others Die:
Spectatorship, Vulnerability
and the Ethics of Being Moved

I launched this second section of the book with the notion, adapted from Elaine Scarry's work, that dying was both inexpressible and unshareable. The framework which this afforded allowed us to review the problem of representing dying within mainstream film culture where it was expressed, albeit distortedly. In the last two chapters I have shown that there is a cinematic language of dying. It is rich and multifaceted but heavily censored nevertheless. It suppresses, still, the banality and brutality of bodily decline to promote the sociocultural and positivist fantasies of late capitalist culture. Such normative fantasies, which cohere in the 'triumph, betterment and futurity' of Hollywood's terminally ill as well as in the not-so-good deaths of others, are hooked, unsurprisingly, on identity politics. As the full ideological weight of these fantasies became clear, their grammar of dying was revealed as fundamentally race bound. Dying is not inexpressible in cinema, then, but the language film forges for it is partial and partisan, and the grammar predetermining it necropolitical.

In this chapter, I move on to the question of the unshareability of dying, of its place as a profoundly personal experience that cannot be communicated to, and shared in by, others. For Scarry, inexpressibility and unshareability were mutually dependent: the inadequacy of language, choked back through pain, through stilted and stifled communication, kept the experience of dying inside, interiorised. If there is a cinematic language for dying – and I hope, at least, that I have shown that there is – if dying is exteriorised within and through this medium, then it follows that film also allows pain and dying to be shared in, on- and off-screen. Given the importance of the affective register to film – how it is a *moving image*, it emotes, is emotive – spectatorship could be thought of as symbolising shareability itself. This is not to switch attention to the affectivity of film or the primacy of the audience – as I discussed in the book's introduction, these shed scant light on my thesis – but to stress the busyness, and with it the agency, of spectatorship, its psychic, contemplative and visceral activity, even within the constrained vocabulary of mainstream film. Just as the cinematic language of dying sustained taboo, and a limited and prejudicial, vocabulary, so its shareability will need to be defined and qualified, as well. Film might be, as Alison Landsberg argued, 'a technology that could generate empathy', but how does it use it?[1] Is empathy enough, as a term and as an experience, to describe the spectator's response to others' suffering, or to bridge the fraught, and constantly reinforced, distances separating the healthy and the frail, those in ascendancy and those in decline, those watching as others die? And what would, or should, this bridge afford or enable? In turning to the question of spectatorship, to the moving image of dying, this chapter explores how film conveys the experience of dying to allow it to be shared in. The emphasis here is on this sense of a *shared* experience, on a relationship between subjects on- and off-screen. What sharing means or could mean will be explored as we reconcile the imbalances – and prescriptiveness – inherent in this relationship to reckon with the necessarily ethical questions surrounding our involvement in others' deaths.

The 'use' of the feelings generated through fiction film's various dealings with death – their productivity for, or foreclosure of, thought or self-consciousness – has been a recurring, if submerged, theme in this book already as I navigated a range of affecting texts for other ends. In these representations of self-endangerment or dying, we saw how sentiment is managed, indeed, finely orchestrated, in the service of the status quo. It was only outside Hollywood, in the resistant aesthetics and relative blankness of *Paradise Now*, that an ethically empathic, rather than prescriptively emotive, spectatorship was gestured towards, even if this spoke more to the truth of subalternism than suicide. Such a spectatorship seemed possible, too, within a post-9/11 sensibility detected in the Hollywood films explored in Chapter 3. But a wider problem of ethical film criticism emerged there. The outrage and empathy generated in and through *Hotel Rwanda* suggested a wrestling with complicity and responsibility but, in its repetition of colonialist and absolutory goals, it might instead be deemed unethical. The problem is with the 'i' or rather 'I' at the centre of ethical: the relentless, the always eventual, return to the same old story, that is, to the priorities and psyche of the Western spectator. This problem isn't strictly what Lilie Chouliaraki calls 'the narcissistic emotion of modern humanism', the caring only for people like us, but a more invidious and no less common version of it: the solipsistic unconscious of modern humanism which cares for those not like us in order, ultimately, to salve or save our souls.[2] This unconscious finds a natural home in Hollywood. Unease with the ethical, a wariness of this unconscious thrall, footnote what follows as they have what's gone before.

If mainstream fiction film disavows, distorts and displaces dying, and if, in doing so, it confirms the values, salves the conscious and the death fear of the spectator, this chapter seeks an alternative. It does this not to slight Hollywood further but to understand more fully what is at stake, and what is possible, in our encounter with dying on screen. With the shifting landscape of film cultures, the ever spreading mediatisation of human suffering, and the remarkable motivational potential of the moving image as evidenced by YouTube's *Kony 2012* – this seems an especially timely pursuit. In seeking this alternative, I focus on films that, rather than turn away from death, rather than deny, deform or degrade its realities, turn towards dying, real dying, and dwell there. This excludes therefore the shockumentaries or mondo films with their 'real' footage of dead people or dying. These attest to the appetite for watching death, an appetite taken to extremes in snuff and, more recently, 'reaction videos'.[3] While mondo has been variously celebrated in its subversion or even profundity my emphasis on the mainstream and, more specifically, on the banal preclude them from study here.[4]

A small group of documentaries of real dying forms the bedrock of my enquiry instead: *Dying* (Michael Roemer, 1976); *Near Death* (Frederick Wiseman, 1989); *Dying at Grace* (Allan King, 2003); *Silverlake Life: The View from Here* (Peter Friedman and Tom Joslin, 2003); and *How to Die in Oregon* (Peter Richardson, 2011). These are not mainstream fiction films and they are not Hollywood products. In the age of 'docu-auteurs' and the documentary as 'global commodity', this doesn't go without saying.[5] They are not marginal films either. Many of them have won awards, are made by directors of note and have been viewed widely, whether at festivals or on television.[6] Neither is this a complete list. The last decade has seen a major surge in the production of made-for-television documentaries on end-of-life issues that centre on dying and even show it.[7] Directly linked to current debates, and legal moves, surrounding assisted dying in the West, this surge sits within a more pronounced addressing of mortality and death practices in the public sphere. This address is a result of AIDS perhaps, and shifts in visual culture, but certainly of demographic changes: extended life expectancy and the social and financial crises attending the expanding aged population.

Though these films are non-fiction, they are not devoid of drama or theatricality or fantasy. At the same time, on the fringes of this group is a number of avant-garde feature films that chronicle real dying even as they employ markedly aesthetic registers to do so. *Lightning Over Water* (Wim Wenders, 1980) and *Blue* (Derek Jarman, 1993) are especially interesting in their blurring of autobiography, biography and fiction.[8] Theirs is not the 'creative treatment of actuality'[9] so much as the 'truth of art'. Indeed, each has been distinguished for its ethical or filmic intervention.[10] We might also note the very occasional fiction film – outside the confines of Hollywood, of course – that provides the highly realistic portrayal of death, even if simulated. Maurice Pialat's *La guelle ouverte* (1974) stands out in its commitment to the bodily and boring detail of dying, as does Mike Nichol's television film *Wit* (2001) in its depiction of the brutalities of hospitalisation. Rather than polarise fiction and non-fiction film here, I am, in the spirit of documentary theory, recognising their 'tangled reciprocity'.[11] I do so not simply to nod to this key genre debate, or to a postmodern fuzziness of category itself, but to locate and reconsider this tangle within each film in its thorny negotiation of 'truth' and fantasy and ethics. Fiction or fictionalisation, here, becomes not a question of simulated or non-simulated death, of ordinary or special effects, but of the ruses and reassurances attending them. Indeed, the mythic or palliative proportions of film pay little attention to genre or industrial divides; a continuum exists instead.

Vivian Sobchack, in her seminal essay on the ethics of filming death, drew parallels between fiction and non-fiction films' evasion of it.[12] Sarah Cooper and Libby Saxton, however, both writing within the recent turn to ethical film criticism, found that each format's treatment of trauma or pain is capable of generating ethical insight and implicatedness.[13] Similarly, Benjamin Noys makes a powerful case for even fiction film's profound exposure of death.[14] In a different vein, Roemer's *Dying* was harshly criticised for repeating fiction films' softening of death in, among other things, its 'sense of tact and good taste in dealing with a taboo subject'.[15] Similarly, the real dying documentaries have also been found to follow redemptive trajectories. Janet Maslin's review of *Near Death* suggested how the difficulty of its issues led to a calmer resolution.[16] King's film has been spoken of in similar terms. Michael Koresky remarked that 'the overall feeling becomes one of tranquillity, even elation', and even likened the journey to Kübler-Ross's model.[17] Geoff Pevere saw *Dying at Grace* ultimately as 'an embrace of life'.[18] The extent to which this sweetened slant on the journey reflects the narrative or the spectator's needs, or minimises the film's potency, will be attended to later where I'll propose a different context for such positivity. Meanwhile, my point here is to argue against the polarity of fiction and non-fiction – 'as if only real things are meaningful' – and for a continuum of spectatorship.[19] It is also to note the spectre of the heroism, grandeur or ineffability of confronting death: how it is often conceived as a virtuous or spiritual, but certainly intense, experience for the film-maker and audience and, as Noys reminds us, even the critic.[20] Sam Adams writes that 'How to Die can be tough to watch, but when it's over, you feel privileged to have taken part,'[21] and Dying at Grace has been considered 'transcendent'.[22] It is precisely this profundity that I am pursuing in this chapter but not without suspicion of the consolation or self-commendation that rhapsodising can herald.

From this collection of documentaries I focus on Allan King's penultimate film Dying at Grace – '[p]ossibly the definitive film on death'[23] – and for a set of what I hope are engaging reasons. Not only does it operate as a counterpoint to both Hollywood and to direct cinema, but it offers an extraordinary commentary on the capacity of film to represent dying, to express it and to share it, and to do so ethically, that is, with an eye or, better still, an ear to the experience of dying and to our (deprivileged) part in its lesson. I have also fixed upon King because of the sheer lack of scholarly attention that his films have been given: redressing this grants this study broader purpose too.

Dying at Grace is one of the five 'actuality dramas' directed by King. A hugely important Canadian film-maker, King is relatively unknown within international film, and film studies, arenas. He has been variously acclaimed, however. Jean Renoir called him 'one of the greatest film artists working today'.[24] John Grierson was an admirer of his work, and his first full-length documentary, Warrendale (1967), has been considered 'revolutionary'.[25] His films won numerous awards and, in his long and productive career, he headed the Directors Guild of Canada and received its Lifetime Achievement Award in 2006.[26]

There are various causes of King's obscurity. Foremost might be that his work and cares were so fixed on the individual, on the local, and on the Canadian. Beyond the familiar marginalisation of Canada within a North American imaginary, and King's 'gentle regional self-awareness',[27] it is clear that his priorities didn't lie with the mainstream film industry or international stage. Indeed, much of his work was made for, and funded by, Canadian television, and received limited alternative distribution.[28] He was always open about his divergence from the aesthetic investments of Hollywood:

> There's a whole body of work that's just pure entertainment, a spectacle, and the Americans are extremely good at it, so I don't know if we should be trying to compete. We've got great Canadian stories – human, personal stories that enlighten viewers about the experience of an individual rather than the experience of an explosive device.[29]

Yet he can also be distinguished from his 'direct cinema' peers. Dennis Lim, who called King 'cinéma vérité's forgotten man', remarked that 'he gravitated to harsher subjects than his American colleagues'.[30] For Michael Koresky, his films 'stand out from the field for their sheer sense of drama'.[31] Firmly rooted in this documentary movement, King's observational style resulted in films with much in common with his socially conscious contemporaries elsewhere. Frederick Wiseman, in particular, made a number of films that, like King's, went inside institutions and used an observational style to record the raw and often unsettling activities therein. *Titicut Follies* (1967), which took place in a mental institution in Massachusetts, was prohibited from exhibition to a general audience for twenty-four years. As Alan Rosenthal notes: '[t]he truths that Wiseman reveals are not always pleasant, and he has thus had to spend a considerable time in court fighting against censorship and for freedom of distribution'.[32] King was, similarly, a controversial figure. Despite being commissioned by CBC, the Canadian Broadcasting Corporation, *Warrendale* was banned for its bad language and wouldn't air on television for thirty-one years. What is more, his methods in *Who's in Charge* (1983) caused an ethics-oriented uproar within the Canadian film community.[33]

The greatest parallel, and distinction, to be drawn between Wiseman and King come with their observational documentaries on dying. Wiseman's *Near Death* is a six-hour epic set in a hospital's intensive-care unit. *Dying at Grace* is far more accessible and commercial. It is feature length and was funded by, and screened on, TVOntario. Though some might disagree that Wiseman's films are anything other than non-aligned, Seth Feldman has argued that, unlike his films on similar subjects, 'there is no case being made, no heroes or villains' in King's work.[34] Adam Nayman, in a similar vein, notes that 'King's films are indeed rife with stolen moments, and yet one never feels (as one sometimes does with Wiseman) that anything is being taken away from the people on screen'.[35] In what follows, I will illustrate how King's non-polemical, non-egoic and non-diminishing treatment of dying, and of spectatorship, distinguishes *Dying at Grace* from his peers and from Hollywood and explore what this distinction indicates for our understanding of the watchability and shareability of dying on film.

Against 3D: Un/Special Effects and Intensive Care

Where denial, distortion and displacement characterised the representation of dying in mainstream fiction film, the opposite is true of *Dying at Grace*. Instead, King provides an unflinching and metaphor-free record of five people's final days at Toronto Grace Health Center. His commitment is to the individual's experience. He captures rather than tames death. His style is confrontal: it faces head-on and up to its topic. This confrontation will prove neither frontal nor solipsistic, in Levinasian terms, nor heroic in its impulse or promise. Instead, it will be shown to provide a rich, even unrivalled, reflection upon the potentiality of our experience of dying on screen: its profound and (un)special effects.

The film starts with titles on a black screen, as prologue and dedication. The first: 'This film is about the experience of dying.' The second: 'Five patients in a palliative care ward for the terminally ill agreed to share their experience in the hope that it would be useful to the living.' The subsequent frames dedicate the film to these five, to their family and friends and to the staff at Grace. As well as redressing what John Tercier calls contemporary culture's 'paucity of experience' when it comes to dying,[36] the first title distils King's intent, and perhaps signature: experience is all here. What the titles make primary is that the experience of dying and its lessons are owned by the dying themselves. This defies the object status usually accorded them: instead, their status as subjects, as sovereign centres of the narrative, and the denial of objectification and dehumanisation underwrite the film.[37] The titles also suggest that the lessons of dying are for the living: they are not for the grieving, for the survivor left behind, but for an unprivileged and unspecified group elsewhere.[38] In this way, *Dying at Grace* embarks with unconventional aplomb: in place of directorial accreditation, the film centres its 'characters'; instead of the trauma of bereavement, dying is to be a gift to the audience. The experience of dying gives and is used: if it is an experience it is a *co*experience. This is not to undermine the authority of the dying individual or to stress, again, the activity of the spectator but to emphasise how dying must be thought of as somehow social. Allan Kellehear, a prolific commentator on the topic, defines it as a 'shared set of overt social exchanges between dying individuals and those who care for them'.[39] One of my objectives here, and in this book more broadly, is to expand the sense of, and forum for, the sharing of these exchanges, and the range of participants involved. I want to instate cinema (at least) and the spectator as noteworthy but also knowing coordinates in this exchange. Cinema has always played a role, albeit mostly derisory, in death's cultural life. It is to its potential as more than a stock house for a 'surplus of representation', that I am aiming.[40]

Implicit in the opening titles, too, is the consent of those dying, to the film that is being made. Consent, and with it fairness and respect, have been the hot topics historically in ethical film-making and documentary theory but my ethical approach is shaped by other things. It aims to move on from these issues to the question of privilege, sovereignty and accountability, to an understanding of how the spectator is implicated in, impacted by, and responsible for the suffering and vulnerability of the other being watched without – and this is crucial – collapsing that under-standing into solipsistic reassurances or discourse. Necropolitically and cinematically attuned, this ethical film criticism is grounded in Levinas's 'first philosophy' which defines subjectivity in its reach to the other rather than the self. In this model, the subject is constituted *through* respond-ing to the other (and, specifically, to his or her vulnerability) and *as* an obligation arising from the other's difference or alterity.[41] This obligation is so formative because alterity underpins intersubjectivity and is inher-ently compromising. This obligation 'arises from our most primary, and unavoidable, implication in the other's potential death: the murderous impulse that frames self-interest'.[42]

Cooper has spoken similarly of this different ethical approach in her focus on films which might 'resist the reflective mechanism that would refer one back to oneself or one's own world', and in her use of Levinas 'whose work is concerned with an inability to reduce alterity to the self-same'.[43] Key here, then, is the way in which King provides the experience of dying as a coexperience, grounded in the intersubjective encounter in which death is at stake and the other is not to be reduced to the same.

After the dedication fades, the ambient sound – of a machine's beep pervading the ward, of work behind doors – kicks in over the black screen before the image appears. A nurse pushes an empty wheeled stretcher along the corridor and enters a hospital room. With another nurse's help, she tags the big toe of a recently deceased patient. The body is zipped into a white plastic bag and four people lift it on to the stretcher which two nurses wheel to the lift and take to the mortuary. These scenes provide the credit sequence but also a second prologue to the film. They bookend the film's narrative and initiate its exceeding of the conventions of taboo, sentiment, and narrative.

The film starts after the film ends: it starts where all its key characters journey to, the period after death and the first step in the disposal of the body. The period before death concludes the film: we watch and wait as Eda's breathing ceases. There is a beginning and end here but a constantly looping one. Death happens but only as part of a cycle. This is taboo-breaking fare in its sighting the unseen and departure from narrative format but there is more to it. We rarely get to see corpses and, when we do, on television at least, they're never old, are always pristine, and rarely in motion.[44] The naked feet and glimpse of grey, as the zip passes over the head, provide neither spectacular nor fetishised corpse: no frightening sight is soothed by a glut of effects or other diversions. Death is introduced through the banality, and menial labour, of disposal, performed by nurses who are also participants in the event. Like the titles before it, this second prologue instates the interpersonal or coexperience of dying. It also, I'd like to suggest, introduces the place of fiction within this coexperience.

As the drawer in the mortuary is closed, one nurse says 'God bless ya' and, as the two women leave, she adds, 'Light out' before the screen goes dark. Though this marks the end of the sequence, and the care of the staff, it cannot help but repaint the events as a putting to bed: the tucking in, the 'God bless you' and the lights out. Sleep, of course, is not what has been achieved, a child is not who was spoken to, and there'll be no waking in the night. But the coexperience of dying constructed here is overlain with a sense of what can be thought of as personal fictionalisation: how the nurse's 'character' draws upon, and forth, a sweetening of things. This maternal moment resonates with idiom yet, unlike Hollywood's treatment of terminal illness, it is subordinated to, not constitutive of, dying. It is held in words and gestures that jar with the setting and event: the cold metallic functionality of this basement mortuary contrasts with the softer-furnished, windowed ward above. There is no spiritual imagery, slow motion or cut-aways, to romance or infantalise the dead further, nor weeping family members dominating, and directing, the swell of feeling as on-screen surrogates. Instead, human labour and sentiment, colloquial, habitual and even poetic, tint the film but never take precedence over its long look at dying.

The screen stays black for a few seconds after this and then the film starts proper with an establishing shot of the hospital exterior at night. This is the first of several cuts to the Toronto setting, to the perseverance of the city, and to the cycle of seasons and day and night. Locating dying both physically and temporally, such scenes repeat the disruption of linearity and again intermingle its poignant and recurring tropes: the enduring with the finite, the universal with the local, the mundane with the poetic, and blankness with simile rather than sentiment. The manoeuvring of truth around watchability is, of course, the challenge of documentary and especially 'direct cinema' with its distinctive claims to veracity. King preferred the term 'actuality drama' for his brand of it, for his twist on fiction in fact.[45] Experience is all but experience cannot be, is not, without human or poetic resonance. Fictionalisation does not contest truth, then, but enhances it. Fictionalisation is borne in film technique from the barest to the most fanciful editing but it is also the imposition of a more figurative film language.[46] This, as I've begun to demonstrate, is subtle and subordinated in *Dying at Grace* but important nevertheless. In addition to its prologues and shots of the cityscape, and its personal fictionalisation, which affords actuality an inner drama without privileging it, there are some other devices in the film.

A nurse's recording of the evening report operates as a quasi- or borrowed voice-over. Though clearly a device, albeit a casual one, and narrative rather than experience driven, its artificiality is undercut by its place in the world of the ward. In other words, it, too, is observational and diegetic. That said, it holds narrative purpose. Furnishing us with important information, the borrowed voice-over keeps the emphasis on palliation, on care rather than cure. This is a major break with the recovery momentum of the fiction film discussed in Chapter 1, and the way that care itself – as acceptance, self-betterment, futurity – provides the cure for dying in Chapter 5. In addition, the emphasis on palliation, on care rather than cure, on nurses rather than doctors, keeps the coexperience in the social exchange of dying ever present. But the borrowed voice-over also operates as a counterpoint to what is going on on-screen; it provides another layer of personal fictionalisation. When the nurse describes Joyce's death as peaceful, we are not convinced at all that this is what we've witnessed. She starts by stating how Joyce was asking for pain relief, and continues with 'in the end it was a rapid decline with respiratory distress, and then a peaceful last breath' over the close-up of the now-dead Joyce's face, which it would be hard to describe as peaceful.

Pointing, inevitably, to the 'paucity of experience' and the relativity of 'peacefulness', the film still strains under the will for a good death. The nurse's final, hope-filled, well-trained and unavoidably inadequate claim cannot but falter alongside the experience that seems far from serene. That is not to say that Joyce's death wasn't peaceful, only that it is impossible to know (and hard to believe). And when this surety combines with the later sight of a nurse fixing the just-dead Richard into a more at-peace repose – closing the open jaw, repositioning the head and body – we are, despite its professionalism, reminded of the more cosmetic and comforting translations of life's close. King reveals the different layers in the coexperience of dying but without them competing and, it seems, without judgement. Neither is the spectator torn by these different takes. Barry Keith Grant suggested of Wiseman's *Near Death* that it 'encourages the viewer to oscillate between conflicting views of Dr Weiss and, by extension, of the entire medical staff'.[47] This is not what King is after, however. *Dying at Grace*'s dramas or fictionalisation do not invite oscillation at all but a steady embrace of different positions.

Commenting on Eda's decline, Marni Jackson has noted a similar tension in the film. She writes that:

> The most uncomfortable moments for me were scenes in which the very kind lady chaplain poured the words of the twenty-third Psalm into the ear of a dying, young-

ish woman who had earlier informed the camera that she had most definitely lost
her faith. I found myself hoping that her hearing had shut down. Toronto Grace is
a Salvation Army institution, and although the staff was all compassionate, kindness
does sometimes come with a rider.[48]

King welcomes such riders, I'd suggest, within his bigger picture but he
neither privileges nor disparages, at any point, the religious context. King
had great sympathy for society's institutions but also railed against them
so, when he titles his film *Dying at Grace*, there are to be a few misgiv-
ings. The peaceful or beautiful death is certainly not what is on offer or
promised either in the hospital or by the film. The title bears the tension
between the spiritual and the banal, the literal and the figurative, which
we find throughout. The title says it how it is but also, of course, points
to a state of salvation attained by its participants, and to the 'gift of God'.
While this spiritual, and spiritualising, interpretation might grate upon a
healthy scepticism of redemptive thrusts, I want, here, to be more open
to what I called earlier the 'potentiality' of cinema in its treatment of profundity, and what King himself, and in a purely secular register, termed
the 'awe' in this experience.[49] I do so mindful of, and reassured by, King's
secularism and committed contrariness. As Feldman put it, '[w]hen we are
in some sort of paradise, King, like Thomas More in the original *Utopia*,
is often cagey about approving of the place'.[50]

There is one pronouncedly figurative moment in the film, where King
includes an additional creative flourish in place of sustained close-ups.
Lloyd Greenway, the youngest on the ward, has been close to death for
some time. In a rare extended sequence in his room, and focused on his
partner, Ned, as well as him, we receive an interminably long, viscerally
gruelling, scene of Ned in distress, Major Bobbit reading from the Bible,
and Lloyd's death-rattle-like breathing. There is a disturbing intensity
here brought about through the convergence of these, and the focus on
the palpable pain of Ned, and struggle of Lloyd. This is the only time we
really witness the suffering of the survivor too. Finally, the film cuts away
from inside the room. The noise of Lloyd's breathing and Bobbit's reading
bridges the cut, however, and continues as another quasi-voice-over as we
view the other patients in their hospital rooms, as well as the corridor.

The cadence of the rasping breath and Bible passage works more like
a soundtrack in this strangely and singularly aestheticised sequence. In
part, we are simply relieved to be out of the soaring and searing emotional
experience of watching Lloyd and Ned. At the same time, the swell of
sentiment isn't allowed to overwhelm the experience of the film. This
overt editing of sequence and sound, then, is a special effect but one that

diffuses, rather than determines, the spectacle, that is, in other words, un/special. The relief provided, however, is not, and neither could it be, complete. The soundtrack continues: the coexperience hasn't stopped, it just moves beyond our face to face with Lloyd's and Ned's suffering to a non-frontal register. We are hearing, now, rather than seeing it but more than this (and not to privilege sound in a simple swap for vision or to replace Lloyd with Richard or Eda) our encounter with dying is located on the ward and with its other inhabitants. This move beyond the face to face is significant in ethical terms too. Though it was never a direct, frame-filling, straight-on look at either Lloyd or Ned's face, the shift of their suffering or vulnerability off-screen and into non-synchronous sound, renders their exposure outside the remit of the field of vision or dominance of the face. For Levinas, the visage of the other, which summoned the self into obligation, is more than the literal or constrained human face: '[e]xpression, or the face, overflows images'; 'the face [is] a source from which all meaning appears'.[51]

In addition, from the long take of the corridor, like the trunk of the ward, the film visits the other dying individuals and thus creates a sense of community. This serves not as the salve of solidarity: the irrevocable isolation of the individuals is made clear as we see each one in their bed reaching ever closer to their own last night. Neither is it, exactly, what Chris Townsend sees as a post-AIDS contemporary culture where 'witnessing death . . . impel[s] the re-imagining of community'.[52] The politicised act of witnessing is not what King's film summons. Rather, though not unrelated to Townsend's point, we have here the connectedness of humanity, a connectedness through shared vulnerability. This connectedness levels, rather than privileges, the individual: it is a community of (estranged) equals.

While we know that '[w]orldly inequalities are in no way levelled at the time of death but persist, permeating every aspect of death and dying',[53] so that who and where you are has a great deal of influence on how you die, *Dying at Grace* seems to contest this. The five individuals have ended up in a hospital that seems intent on making social identity irrelevant.[54] There is no real background story to the characters other than snippets revealed through their conversations. This tightened focus is supported by the only attention to their 'families' coming purely in their presence. The differences in class and circumstance are evident among the individuals and, while this might prove Grace's mission, it also adds another layer of fictionalisation to the film, more public this time – the fantasy of equality in death.

The un/special sequence of Lloyd and Ned also contains a powerful and rarely seen message of religious tolerance, for it is the dying gay man and his partner who benchmark dying at Grace, who most explicitly animate the convergence of the personal and grand narrative. Prominent for the reasons already stated, this sequence also represents the hub or midpoint of the film for Lloyd's is the third of five deaths. More than this, though, its distinction defuses the rider Jackson had noted, for here we have a firmly religious man – Lloyd was the pastor for the Metropolitan Community Church – and, in the absence of homophobia, an emblem of the best side of religious 'kindness' perhaps. King's community and coexperience of dying, and the heights of his moving image, are anchored, again, in an embrace of difference. While it cannot be forgotten that Lloyd is, in many ways, the most conventional member of the ward – white, Anglo-Canadian, middle class, religious, 'married' – his normativity is offset by the range of circumstances represented by the others: the 'outlaw' Richard, the tragic Joyce, the Italian-Canadian Carmella, and the non–nuclear families of all.[55] The centring of Lloyd, here, is also offset by the fact that, unlike each of the others, he is too ill to speak and, in this way, rather than having a privileged voice is the most 'absent' throughout.[56]

The Moving Image

Dying at Grace provides no centred or privileged character or viewpoint. Instead of identification with, or objectification or abjectification of, the dying, we are simply moved through and, most importantly here, moved by what is going on. This moving image reaps its return not through string playing or pulling but through something slower, stiller and, like dying itself, less regulated. Eda seems to be recovering over most of the film's course and then suddenly declines and dies: 'dying follows its own stubborn narrative' says Jackson of the film, it 'won't be "directed"'.[57] Neither is there, then, a centred, rarefied, creative voice: the accoutrements of authorial imprint are dispatched, and overwhelmed, by the precedence of as raw a record as possible.

Our being moved by the film isn't a signal of sympathy or empathy, of distant care or compassion. And it isn't a vehicle for sculpting sentiment in the service of ticket sales or public opinion or political ends. Such things, as I'll continue to clarify below, are the armaments of unconscious solipsism, of the constant return to the concerns of the Western self, cautioned against above. Instead, this moving image is an encounter with what I want to call raw life, but how best to interpret it? In this final section of the chapter, I want to consider a number of ways that this kind of encounter has been thought about in order to assemble a term or terms that afford us greater insight into the capacity of cinema to share death with us. With the ever-spreading mediatisation of suffering, and its critique, this seems a pressing concern for film studies. Such a term must avoid commending or comforting the spectator, or returning him or her to the concerns of the self rather than of the other. It must, in other words, be ethical. Such a term might provide intimacy but not at the expense of objectivity. It might be subjective but never exclusive: universal and always particular. It might also, ultimately, speak to the specificity of film and therefore contend with cinema's conventional rhetoric as well.

In speaking of *Dying at Grace*, King made clear that the experience and the lesson of dying were inherently linked, that one must '[put] oneself into the experience in some emotionally vivid way, so one can come to terms with it'.[58] We are put into, we enter, the experience through the observational mode. The paring down of film-making into long takes and close-ups with broad access to rarely seen events immerses us in the world of the ward and the dying individuals. We are privy to highly personal events but with discretion: recalling my discussion in Chapter 4, the bodies here remain intact and retain their dignity but without precluding their embodied vulnerability. There's no suppuration or stench but the film is corporeal: the close-ups and long takes chronicle the hair on Richard's face, the stroke of Carmella's hand, each inhalation of Eda's until her last. This intimate but disinterested engagement with the individuals – bar the extended sequence of Ned and Lloyd, the film resists singularising suffering and even this scene is consciously curtailed – is 'emotionally vivid' because of the place of the personal and un/special effects within it: the fictions emerging through the nurses' and Major Babitt's speech, and other, edited, sequences of love and care.

Intimate but disinterested, the experience of dying on-screen does not become our own; it is not prosthetic. This negotiation of distance and absorption without co-option is fundamental. Indeed, its critical import is an ongoing, as well as historical, theme.[59] Our own dying is promised, of course, in the wages of time, in the cycles figured by the second prologue's corpse, by the seasonal shots of Toronto and passage of night and day, but also by the machine's beep punctuating the film with false infinitude. But the experience of dying does not become our own for to do so would be to reduce their experience to ours: we can share in it without identifying with it or owning it. It is a coexperience though we have very different parts to play. It is an embrace, not a levelling, of difference. In and through that embrace, through 'the mix of distance and compassion that became [King's] trademark',[60] we feel the magnitude of the events without training them to our own interests.

Hollywood, in contrast, strives for sameness in its protagonists: we draw close to, identify with, them in their familiarity. Alison Landsberg has made some interesting points about sameness and 'deep feeling' in her distinction of spectatorial empathy from sympathy. Empathy for her is ethical because it operates 'beyond the immediacy of one's own wants and desires'.[61] It is encouraged by what she calls 'prosthetic memory', the way in which the cinema spectator, as the key example in modernist culture, 'sutures him or herself into a larger history . . . [and] takes on a more personal, deeply felt memory of a past event through which he or she did not live'.[62] Sympathy, however, does something else and is less ethical for it. It is worth quoting Landsberg at length here for she makes clear the political reverberations of these responses:

> Sympathy, a feeling that arises out of simple identification, often takes the form of wallowing in someone else's pain. Although it presumes sameness between the sympathizer and her object, whether or not there is actually a 'sameness' between them, an actual shared experience, matters little, for in the act of sympathizing, one projects one's feelings onto another. This act can be imperializing and colonizing, taking over, rather than making space for, the other person's feelings.[63]

Where Landsberg warns of sympathy's reflexive mechanism, empathy, as I've suggested already, achieves the same kind of co-option but on a different schedule. It is not immediate: indeed, it is delayed and deeply contextual but the focus rebounds eventually regardless. Where sympathy's return to self is effusive and transparent, empathy's, as we saw in the discussion in Chapter 3, is quieter, refigured, charged, instead, with neo-imperialism or neocolonialism. Sympathy wears its self-indulgence openly, is more blatantly narcissistic, but empathy is solipsistic still. The socio- or geopolitical price is the same. For Landsberg, these new prostheticised memories 'might serve as the grounds for unexpected alliances across chasms of difference' yet this book has argued that, while true, these alliances are still, if not more, problematic.[64]

Striving for the universal, I've delayed ideological analysis in this chapter, though it goes without saying that ethical film criticism is inherently political. Levinas's first philosophy, a first politics if you like, marked the violent stakes of the inevitably *inscribed* difference between the self and the other. In more common terms, we might remember the constant 'asymmetry of power between the comfort of spectators in their living rooms [say,] and the vulnerability of sufferers on the spectators' [cinema or] television screens'.[65] Watching others die always involves a pronounced imbalance: the gaze may not be presumed healthy – *Dying at Grace* does not construct the well gaze of fiction film, and King anticipated an audience in palliative care – but neither is it on this cusp of death.[66] I am pointing here to how the (ostensibly normative) dying individuals in King's film receive excellent treatment which they are extremely privileged, in the bigger picture, to have access to. Theirs is hard to see as a 'place in the sun' – that place of the subject, in Levinas's first philosophy, which always depends on the 'usurpation of spaces belonging to the other man whom I have already oppressed or starved, or driven out into a third world'[67] – but it is a much better experience, if not death, than so many have (from starvation, civil war, abuse etc.). So, while *Dying at Grace* confounds the cinematic language of dying, rife in mainstream fantasies, it still provides a forum for seeing death, and experiencing it, untroubled largely by class, or nation, or race, or gender or other social specifications. This kind of coexperience is always already political therefore, and, always already ethically charged.[68]

Theirs is not 'bare life', either, though I'm mindful of the echo. Giorgio Agamben made the important distinction of the abject figure of the 'living dead' in his theses on the deathly workings of sovereign power.[69] Describing the Muselmann of the concentration camp he wrote: '[m]ute and absolutely alone, he has passed into another world without memory and without grief'.[70] While the five dying individuals in King's film inhabit a similar space, and also, as I'll argue below, one ripe for ethical interpretation, theirs is not a 'life that does not deserve to be lived',[71] (or, to be grieved, as Butler has put it).[72] They have not been reduced to this state by others, are not afflicted from elsewhere. Neither has the (necropolitical) system cast them out, removed their worth and rights and rendered them inhuman. Raw life, then, echoes this other inherent asymmetry: not just between the spectator and the near dead in *Dying at Grace* but between them and the near dead of, say, the Holocaust. In this way, 'witnessing', the ethical outcome of attention to bare life, and its political project, is *not* the modus operandi of *Dying at Grace* or what spectatorship enables here. The five people in King's film are 'just' dying from terminal illnesses. The imprint of sovereign power does, of course, mark the dramas of dying of even the 'oldest' citizens – life is always subject to it, hence the critical valency of Agamben's work – but, crucially, by degree.[73] Politics, though always already at play, recedes, and the full weight of the potentiality of the moving image can come to the fore.

With sympathy dispatched, empathy flawed, and asymmetry recurring, what further ways might there be of understanding the powerful feelings engendered, and the borders crossed, by watching others die in popular film culture? Chouliaraki, in her Luc Botanski-influenced work on representations of suffering in Western news media, promotes 'connectivity' and 'solidarity' to describe an optimal, ethical, spectatorship.[74] Though she speaks in similar terms – of pity, reflexivity and narcissism – she has a specific focus and agenda. Her analyses of news reports of 'distant suffering' refigure the public sphere in order to proliferate humane responses to global calamity. *Dying at Grace*, however, is not a window on distant suffering, on a geopolitical elsewhere, but the question of the distance between the sick and the well, the subject(s) on-screen and off, remains fundamental. Indeed, though the genre and goals differ, the shared landscape of the ethics of watching others die renders Chouliaraki's, as well as others' work from different disciplines, both compelling and compulsory frames.[75]

'Connectivity' usefully bridges the distance between individuals, without prejudice or priority, and 'solidarity' lends it the political and emotive edge, even as it keeps things fairly clinical. But Chouliaraki warns, too, of the by now familiar problem of one circuit of connectivity being privileged: 'It is not connectivity to the "other" seen on the screen that counts as the purpose of mediated experience, but the connectivity to fellow spectators . . . [a] self-referential loop.'[76] In response, she ponders a more impersonal pity that might stall the narcissistic folding back of humanitarian response to self-same concerns and construct, instead, a cosmopolitan public as her ideal. 'Far from being a denial of pity, impersonality is a necessary condition for the cosmopolitan disposition in so far as it prefers the value of detached judgement to the intimate reflex of communitarianism.'[77] As I discussed in relation to Ned and Lloyd's big scene, King's communitarianism is forged in detachment *and* intimacy – a navigation of absolute aloneness and inclusive experience – and rejects reflex as well as judgement. In this way, Chouliariaki adds the crucial broader context to the affectivity of Landsberg's discussion but sustains barriers that King's film, and our growing description of spectatorship, want to transcend.

In her meditation on the ethics of vulnerability, Anat Pick also utilises connectivity, but an embodied connectivity, to propose a 'creaturely poetics' of film and literature. For Pick, 'creatureliness' is the term of choice for the material vulnerability describing connectivity.[78] She draws on Simone Weil's work, and specifically her notion of 'contact', to designate our connection 'with the flesh and blood vulnerability of beings'.[79] Though her interest in the troubled vulnerability of life (and the genocidal passions associated with it) is focused on the human/non-human distinction, and mine looks not to interspecies but intraspecies, intrahuman, necropolitics, her discussion is illuminating, nevertheless. It also recalls Laura Tanner's emphasis upon the 'shared vulnerability of embodiment' customarily disavowed in Western culture but exposed through the defence-lessness of the dying.[80] Where the terminal illness films of Chapter 4 were shown to confirm this disavowal, *Dying at Grace* possesses the potential-ity of connected vulnerability or exposure that Pick and Tanner allude to.

For Pick, the embodied contact of connectivity is achieved through an 'attentive gaze' which reveals our common creatureliness and 'cannot help being "innocent" to the extent that it sees while remaining unattached to (uninvested in) its object'.[81] This attentive gaze, then, is relatively neutral: implicitly impersonal and outside asymmetry, yet forged in a shared embodiment. Where I argued previously that spectatorship was never neutral, here the will to neutrality comes not at the expense of the body, politic, or self-cleansing soul. Neither well, nor male, nor objectifying or abjectifying, this gaze contravenes conventional looking. Its mode of con-nection is beyond the normal regimes of sentiment, and power, and vision, but makes corporeal contact nevertheless. Such contact, in *Dying at Grace*, comes with those facial close-ups, the caress, the tears and breathing: an attention to detail that is professional and affectionate, corporeal but not sensorial.[82] And it exceeds the contours of life, as the second prologue makes clear. The nurses' touch continues beyond the individual's capac-ity to register it, whether in brow smoothing the near dead or that early 'God bless you' in the mortuary.[83] It is, in this sense, unrequited. Such contact also exceeds the contours of narrative, for the film starts with the endgame.

Where sympathy is feeling as the other, and empathy is feeling for the other, we are edging ever closer to this sense of feeling with or towards the other. This feeling involves connection plus emotion without narcis-sism *and* with shared vulnerability or exposure. *Dying at Grace*, I believe, achieves this final step as well. It does this through what I want to call its decinematicism. Previous discussions of the ethics of spectatorship, including my own, have focused on the metacinematicism of contempo-rary films about suffering and how they render the spectator self-conscious and accountable through disrupting the seamlessness, and seemliness, of narrative. Such tactics have been shown, too, to afford a celebration of cinema or the individual (as the earlier discussions of *My Life* and *Bucket List* made clear). Dependent, as they are, on self-reflexivity, this is, by now, unsurprising. Decinematicism, in contrast, is not replenishing. It dismantles the spectator's safety nets in moves that are far more radical. *Dying at Grace*, as illustrated above, breaks with numerous filmic conven-tions, not least those attending death, but it also involves a pronounced undoing of film's basic or ontological tenets.[84] In capturing dying, dying as

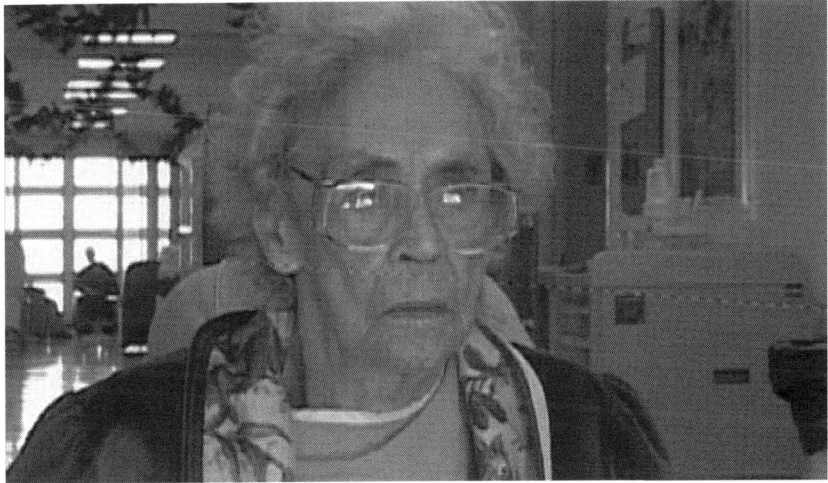

Figure 6.1 The unmoving image of Joyce.

a coexperience, but also and most importantly now, death as process, the film unravels the very contract of cinema underlying spectatorship.

Sobchack suggested that documentary film fails to secure and record death but, in *Dying at Grace*, it is not just the final moment that is captured that constitutes death but a longer and gradated journey.[85] The individual's exit from the world of the living is, in other words, a process. It happens in stages but, more than this, as the terms 'deathwatch', 'brain dead', 'being kept alive' or even CPR (cardiopulmonary resuscitation) attest, it possesses a degree of indeterminacy (rather than ineffability). In *Dying at Grace* death is the 'won't be directed' decline of the individual with bad nights and with 'rallying' en route. It is also a *final* final furlong that is marked by the cessation of cognition, when the dying individual ceases to be able to engage with others, when communication, awareness, agency and even subjectivity recede.

We receive various visions of this state of raw life in *Dying at Grace* but it is especially marked in two key scenes: the decline of Joyce and the death of Eda which closes the film, where the former works as a kind of prerequisite for the latter. As Joyce journeys ever closer to death, her gaze becomes more fixed and blank. In the middle of the film, we sit with her for quite some time and this progression is clear. The camera is positioned so that the emptiness and impenetrability of her gaze are enhanced by the reflection of the window's light in her glasses.

Immobile and opaque, this shot endows Joyce with an automaton-like presence, compromising her human subjectivity further. Compromised but not evacuated, the defamiliarising of Joyce doesn't dehumanise her or the dying subjects here: we are too soldered on the coexperience, the cycle, of living and dying to fall for that. But it does '(positively) awaken [us] to human uncanniness'.[86] Where, for Pick, this product of the blank gaze is integral to a creaturely connectivity, here the defamiliarisation affords, after Victor Shklovsky, a productive estrangement from the otherwise known.[87] It enables us to see and feel again and afresh – beyond what we assumed and the tyranny of vision – as the very potentiality of cinema that I'm pursuing here.

The blank and blind state of raw life in *Dying at Grace* is inevitably affected, if not determined, by drug treatments. The perhaps 'medicated blankness'[88] is, however, potent not simply as a counterpoint to Hollywood expressionism but as the individual's involuntary internality, a withdrawal that ruptures the conventional presuppositions of cinema. What I mean by this is that our long stare at raw life contravenes and confounds the unconscious and, one might add, ethical, contract underpinning spectatorship: the spectator and the film have been defined, historically, by a relay of looks and suspension of belief but this ceases to hold true in King's film.

Foundational film theory in the 1970s saw spectatorship as a tacit agreement, a kind of contract, between spectator and film spectacle: the spectators 'forget' they are watching a film, and the film, and its actors or characters, 'forget' they are in one. In more explicitly psychoanalytical terms, both parties disavow the fantasy – they cover over the absent real with a set of appealing and distracting images – to indulge in it fully. According to Christian Metz, the principle player in this call for the fetishism of cinema, the unconscious agreement runs in the two directions: 'I watch it, but it doesn't watch me watching it. Nevertheless, it knows that I am watching it.'[89] In this way, the relationship between the spectacle and the spectator is revealed as '[an] active complicity which works both ways'.[90] This contractual dynamic, and active complicity, on the part of the film's subjects, translate, overtly and ethically, in *Dying at Grace* into the consent of those dying to the film being made, as well as the choice of the spectator to watch. And the anxiety underpinning fetishism, translates from the general fear, hence disavowal, of death in mainstream fiction films, to the overt 'coming to terms' with it here. To agitate the question of consent further, we are reminded by Sobchack that the spectator's consent is especially, and ethically, heightened when watching someone die: '*Before the nonfictional screen event of an unsimulated death, the very act of looking at the film is ethically charged*'.[91]

In *Dying at Grace* what happens in these moments of raw life, of withdrawal, of blankness, is that the dying individual stops 'knowing' that I'm watching. In so doing a chasm opens up between the contractual obligations of the film, the coexperience and the process of death. The contractual dynamic falters, the reassuring (fetishistic) mutual complicity ends. The spectator is left without psychic or ethical scaffold. This chasm affords a space which is soon filled by possibly scandalous pleasures in exploitation cinema but operates here as the very site of the potency and awe of exposure.

What is more, the dying individual stops being able to acknowledge the spectator's, or my, look to reciprocate in a more conscious way too. The light bouncing off Joyce's glasses is a forceful image of this. In her discussion of the rare documentaries that actually provide an ethical vision of real dying, Sobchack singled out the 'humane gaze' of Roehmer's *Dying* and Friedman and Joslin's *Silverlake Life*. 'Marked by its *extended duration*, the humane gaze . . . engag[es] itself directly with the direct gaze of its dying human subject, who looks back.'[92] The takes are long in King's film but the dying individuals in this observational documentary never address the camera directly. They are also often shot in profile, or asleep, and rarely, centre-frame or frontally. In the concluding long take of Eda reaching death, her ability to sustain life, rather than cognition which has long passed, contracts so that even the rebound of breathing ceases. This scene provides an intense culmination to the film and realisation of the point, and poignancy, of 'no-return'. There is, however, more than 'an agreed-upon *complicity*' between the dying subjects and the film-maker.[93] Indeed, King does not depend upon this humane looking back for his ethical approach. His purchase on humanity exceeds Sobchack's distinction of the two films and, more importantly, an ethics proven, or at least heightened, through consent-as-reciprocity. Arguing for the creatureliness of the blank gaze, Pick locates the returned look within the 'narcissistic economies of looking'[94] and, in so doing, reminds us of the larger stakes, and broader sweeps, of mainstream culture: 'Humanity and personhood in film are partly constituted via . . . the network of visual commerce by which the self replenishes its powers through another's look.'[95]

The spectre of solipsism lingers still. This is not to devalue Sobchack's discussion at all, not least because it appeared before the surge in documentaries about dying that King's film was part of. What is more, *Silverlake Life* was, in many ways, the breakthrough film, and now has been widely acknowledged as such.[96] But where Sobchack focuses, necessarily, on how humanity is ethically constituted through that direct gaze back, King's film represents an exciting possibility of cinema providing something else. Something not so much 'revelatory'[97] as unconditional in its crossing the additional frontier between the subjects on- and off-screen, taking that aforementioned final step and then some: of feeling towards but *without* the other.

> In opposition to the humanist demand that the other look back at me as the condition for her claim to recognition and power, ethics perhaps begins with the blank gaze. For what is ethics if not my seeing without being seen – my unrequited attention?[98]

Where, as Peggy Phelan argues of *Silverlake Life*, the representation of dying 'allows us, at last, to learn a richer vocabulary for the present tense',[99] for Butler this 'keener sense of the value of life, all life, [must] take hold . . . in order to oppose violence'.[100] This chapter has revealed the potential of cinema to share dying with us, and in a way that is meaningful in interpersonal, humanistic and, therefore, ethical terms. Such terms recognise the inevitable place of politics within this – the price of 'my place in the sun'; the 'different ways in which human physical vulnerability is distributed across the globe'[101] – and the necropolitics that flourishes in their absence. And so we come back to Scarry who sketched a very similar sense of the high stakes of the expression of pain and, I'll still add, of dying: 'The failure to express pain [and dying] . . . will always work to allow its appropriation and conflation with debased forms of power; conversely, the successful expression of [them] will always work to expose and make impossible that appropriation and conflation.'[102]

Dying at Grace, like other documentaries of real dying, operates in stark opposition to this necropolitical appropriation and conflation but also to Hollywood which is attributed, therefore, and again and in contrast, a debased form of power. Though this seems a harsh indictment of its saccharine but cathartic efforts, or of the palliation underpinning much of its output, the shoe does fit and especially with those films that so explicitly incant the grammar of dying, such as *Monster's Ball*. In King's film, instead, death is 'stripped of all its pornographic fictional trappings . . . [and the film] offers an oblique critique of our ritualized, pop-culture denial of this primal human event'.[103] *Dying at Grace* opposes the 'debased powers' of the idiomatic and redemptive trajectory too. Instead of evading and mystifying death or sustaining its wondrous ineffability, it renders it 'natural and nameable' and even knowable.[104] It offers, perhaps, not a debased but a 'sort of sacred recognition of life's value as material and temporal'.[105]

Dying at Grace confounds consent and the humanity of the gaze, confounds them in order to rescript and revitalise them. Where the unrequited act of the dying individuals, the 'gift' noted of those opening titles, was the prelude to the film, the spectator of *Dying at Grace* reciprocates in kind. This ethics of spectatorship as sharing, post-consent and unconditional, represents a zone of raw contact between the self and others where cinema affords individuals an unscripted sense of their place in the world and in relation to the rest of humanity: the awe of exposure, self-conscious but never self-indulgent. It also represents a radical departure from previous debates. It squares with Levinasian analysis, which prioritises communion beyond the visual or frontal field, and depends upon an always already political consciousness. But it also breaks with such works, by Butler, Cooper, or Saxton, say, in that its focus lies with watching the natural, neutral or 'unexceptional' vulnerability of others rather than that animated by atrocity, necropolitical violence or interpersonal pain.[106] In this way, the ethics of spectatorship and the potentiality of cinema it illuminates root the representation of dying unsolipsistically within the truth of art rather than the traumas of history or politics.[107]

Part III
After – Responding to Death

CHAPTER 7

At Last:
Towards a Cinema of No Return

The alluring, even jolting, spectacles so central to early film's 'cinema of attractions' and its developing trade in verisimilitudinous and vicarious experience occasionally provided a glimpse of what happened after death.[1] Where the train only approached in the Lumière brothers' classic sequence which inaugurated Part I, and Topsy merely tumbled for Edison's camera at the start of Part II, in this concluding chapter Cecil Hepworth's trick film *How it Feels to be Run Over* of 1900 takes us further. A fixed camera in the middle of a rural road records the approach and passing of a horse and cart. A motor car, however, hurtles towards it and, following the collision, a black screen spells out, one word at a time: '!!! Oh! mother *will* be pleased'. Hepworth, the pioneer of British cinema, using what are considered the first examples of intertitles, had the victim 'speak' from beyond the grave.[2] Inventive and playful, the film is typical of the period in opposing tradition and progress, movement and fixity, and in its device-determining narrative. It also joins other more vivid conjurings of death and the afterlife common to the silent era: the puffs of smoke, double-exposed ghosts, and hauntings found in the films of Georges Méliès, J. Stuart Blackton, and G. A. Smith.[3] This early gesturing to a realm beyond the finitude of life functioned simultaneously, just as it did with regard to self-endangerment and to dying earlier, as the achievement of technology and the wonder of film.[4] It also points, however, to the dominant mode through which what happens after death has been navigated by cinema, a mode characterised, inevitably perhaps, by denial and lavish fantasy.

Mainstream cinema's 'afterlife film', in its elaborate and frequently Judaeo-Christian visions of ghosts, heaven and purgatory, provides yet another set of images and narratives that delight and reassure the spectator with their ultimate 'recuperation of absence as presence'.[5] The afterlife film's recovery momentum is so extreme that even death is curable: no wonder Richard Striner would call it a '*therapeutic* genre'.[6] But it also provides another site for deflecting attention away from the vulnerability and limitations of the body to redeem and centralise, and for eternity this time, mainstream cinema's 'favourite subjects'. In the majority of mainstream afterlife films, from *A Matter of Life and Death* (Michael Powell and Emeric Pressburger, 1946) or *Vertigo* (Alfred Hitchcock, 1958) to *Always* (Steven Spielberg, 1989) or *Ghost* (Jerry Zucker, 1990) to *What Dreams May Come* (Vincent Ward, 1998), or even *Wristcutters: A Love Story* (Goran Dukic, 2006), and through the three filmic incarnations of *Heaven Can Wait* (1941; 1978; 2001),[7] love conquers all for their sympathetic, daring, and persistently, rather than ostensibly, white male protagonists. Where, in Chapter 5, cinema's 'magical negro' afforded a supernatural occasioning of the racialised grammar of dying, something very different is going on here. According to Hollywood, ghosts or the temporarily reincarnated are predominantly male and nearly always white. Other ethnic identities are excluded within the pervasive whiteness of the afterlife, and these films still centre and celebrate the sovereignty of the same old protagonists.[8] So strong is the prohibition, then, that, on the rare occasion where black angels or ghosts are shown, they are 'actually' or eventually white. This is certainly true of *Ghost*, *What Dreams May Come* and *Down to Earth*. In the last, not only does African American Lance (Chris Rock) translate from the white character of the original *Heaven Can Wait* but he's also reincarnated into a white body for much of the film.

Cinematic ghosts, lest we forget, 'have a variety of motives, benign and sinister'.[9] A far less becoming set of spectres joins the afterlife romances just mentioned. Mainstream horror's monstrous resurrections are conservatively and theologically wrought, too, even as some theorists have argued for their more radical, feminist and queer potential.[10] This conservatism, then, is tempered by independent examples, new subgenres and the capacity of the horror film to break new ground, as it were.[11] It can serve only as an inadequate gloss here on an expansive and rich range of material – another potential book, even – on the meaningfulness of cinema's post-dead. I have, aptly, perhaps, run out of time and space, however.

In the embers of this study, I want to consider how, in mainstream cinema, the dead might speak from beyond the grave in a manner that fails to benefit the three abiding categories of death's filmic role in this study: sensationalism, sentimentality, and the status quo. I want, in other words, to build upon the momentum of the previous chapter, and specifically its sense of the potentiality of film, to do something different with, and through, its dealings with death. This 'something' is not separate from what has gone before, from the ideology, iconography and I of mortality in the moving image, but responds to it. And this 'something' is specifically not solipsistic – and we might add solipsism as a fourth, or umbrella, category uniting those other three. It roots the representation of death and dying within a truth of human vulnerability and an ethics of spectatorship that necessarily reach beyond, rather than return us to, the exceptional qualities and needs of the self or the state. For this reason, yet again, and despite our focus on the pain of loss, 'trauma' will not preoccupy us here. Lauren Berlant describes trauma as 'the primary genre of the last eighty years for describing the historical present as the scene of an exception'.[12] It is precisely this scene that this book is seeking to exit.

In Chapter 6, and in contrast to the mortal economies of mainstream movies, I distinguished and prioritised a non-solipsistic treatment of death in film, in spectatorship, and even in film studies. In so doing, that ethical potential of the medium and of its interpretation was mapped out in contrast to the necropolitical grammar of Hollywood. In keeping with the critical, even civic, preoccupations of this book, this potential appeared most realisable in the relatively unrarefied space of a television-funded documentary targeting a mass audience. The question that remains, that nags and is even irksomely redemptive in its intent, is what of the fiction film? In what follows, and as a conclusion to this study, I want to consider how the mainstream feature film, how mass culture, might deal with death differently. Put another way, how might such a film provide us with moving images of death that push us to think differently in our relation to others rather than only to feel better in relation to ourselves and to our mortality? How might we be enjoined, therefore, to engage more fully and fairly with what it means to be alive?

In Tommy Lee Jones's directorial debut of 2005, *The Three Burials of Melquiades Estrada* (*Three Burials*), the eponymous character is killed and his Texan friend, Pete, played by Jones, fulfils a promise he made him that he'd take him back to his home to be buried should he die 'on this side' of the Mexican–American border. Melquiades (Julio César Cedillo), a 'wetback', an illegal Mexican immigrant, is shot, unwittingly, by thuggish border patrolman Mike Norton (Barry Pepper). When Pete finds out that Mike is responsible, he abducts him, has him dig up Melquiades's body, and sets off with them on the journey south to his friend's home town.

This film provides an extraordinarily powerful and ethical evocation of the 'moving' image. It provokes feeling for, and care of, others and, in so doing, it breaks with the contingent or conditional terms of personal engagement represented and solicited elsewhere. And it does it precisely within the auspices of Hollywood, with a 'star' director and industrial machinery propelling this more peripheral project, and within the domain of 'fiction'.[13] More than this, though, the film works as a culmination of all the themes that have emerged in this book thus far. Through revisiting these I want to venture a more comprehensive sense of the necropolitics, but also the ethical possibilities, of death and the moving image.

The Mad and Maverick Hero

As a 'revisionist Western', *Three Burials* rescripts the mythic, moral and iconographic implications of this 'quintessential American genre', while inevitably reiterating its exemplariness. The maverick protagonist's self-risking and slightly crazed acts identify Pete with the recklessness of the long line of action heroes and damaged men mentioned in Chapter 1. Like them, he is propelled by loss and pluck. But his pain and sense of obligation prove key here, not to the narrative's recovery momentum but, instead, to a productive rejection of conventional closure.[14] Like the body of Melquiades and the film's very title, the narrative strives for alternative resting places.

Death is close by in *Three Burials*. Such is the landscape of the western, the legend of the cowboy and the reality of the borderlands.[15] The film's hero, Pete, is the archetypal self-governing 'American' adventurer and self-endangerer, for 'the American propensity to venerate folklore has enshrined [the cowboy] as a creature beyond and above the law'.[16] Nonconformist and crusader, Pete follows his own code and achieves the improbable: crossing the border without detection; evading the extensive state forces pursuing him; finding, or perhaps inventing, Melquiades's home and burying him there and 'enlightening' Mike. But, whatever romance or allure accompanies such legendary figures, it is absent here. Pete's wizened features, melancholic resolve, and increasing imbalance are a long way away from the magnetism, and eventual taming, of Riggs/Gibson or Maverick/Cruise (or the other heroes populating the action genre).

We glimpse Pete in better times: snapshots of his developing friendship with 'Mel' have a *Brokeback Mountain* (Ang Lee, 2005) naivety to them but this is all in the past and in flashback. Instead, in their place, are Melquiades's decomposing corpse, Mike's beaten-up face and Pete's weathered integrity. Pete is called mad from the start. When he asks the sheriff to give him his friend's body, at the start of the film, Belmont (Dwight Yoakam) says 'I can't do that. Are you crazy?' Pete's slow, sober response, 'No. I'm not,' stands as a subtext to the rest of the film which weighs in, albeit quietly, on his wisdom or waywardness. He does appear to unhinge towards the end, as Melquiades's story and his romantic investment in it are undone. But Pete's no 'psycho son of a bitch', his lawlessness, are thrust upon him by a higher order. More than this, these fantasies – his and Mel's 'personal fictionalisations', if you like – are insignificant in the scheme of things, in the call to care for others. Indeed, like those more figurative elements in the documentary discussed in the previous chapter, they enhance, rather than contest, the film's import.

Of ever sharpening contrast to Pete, is the lawkeeper, the border patrolman, Mike. Mike's experience of 'dutiful' danger arises from the unnecessary violence he directs at others. When we first see him on the job, also in the film's first ten minutes, he chases fleeing illegal immigrants. He kicks a man on the ground and punches an already halted woman in the face. (This same woman will save his life later on but not without breaking his nose and many clichés of righteousness.) 'You're way over the line,' says Mike's superior, converging the geographic, professional and moral boundaries we know to be at stake.

The Dead-already

Three Burials revises the flirtation with death that permeates mainstream fantasies of masculine, and invariably nationalist, adventure to instate in its place the reality of death's proximity for certain social groups. The romance of the range, as Melquiades checks on his goats and then shoots a fox that threatens them, is interrupted by the bullet from nowhere that cuts down the Mexican. As a 'wetback', his life is always at risk from people like Mike. His exhumed corpse, lugged from one untimely grave to another, is a constant reminder of this inheritance. It is also a crucial rejoinder to the niceties of death, and the grammar underlying them, found elsewhere in film. I'll come back to this below but, for now, what matters is that the fantasy of self-risk, the aggrandising of cinema's favourite subjects, are undone. Instead, determining the action here, are the mortal economies of mainstream film/culture: the reinforced and replenishing structural logic that keeps subordinates in their place.

Like *Paradise Now* (Hany Abu-Assad, 2005) of Chapter 2's thesis, Jones's film illustrates this logic in order to challenge it. In that earlier chapter, two mortal economies underlying the system of cinema were distinguished. These hinged upon 'either' gender or nation/race and the deathly coordinates of both the male and imperial gaze in film. (I say 'either' for these are not discrete structures or gazes though they might try to pass as such). First, then, there was the representational logic of visual pleasure which was bound by the persistence of a cultural 'necromanticisation' of femininity fuelling the enduring construction of the exquisite 'to-be-dead' woman. Such a construction reaches its apotheosis in films of

Figure 7.1 Lassoing the cattle I

female suicide, such as Coppola's *The Virgin Suicides* (1999), dwelt on in Chapter 2, but still celebrated in Darren Arronofsky's *Black Swan* (2010) and its reiteration of the ecstasy of white, Eurocentric, high culture. It also, inevitably, frames all aestheticisations of fatal or fated femininity. Though sexist cliché abounds in *Three Burials*, its implications for women and their choices are not thoroughly foreclosed. Despite their routine of dodgy sex, dirty talk, and daytime television, the two seemingly restless wives have options, and their lives are, anyway, peripheral to the plot. Entrapment, according to this film, is relative.

In *Three Burials* the mortal economy that dominates is the representational and structural logic that frames the illegal immigrant, or unwanted resident, as dead–already. The literal dead–already–ness of Melquiades is announced in the title of the film, enforced in its opening scenes, and replenished in his body's persistent presence. But he is also figuratively dead–already, in a manner similar to Said in *Paradise Now*. When we meet Melquiades, in Pete's first flashback at the start of the film, he has arrived on the ranch where Pete works. The ranch hands are in a barn practising lassoing a makeshift cow. The camera is positioned at ground level and the shaded interior is offset by the bright sunlight from the open doors. It is into this frame, behind the symbolic trapped animal, that the Mexican enters. As the conversation between him and Pete starts, the camera moves on from aligning him thus, first to the shot reverse shot of their conversation and then to a high–angle shot from the back of the barn.

Theatrically positioned centre stage, the film initiates, but then resists, the stranger's alignment with the cattle. Mel is at first located through the image's structuring symmetry to a place regularly reserved for the subaltern: the place of the captured, of the latently lassoed. In Chapter 2, we saw how the closing scene of *Paradise Now* fixed Said forever in this location. Unlike Said, however, Mel's communion with the other cowboys immediately shifts him from this position. What is more, intensely backlit, this interloper stands out from – is not absorbed by – his horizon: there is no vanishing point here. Not in this scene, at least. When the film cuts directly from the close-up of Melquiades's face softly smiling as he looks around with recognition and say's 'I'm a cowboy, nothing more', to the image of Mike dragging his bloody body into a makeshift grave, the foreclosure of the illegal immigrant's fate – his dead-already inheritance – overwhelms its revision in the previous scene. In the ensuing narrative, Pete attempts to restore this state of communion and revision, and, via Mike, atone for the unthinking and self-indulgent practices that revived Melquiades's dead-already-ness. Not unlike the occupying forces in Palestine, Mike represents the death-dealing immediacy of that most brutal exercise of sovereignty: necropower. Yet, unlike those unflinching forces (and context remains everything) *Three Burials* makes it clear that Mike is 'out of line' in this, that his gunshot was in error, and that he might in fact be reprogrammable. But the problem of his redemption, of Pete's benevolence, and of this 'American dream' in which both Melquiades and Mike aren't so simply trapped by fate, cannot be ignored.

Ethics in/as Context

In the revisionist western, the classic genre's 'two visions – the epic and the morality play [no longer] support and enrich one other . . . [but] collide'.[17] As Philip Skerry continues, the traditional and highly racial distinction of villains and heroes reverse in this subgenre, making 'white Eurocentric imperialism . . . the evil force'. It was exactly this evil force that surfaced in the conflict and complicity film of the mid-2000s that I discussed in Chapter 3. Where the appearance of revisionist westerns has been shown to correlate historically with United States foreign policy,[18] the same was found to be true of these, what we might call here, revisionist war films which I argued were responding to the 11 September terrorist attacks in the United States in 2001 and the ensuing, and controversial, 'war on terror'.

Released around the same time, *Three Burials* might appear to have a lot in common with the conflict and complicity films but they, like the revisionist westerns, are not quite so revisionist after all. In particular, in the earlier discussion of the conflict and complicity group, I distinguished what I called their pseudo-ethics. The unassuming heroes of these powerful tales of human atrocity sacrificed themselves for others' lives in a manner that seemed distinctly Levinasian. They were summoned into a position of responsibility for others' suffering and responded to the call. But, in perpetuating racist and imperial myths at the same time as saving and salving the same old souls – whether the Western or Westernised protagonist or spectator – films like *Hotel Rwanda*, *The Constant Gardener*, *Blood Diamond* and even *Children of Men*, ultimately worked to reinforce the centring of white Western needs and Eurocentric concerns.[19]

Unlike these four films, *Three Burials* is not about armed militia or civil war nor channelled through a reluctant hero in a distant land. It shares their explicit focus on personal obligation and unconscionable acts, and also pits the individual against the state, but Pete immediately adopts his position of obligation in relation to his dead friend, he doesn't have to be turned. What is more, the film profoundly and self-consciously locates its sites of conflict and complicity in the lived experience of the southern borderland of the United States. In other words, its ethical engagement is rooted in an ethos of instinct not reluctance, familiarity not distance: 'Born in and formed by the border world, Jones is striving here to incarnate its spirit, document its culture and describe its pain'.[20] *Three Burials* also shares in the transnational aesthetic that I attached to the conflict and complicity films' cross-cultural exchanges on-screen and off-. Unsurprisingly by now, however, it seems much more genuine in this: indeed, it performs 'an extraordinary feat' in its dogged 'multi-cultural balance'.[21] Such a balance flows from its soundtrack which 'echoes both Texan C&W and Latin sounds native to the region' and 'from the film's shared authorship' and subsequent acclaim of Tommy Lee Jones and Mexican screenwriter Guillermo Arriaga.[22]

Three Burials intervenes in, rather than replenishes, racist myths but it also, crucially, prevents or, at the very least, complicates the redemption and absolution of its characters and audience. The narrative traces Pete's physical and emotional journey as he fulfils his promise to his dead friend. Though his motives seem always simple and unselfish, he does not 'find himself' or 'the light' through his quest. Indeed, when he discovers Melquiades's photo of his family to be false – his 'wife' tells Pete she'd never met him – the story becomes ever less 'goal' oriented (and heroicising). For Camilla Fojas, such a quest was always fallacious with 'Melquiades' permanent grimace [as] a half-mocking smile at the increasingly ridiculous antics of Tommy Lee Jones' character'.[23] What is more, the film's denouement is decidedly anticlimactic. Pete simply rides away, not in triumph or into the sunset or homeward bound. More problematic, then, are Mike's deliverance and what Melissa Anderson sees as Arriaga's 'facile ideas about salvation and forgiveness'.[24]

Unlike Pete, Mike's is a recuperative moral journey which he embarks on not just reluctantly, like our protagonists in Chapter 3, but kicking and screaming. Such resistance doesn't accentuate the nobility of later acts, as it did for them, for the emphasis in this film is on Mike's relentless refusal to take responsibility and make amends, until the very end. There and then, he weeps with contrition at Melquiades's photo of his fictitious family that Pete pins to a tree by the ruined village where they bury the body. Begging for forgiveness, Mike appears finally to be fully conscious of his selfish, foolish and destructive ways. He has grown into this position, steadily crumbling under the weight of Pete's harsh gaze, others' unexpected kindness and the very slow dawning of his responsibility via these. When Pete takes his leave the next day, Mike is surprised: he thought he'd kill him. But Mike won't substitute for Melquiades's death: there is to be no equilibrating exchange here, as there was in the conflict and complicity film, no 'cunning' sacrifice whereby the individual '[throws himself] away in order to preserve' or ennoble himself and what he stands for.[25] This, too, is part of the lesson of the film: the third non-burial of Mike Norton. From the opening gunshot, which Mike mistakenly took to be at him, to his 'fatal' snake bite that he is saved from, and now to this avoided death, Mike survives against these odds. Mike Norton, Mike of the Northern town – rather than Mike merely as white trash, suggested throughout the narrative – gets to live on in the knowledge of the injustice of his survival. His acceptance of his responsibility in this final scene operates as knowledge of his 'place in the sun', as Levinas put it, of how his being and survival come at the expense of others, others whom he has precisely driven out and usurped.[26] The dynamics of this driving out and usurpation are animated not only by Mike's egregious acts but also by the particular fraught history of the southern borderlands of the United States and Mexico.

Does this ending mark Mike's salvation, or his submission and survival-for-now and only now? He is 'enlightened' but the recognition characterising this final scene is far from inward looking, depoliticised, or even self-conscious. Kneeling before the photo, he cries his regret to Melquiades; he names the nameless 'wetback', 'documenting the undocumented worker'.[27] Most significant for me, the marker of Mike's enlightenment is not to be attached to his abject apologies but his potential, realised here for the first time, to break the cycle of his own concerns and care for others, not just through acknowledging the crimes of his past but as a gesture of change. The last words of the film, and the first ones to suggest Mike's genuine extension of care beyond his own needs, are his calling after Pete 'you gonna be alright?'

Jim Kitses, Marianne Gray and Edward Buscombe also queried the film's redemptive thrusts: 'Jones' multi-culturalism is old-style Hollywood liberalism; a white male's rescue and affirmation of a minority identity. Yet his film smacks not of insincerity but of ferocity and personal passion.'[28] But, and as this book has argued – through *Bucket List* and *Monster's Ball* especially – it isn't insincerity that enforces the passive racism of films or film-makers (or film theorists). Instead, a seemingly entrenched, inherited and even institutionalised distance from the topic combines with what we might think of now as the compulsive repetition of the symptoms of a faux post-racism. What Jones enacts, which is neither facile nor passive, is a committed and deliberate undercutting of such symptoms, of the tropes of redemption and white liberalism. *Three Burials* inevitably focalises the white man's experience but, unlike so many other films, not least those discussed in this study, it derails these salvific and repressive impulses. What is more, though Pete's experience is centred, albeit understatedly, Melquiades's does not disappear beneath it. Conjured in flashbacks, and not restricted to Pete's memories alone, Melquiades achieves the status of subject in the narrative. We are regularly reminded of episodes from his recent life, events he shared with Pete but also some without him. More than this, he becomes Pete's and Mike's constant companion. In stark contrast to the usual treatment of the dead and dying, in cinema and culture more broadly, Melquiades's dead body does not suffer objectification, abjectification, or alienation, not strictly anyway, but remains instead corporeal, communed with and even cared for until finally laid to rest.

Eloquent Bodies

In the second part of this study I sought to lay bare a cinematic language of dying and death and the ideological grammar preceding it. In Chapter 4, via the terminal illness film and epitomised by *Dark Victory*, a lexicon or 'holy trinity' was identified: the triumph, betterment and futurity characterising the depiction of bodily failure in mainstream cinema. In contrast to the mainly Hollywood case studies, I isolated some examples that resisted or slurred this lexicon. Such films privileged the graphic, embodied and mundane dying more reflective of the physical, economic and demographic realities of the contemporary deathbed, and of our 'shared vulnerability' that would prove so central to the ethical perspective crystallising by the end of the section.[29]

The niceties of terminality found in mainstream fictions saw the body sanitised, even beautiful, and its deathbed sacred. In the more realistic or resistant examples, its porosity, banality and helplessness were revealed through what I called the films' extrasensorial dimensions. These, the unusual use of, say, smell or sound and film-making technique in *Hilary and Jackie*, *Wit*, *The Diving Bell and the Butterfly* and *The Death of Mr Lazarescu*, breached the distances between the declining body and its surroundings, distances so fundamental to the common sequestering of death from the public realm (and rife in Hollywood). In *Three Burials*, though Melquiades's body is already dead, the manner in which it is depicted, and structured into the narrative, speak very powerfully to the 'truth' of the body and to those taboos and conventions surrounding mortality which it similarly works to rupture. But the film also intensifies their ideological underpinnings, revealing what else, or what othering, is at stake in the objectification and abjectification of the dead and dying.

Melquiades's death is first and foremost a bad one which only gets worse with each new perversion of funerary practice that follows. 'Gunned down', as the sheriff surmises, Melquiades's lung bursts and the ensuing 'severe haemorrhaging' would, we're told, take fifteen to twenty minutes to kill him. Buried by Mike in a shallow grave in the desert, the week-old cadaver is being eaten by a coyote when first discovered. The vomiting of Pete in the county mortuary, and retching of Mike as he digs Melquiades out of his second grave follow the involuntary gasps of the men who first encounter the corpse. The stench of death is both very literal and very figurative here. It is not that Melquiades's body simply 'intrudes upon public space' resisting those self-protective statutes of the sanitary with its potent smell and carrion effects – Pete must keep ants and other critters away – but that it also intrudes, and keeps intruding, upon public conscience too.[30] The sheriff will bypass protocol, and Pete's insistence, to have Melquiades buried, lying to the pathologist that he has no family. But the alternative code of practice imposed by Pete will eventually gain Mike's adherence and even see the sheriff, who at one point has the fleeing posse in his line of fire, hold back.

The principal manifestation of this double intrusion is the near-constant presence of Melquiades's corpse: slung across a horse, propped up across the campfire and, finally, 'reclining' at home. Pete ministers to his decaying flesh both to prevent its disintegration and to retain his camaraderie. He burns him and fills him with antifreeze; sits with him and combs his hair. The profound care Pete takes of his friend bespeaks his refusal of Melquiades's object status before and after exanimation. As we saw above in the scene in the barn, the sense, or rather economy, of the 'wetback' as cattle, chattel, the latently lassoed, haunts but is adjusted in that first encounter of the two men. Later, however, Mike comes to occupy a similar location, dislodging Melquiades's subaltern status once

Figure 7.2 Lassoing the cattle II

more. Again, the potential denigration of the white trash male is evident
but overwhelmed by a bigger picture.

The impact of Melquiades's death does not only determine and structure the narrative of *Three Burials* but his corpse entreats Pete and, less
swiftly, Mike to do the right thing. It cannot be refused or buried but
speaks, as it were, and keeps speaking, from beyond the grave. Neither
can it be displaced. As I emphasised above, Mike doesn't substitute for
Melquiades. And, though Pete might reduce him to, or reveal, the inhumanity he already betrayed in the first scenes of the film, this is part of the
lesson, not its resolution. There may be a paralleling of the two men but
no equivalence. Cathy Waegner has seen their 'exchange of bodies' as the
'main trope of the film' but it is their enduring imbalance, Mike's eternal
usurpation of Melquiades, and the film's rejection of reciprocity that are
key, instead.[31]

The main displacement technique of mainstream melodramatic death
was that of reproductive futurity. All the swooning into saintliness in the
terminal illness films invoked children in some way, covering over the
degeneration of the body with regeneration elsewhere. *Three Burials* has
a distinct lack of children but also actively dismisses such wishful thinking. The film closes both with Mike's prostration in front of Melquiades's
invented kids and Pete suggesting Mike returns to his wife who, unknown
to them, has already left town. Melquiades's dead body isn't masked,

or closure guaranteed, or human fallibility overwhelmed, by dynastic promise here. Crucially, though these children are not his children, they are the sons and the daughters of someone else. They are not, in other words, dead.

When discussing the ideological grammar of dying in Chapter 5, I emphasised how black characters in Hollywood are not just death-bound but had no future The futurity characterising the good 'white' death in the terminal illness film in Chapter 4 became the progenicide of post-racist filmic fare. Indeed, white redemption in cinema was shown to depend upon the literal or figurative death of black children more broadly. *Three Burials* once again undercuts the cinematic symptoms and tropes of (post-)racist and white liberal compulsion not by ignoring them but by revising/revealing their tokenism and totemism. Pete's quest is sited ever further away from redemption once Melquiades's children cease to exist. More than this, though, the film's repetition of Melquiades's nec-ropolitical inheritance (the denial of his life and legacy) and his interracial relationship with Pete do not foreclose the possibility of intervention or innovation as it did in those, what we might call, slave films, following Frank Wilderson's lead, like *Monster's Ball, Green Mile, Bucket List, The Help*. In other words, the borderland of *Three Burials* possesses a poten-tiality lacking as yet in those (white-authored) tales of African American experience which are destined, despite corrective intent, to sustain black evisceration as their epicentres, their ground zero, their glass ceil-ings. What is more, where 'much of contemporary ethnic literature in the United States is characterized by ghosts and by hauntings [as] . . . the objects and subjects of national melancholia' this is yet to translate to the big screen.[32] In *Three Burials*, however, the borderland, that zone of inter-activity, porosity and pseudosegregation, is a potent site for this possibility of intervention and innovation which have, in the uninterred Melquiades, a perfect and even unique icon.

According to Diana Fuss, the longstanding 'corpse poem', in which a cadaver is 'endowed with the power of speech', became political in the twentieth century.[33] Such poems, specifically those focused on African American history, had the 'aim to correct a social injustice'.[34] Most power-ful, she notes, are the corpse poems of slave experience, such as Richard Wright's 'Between the World and Me' (1963), which simultaneously 'portray the radical dehumanization of the lynching victim but also . . . rehumanize the dead through the agency of voice'.[35] *Three Burials*, I'd suggest, uses Melquiades's body to speak political injustice and reveal the dehumanisation–rehumanisation of the 'wetback'. It is not strictly a 'corpse film', however, though the term unsettles the fantasy of the cinematic afterlife well. Film does not, after all, speak through words alone, and the kind of speaking that I am referring to here is, in any case, more philosophical than that addressed by Fuss. It recalls, in fact, Judith Butler's comment that launched this study that something beyond the 'face' or conventional language would reveal 'the precariousness of life that is at stake'.[36] What is more, the rehumanisation of Melquiades rests not with the agency of his voice but with the subject status accorded him by Pete/Jones/Arriaga before and after his voice is silenced and his body, in its eloquent entreaty to human obligation, takes over.

Against Solipsism: Ethics as/of No Return

Three Burials animates the ethical approach to the representation of human suffering on film that has been my task to unfold throughout this book. It performs the Levinasian ethical encounter, one based on an understanding of the inherent power dynamics, even deathliness, of human relationality. Not only does it detail personal obligation beyond the confines of noble deeds or normative duty but it does so against the ideological backdrop of necropolitics, especially that of mainstream cinema, which this book has been at pains to reveal. In Chapter 6, seeking to understand more fully how film could be moving without foreclosing where such movement might lead, I pushed this ethical film criticism further still through a number of additional aesthetic as well as postcolonial coordinates. These coordinates were specifically antisolipsistic: they refused a return to the same old subjects, priorities or channels of feeling; they resisted underwriting concern for others with one's own interests. Might mainstream fiction film's representation of human suffering move us, then, towards the needs of the other and beyond the needs of the self same? Might it eschew the fantasy of symmetry or recovery of balance, and the conventional and closed circuits of thinking and feeling? In these final paragraphs I want to apply this refusal of solipsistic return to *Three Burials*.

Three Burials is an afterlife film that defies the resurrectional principles normally associated with this genre 'of second chances'.[37] Where, in films as diverse as *Always* (Steven Spielberg, 1989) or *After Life* (Hirokazu Koreeda, 1998), the deceased appear again, as if alive and well, Melquiades is simply dead and gone . . . ish. Though lacking spiritual or romantic vigour, he remains present and central to the film's narrative. But his corpse is a sign of corporeal finality: the dead do not return here to nurture us in our grief or reassure us of their/our or even God's significance.

Melquiades's corpse is the perfect testimony or foil to the unconditional acts of Pete whose steadfast commitment to his dead friend places selfless-ness centre stage. This was not without precedent. In one of the flashbacks to their friendship, we see Melquiades give Pete his horse. When Pete protests at the generosity of the gift, Melquiades says 'mine, yours . . . what's the difference?' The bond between the two men is forged in the irrelevance of reciprocity, that 'towards but without' of being moved by film so resonant in the previous chapter. This active absence of reciprocity perseveres in *Three Burials* privileging the one-wayness of obligation and unrequitedness of care.[38] In complete contrast, Mike rejects reciprocity for very different reasons. His self-serving, onanistic place in the world is epitomised by the cold, one-sided sex he has with his wife (ignoring her 'stop it', his swift pleasure-taking barely interrupts her view of the television) and his repeated attempts to 'jerk off'. Indeed, his unwitting shooting of Melquiades arises directly from his getting out of his jeep to masturbate. To reiterate: his, and the narrative's journey, are marked by his eventual doing for others rather than doing only (for) himself. Firstly, he'll join a circle of people shelling corn when asked if he wants to help but, finally, he appears not to need to be asked to rebuild Melquiades's home with Pete at the film's conclusion. He does it with a diligence and delicacy previously unrecognisable. It is hard to know for certain whether this constitutes care on Mike's part or his fear of Pete's increasing distrac-tion but, passing Pete a bottle as they admire their handiwork, his surren-der to an obligated connectivity rings true in the end. That the film's final words are Mike calling after Pete 'you gonna be alright?' solidifies this turning outward and breaking away from a masturbatory, solipsistic past.

When the dead body of Melquiades Estrada entreats Pete, and finally Mike, to do the right thing, we're a long way from the 'face' that summons responsibility in more consumable, compassion-igniting images of human need, and deliberately so. Indeed, there is nothing fresh, frontal, or par-ticularly facial about the men's ethical encounter with the corpse. For Levinas, the visage of the other, which called the self into obligation, is, as I noted in the last chapter, always more than the literal or limited human face: it produces all meaning; it 'overflows images'.[39] Meaning moves from beyond the face-to-face, symmetrical, or even (a)live encounter, and never more poetically than here as Melquiades's visage becomes steadily more emptied of life yet full of import. Deposing the conventional dominance of the eye as the window to the soul and the 'returned look' as the site of reciprocity and alignment, *Three Burials* exploits alternative channels of connection.

Melquiades's lingering presence also provides perpetual reference to the disenfranchisement of the illegal 'wetback', to the 'bare life', as

Giorgio Agamben called it, of the individual living beyond the law's protections.[40] Agamben distinguished this concept via the Muselmann of the concentration camp but it has been applied more broadly to other abject figures whose lives do 'not deserve to be lived', or remembered, or mourned.[41] Cast out by the necropolitical system of the camp, the 'living dead' had their worth and rights removed and '[passed] into another world without memory and without grief'.[42] In the discussion of the documentary *Dying at Grace* in Chapter 6, the 'natural causes' of the 'dying lives', rather than living dead, on the hospital ward in the film were framed by the (potentially perverse) privilege attending old age or palliative care or a Western welfare system. Bare life became the benchmark for instating the racial, class and geographic coordinates of those approaching death, for entrenching the relativity or 'comparativity' – rather than closed circuit – of sociocultural critique.

Neither the living dead, nor a dying life, Melquiades's intermediary state between presence and absence, dead and buried, resonates nevertheless with the politico-ethical 'threshold' of bare life, the state of exception enforced by sovereign power.[43] *Three Burials* contests this enforcement while revealing, rather than repressing, its deadly logic. It restores to Melquiades both memory and grief which the institutions – the border patrol agency and the police – denied him. Pete's reminiscences, loss and even love, flood and fuel the narrative, working against the state of exception imposed by both Mike and the sheriff. Pete/Jones makes of Melquiades's a 'grievable life', for Melquiades but crucially for Mike, and by extension for the audience. This is not just to satisfy his own desires, though these are invariably at play, but to destabilise further the sovereignty of trauma as the privileged framework for understanding suffering, to deprioritise Pete's pain as explanation for obligation and connection, and to train what is moving about the film away from the familiar grooves of seemingly compulsively repeated treatments of death (both as trauma and as passive racism). Instead, undercutting, still, those redemptive structures that would bring it all back to Pete, his memories enrich Melquiades's subjectivity and the strength of their relationship. Indeed, the men's inherently imbalanced connectivity endures beyond the bounds of necropower or even life. When Mike beseeches Melquiades to forgive him at the film's end, he is acknowledging a similar connectivity. This connectivity is hooked on the unsolvable and unsalvable imbalance between Mike and the man whose clothes he wears and life he's usurped. And it is crucial, in its dissymmetry, to the ethical, postcolonial project, to a 'radical human vulnerability' which, as Malini Johar Schueller explains, can only be 'transformative . . . [if it] does not, in fact, depend on the erasure of unevenness that has been the basis for a West-centred human-ism'.[44] Though profound and deadly, such an imbalanced connectivity is outed in order to interrupt, at the very least, the necropolitical holding pattern.

Forged in the dissymmetries of illegal acts, necropolitical inheritance and infinite alterity, the geographic, political and corporeal borderlands of *Three Burials* stage formidable acts of obligation. The bonds between its male characters overwhelm the confines and conventions of the normative: they cross barriers of age, place, culture, expectation, mortality; they resist the redemptive, absolutory, reciprocatory cycle of return. These bonds and this ethos I want to call queer. This is not to privilege the homoso-ciality and romance of Pete and Melquiades's relationship, though they are in evidence, or the film's dismissal of reproductive futurity, though it remains for me a far more telling concept in terms of race than sexuality. Rather, introducing this term points to its broader radical meaning. Queer is most commonly understood as a means to defamiliarise the familiar but its more critical charge, of particular relevance here, is to defy the cen-tring of privileged identities and narratives. It defies, in other words, the normative, sovereign or solipsistic logic behind the mortal economies of mainstream cinema/culture that I have outlined in this study.

That queer re-emerged as radical theory and activist battle cry in response to the AIDS epidemic and the genocidal dimensions of, in that case, homophobia, welds it, unsurprisingly perhaps, to questions of the ethical, to a consciousness of the death-dealing encounter with alterity, to the power imbalances of human relationships. Though I can only point here to its resonance for further work, the link between queer theory and ethics and its high stakes remain an ongoing and ever more important theme. Michael Warner speaks of the ethics of queer life as representing '[a] relation to others' which '[a]t its best . . . cuts against every form of hierarchy you could bring into the room'.[45] Douglas Crimp refers to 'the removal of grounds . . . [initiating an] authentic responsibility' that he called queer.[46] These authors would later be taken to task, quite rightly, for the white, western and male privilege inherent in their wider levelling of queer experience but their emphasis on obligation's origins with, and always in relation to, the cast out, is key. Judith Halberstam, David Eng, and José Estaban Muñoz, in reckoning with 'What's Queer about Queer Studies Now?', would draw upon Judith Butler, and invariably Levinas to whom Butler's ethical appeals are indebted, to claim an 'ethics of humil-ity' as underwriting a decentred and anti-unilateral, what we might call, a postcolonial queer critical perspective.[47]

With *Three Burials*'s representation of death, mainstream cinema, I have wanted to suggest, 'removes grounds', cuts against hierarchy and knows that the future is at stake. This moving image pushes towards an understanding of our place in relation to others' suffering and vulnerability, how we might be compelled to reach towards the other, unavoidably, unconditionally, with such care one might be inclined to call it an unrequited capacity to love. Such a love evades the bribes of futurity that undergird our world and that mask the social violence confounding hope elsewhere. Such a love gestures instead to utopian, even queer utopian, life.[48] It is no wonder, perhaps, that Pete's quixotic journey to his friend's home sees him find, or create with Mike, this non-existent village, this 'most beautiful place on earth'. As Melquiades entreats: 'If you go to Jimenez, I swear to you, your heart will break with so much beauty.'

Notes

Introduction

1. Becker, *Denial*.
2. Ariès, *Western*.
3. For discussions of death in eighteenth-century/Victorian culture, see, for example, Frank, *Representations*; Ruby, *Secure* and Strange, *Death*.
4. Ariès, *Western*, p. 85.
5. See, for example, Dollimore, *Desire*, pp. 59–70, 119–27.
6. Freud, 'Attitude', p. 291.
7. Ariès, *Western*, p. 94.
8. For Tanner this split exists between 'competing discourses of objectification and transcendence', *Lost*, p. 221.
9. See Gorer, 'Pornography'.
10. Gorer, 'Pornography', p. 75.
11. Rank, *Will*, p. 130. Quoted in Becker, *Denial*, p. 99.
12. Killilea, *Politics*, p. 6.
13. Freud, 'Economic', p. 418
14. Studies abound on this topic too, especially with regard to horror, but see, for example, Slocum, *Violence*, Stringer, *Blockbusters*, Batchelor, *Cult*.
15. Black, *Aesthetics*, p. 3.
16. Mbembe, 'Necropolitics', p. 11.
17. Ibid., p. 14.
18. For an alternative take on death's narrative role, see Russell, *Narrative Mortality*.
19. Tanner, *Lost*, p. 211.
20. Tercier, *Contemporary*, p. 22.
21. Ibid., p. 212. Bazin called the representation of real or imagined death obscene, too, in its 'violation of nature' ('Afternoon', p. 30).
22. See Williams, *Hard*.
23. See Azoulay, *Contract*; Chouliaraki, *Spectatorship*; Cooper, *Selfless*; Modlinger, *Other*; Saxton, 'Fragile'; Sobchack, *Inscribing*; and Wilson's recent publication which addresses 'moving image artists' (*Love*). My approach also contrasts with another recent study on death and film which traces the relationship between philosophies of death and classical Hollywood narrative structure (Hagin, *Classical*).
24. Aaron, *Spectatorship*, p. 122.

25. King, *Washed*, p. 12. For a discussion of the potential Eurocentrism of the affective turn, see Gunew, 'Subaltern'.
26. For a detailed critique of affect theory, of, for example, its 'circular logic' or closed 'circuit of feeling and response', see Hemmings, 'Invoking', pp. 548, 552.
27. Ramazani, *Writing*, p. 2.
28. Wailoo, '*Katrina's*', p. 2.
29. See Barthes, *Camera*.
30. Tercier, *Contemporary*, p. 210.
31. Field, *Gender*, p. x.
32. West, 'Matter'.
33. Jennings, *Benjamin*, p. 151.
34. Frank, *Representations*, p. 4; Strange, *Death*, p. 19.
35. See Dollimore, *Desire*, pp. 121–3.
36. Ibid.
37. Aaron, *Spectatorship*, pp. 51–86.
38. See Althusser, 'Ideology'.
39. Townsend, *Art*, p. 9.
40. Kellehear, *Social*, p. 251. A principle text within this explosion of interest was Bronfen, *Death*.
41. Radstone, 'Trauma', p. 9. These other texts include Usai, 2001; Dixon, 1999, 2003, 2004; Brottman, 1997, 1999, 2002; Dika, 1990, 2003; Farrell, 1998; Hallas, 2009; Lewis, 2001; and many others.
42. Sturken, *Tangled*; Grainge, *Memory*; Radstone, *Methodology*.
43. See, for example, Dixon, 1999, 2003, 2004; Brottman, 1997, 1999, 2002; Dika, 1990, 2003; Farrell, 1998; Hallas, 2009; and Lewis, 2001.
44. Gabbard, *Magic;* Diawara, *Black*, p. 3.
45. Wallace, *Dark*, p. 121.
46. Bradbury, *Representations*, p. 1.
47. Kramer, 'Anatomy', p. 27.
48. Berns, *Closure*, p. 12.
49. Clark, 'Oncology'.
50. Globalisation or the internet/digital revolution of the 1990s sustained enduring imbalances, as Holmlund puts it, the 'marked digital divide partitioned the world into those with access to computers and those without' (*American*, p. 1).
51. Ricciardi, *Ends*, p. 3; Williams, *Hard*.
52. Gibson, 'Death', p. 423.
53. Gilbert, *Door*, p. 229.
54. Bersani, *Culture*; see also Suleiman, *Risking*.
55. Butler, *Precarious*, p. 151.

Chapter 1

1. According to Bean this connection endured. For a discussion of the risk characterising nickelodeon action films see her '"Trauma Thrills"', pp. 17–30.
2. *Fearless* was certainly the more noteworthy film, and Rosie Perez was nominated for an Oscar and Golden Globe for her supporting role and won at some other festivals. *Mr Jones* mustered less enthusiasm.
3. Breuer, 'Hysterical', p. 57, original emphasis.
4. Laplanche, *Language*, p. 78.
5. Freud, 'Remembering', p. 151.
6. Ibid., pp. 155–6.
7. Ibid.
8. His repression of the trauma is evident in the sharp contrast between his retrospective idealisation of the catastrophe and his place within it, and the sheet-soaking trauma of his nightmares that he does not admit to himself or to the therapist assigned to him.
9. See Kawin, *Mindscreen*, p. 10.
10. Macnab, *Mr Jones*, p. 51.
11. Kemp, *Fearless*, p. 42.
12. For a discussion of the 'ideological tendency of death as closure' in mainstream film, and how it is split from closure in new wave cinemas, see Russell, *Narrative Mortality*, p. 2. See also Neupert's *The End* on the varying degrees of closure in film.
13. Bordwell, *Film Art*, p. 65, original emphasis.
14. Propp posited a universal structure of popular narrative through his study of one hundred Russian folk tales. Regardless of the numerous differences in their stories, the tales shared a fixed group of functions. While evidencing an irreducible structure to the tales, these functions charted a highly moral or social imperative in the struggles between, for example, good and evil as hero and villain. These struggles were implicit to the narrative and fortified in closure. See Propp, *Morphology*.
15. See Todorov, 'Principles', pp. 138–9.
16. See Arroyo, *Action/Spectacle* and Tasker, *Spectacular*.
17. See Tasker, *Action*, Jeffords, *Hard*, and Stringer, *Blockbusters*, pp. 45–113.
18. Two come to mind: Philippe Petit's 1974 tightrope walk between the Twin Towers of New York's World Trade Center and, more recently, Nik Wallenda's across Niagara Falls.
19. Freud, 'Economic', pp. 413–25.
20. See Aaron, 'The Pleasure of Unpleasure' in *Spectatorship*, pp. 51–86.
21. Holmlund, *American*, p. 2.
22. The noticeable absence of graphic death or of bodies corresponds to the film's endorsement by the United States government – necessary when a film requires the loan of military facilities and equipment – and led to a rise in recruitment.

23. The chief stuntman, Art Schoot, died while filming a reverse dive during the filming of *Top Gun*. See the video *Danger Zone*.
24. Moose's is the only dead body we see. His is also the only live body not objectified within the film. In the infamous volleyball scene, he wears a T-shirt in contrast to the buffed-up self-display of his peers. This confirms the invulnerability of the 'potent' male hero but also points to the impossibility of sexualising male death. The relationship between gender and death will be taken up in the next chapter.
25. Conlon discusses the film's alignment of Maverick's status as fighter and lover: as predator in both environments, see 'Making Love', pp. 18–27.
26. This muddiness or murkiness is emblematic of the problem of 'suicide' but, more than this, of the 'value' of social existence. It speaks perhaps of the ambivalence surrounding 'duty' or even purpose in postmodernism or late capitalist culture.
27. This haunting links to Aldrich's 'anti-authoritarian' or ambivalent stance towards war; see Williams, '*The Dirty Dozen*' in Tasker, *Action*, p. 351.
28. *The Bourne Identity* (Doug Liman, 2002); *The Bourne Supremacy* (Paul Greengrass, 2004); *The Bourne Ultimatum* (Paul Greengrass, 2007).
29. For Bond's historical and contemporary relevance see Comentale et al., *Ian Fleming*, and Lindner, *Phenomenon*.
30. See Tasker, *Spectacular*, Chapter 1.
31. Tasker, *Spectacular*, p. 20, emphasis in original.
32. Cruise was also an emerging sex symbol at this point. Part of his star persona, enduringly, has been an often semi-maniacal relationship with self-risk. See Deangelis's discussion of the two stars as 'entrepreneurial rebel[s]' ('Mel', p. 95).
33. See ibid. p. 88 and Wood, *Hollywood*, p. 241.
34. For discussion of the racial politics of mainstream cinema, see Guererro, *Framing*.
35. While war films would seem to suggest a more understated, or unconditional, heroism, there is a vanity at play, relatively too in *The Great Escape* with the contrast between the exceptional allied heroes and the uninspiring Germans.
36. For a brief discussion of the anxious relationship between American and Japanese notions of sacrificial honour see Hirano, *Mr Smith*, pp. 74–5.
37. In the film *The Last Samurai* (Edward Zwick, 2003) a young warrior has his topknot cut off by the army as a mark of utter belittlement.
38. For a full discussion of this, see Pinquet, *Voluntary Death*. Clint Eastwood's companion pieces in 2006, *Flag of Our Fathers* and *Letters from Iwo Jima* provide fascinating counterpoints on the cultural specificity of dutiful sacrifice, albeit as Hollywood 'doing' Japan.
39. Indeed, 'Tom Cruise' will learn this important lesson in *The Last Samurai* in yet another celebration of the white American hero by Edward Zwick.

40. Deangelis, 'Gibson', pp. 88, 78.
41. See Nye, *Bound*.

Chapter 2

1. Homicide and Suicide Rates – National Violent Death Reporting System, Six States, 2003 http://www.cdc.gov/MMWR/preview/mmwrhtml/mm5415a1.html; Leading causes of death, 1991–2006; http://www.cdc.gov/violenceprevention/suicide/statistics/leading_causes.html
2. Its taboo status leads to its misrecording, as does the difficulty of distinguishing it from accidental death or death from misadventure.
3. Taylor, *Durkheim*, p. 159
4. Ibid., p. 159.
5. Durkheim, *Suicide*.
6. Hill, *Ambitiosa*, p. 6.
7. The language is also telling in this regard. One gives one's life in heroic self-sacrifice: one takes one's life in un-heroic, unjust acts: one takes what is not one's to take. Our lives are ours to give, but 'God's' to take.
8. Althusser, 'Ideology'.
9. Increasingly 'freedom fighters' or suicide bombers are female, see Bloom, 'Female', pp. 94–102.
10. The red-hatted 'child' is one of *In Bruges*'s many references to *Don't Look Now* (Nicolas Roeg, 1973).
11. The early German film is especially interesting in that it was seen as its Nazi director garnering support for the Third Reich's euthanasia programme. Similarly, the more recent surge in euthanasia films can be connected to the AIDS crisis and the increasing public debate on assisted dying.
12. Brown, *Art*, p. 193.
13. Ibid., p. 193.
14. The irreverent recent comedy, *Wristcutters: A Love Story* (Goran Dukic, 2006), which is more engaged with the fantasy of the afterlife than the drive to suicide, also follows a conservative trajectory with its happy ending of heterosexual union and defiance of death
15. See the documentary, *Jonestown: The Life and Death of Peoples Temple* (Stanley Nelson, 2006); the television specials, *Jonestown: Paradise Lost* (Tim Wolochatiuk, 2007) and *Witness to Jonestown* (Stephen Stept, 2008). For Masada, see, for example, the television series, *The Antagonists* (1981) and the television special *Masada* (2002).
16. It provided the storyline for 'Shooting Stars', episode 6, of season 4, of the hit US television show *CSI: Crime Scene Investigation*, first screened 13 October 2005.
17. Chris Morris's satire, *Four Lions* (2010) – an absurdist comedy about suicide terrorism – certainly confounds these categories, and others, too.
18. See Durkheim, *Suicide*.

19. Baechler, *Suicides*, p. 63.
20. The film's politics are problematic in this regard for, as I'll discuss of similar films in the next chapter, it is the white French liberal who is actually, and solipsistically, redeemed through its 'lesson'.
21. Suicide is present in other national cinemas, especially Indian, Nigerian and Japanese. See, for example, Shah, *Indian*, and Haynes, *Nigerian*, p. 235. Most texts on Japanese culture make reference to the place of suicide within it.
22. For a discussion of Kiarostami's 'western mirror', see Cheshire, 'How to', p. 12.
23. Dönmez-Colin, *Cinemas*, p. 50.
24. These two are: *And Life Goes On* (aka *Life and Nothing More*, 1992) and *Through the Olive Trees* (1994). See, 'Akrami', *Taste*.
25. Lippard, 'Disappearing', p. 35.
26. Chaudhuri, 'Open', p. 47.
27. Lippard, 'Disappearing', p. 36.
28. Mulvey, 'Kiarostami', p. 25.
29. The film starts with an extraordinary sense that Mr Badii is soliciting for sex rather than for someone to assist him post-suicide. In this way, the film embarks upon a dialogue with the 'unsaid' rather than with suicide per se.
30. Brunette, *Haneke*, p. 12. This middle-class 'death in life' can be seen to contrast dramatically with the colonised dead-alreadiness, discussed later.
31. Haneke, 'World', p. 30.
32. Cowan, 'Between', p. 125.
33. Wheatley, *Haneke*, p. 56; Saxton, 'Close'.
34. For a discussion of *Paradise Now*'s anti-abject suicide, see Morag, 'Living', pp. 3–24.
35. Brunette, *Haneke*, p. 21. It is worth noting how the most assaulting image in the film was considered to be the flushing of money down the toilet. Haneke could be seen to use such assaultive imagery for postcolonial critique, too, though more commonly and convincingly, this is seen as reinforcing neocolonial norms. See, for example, Celik, '*Caché*', pp. 59–80.
36. See Tolstoy, *Karenina*; Chopin, *Awakening*; Flaubert, *Bovary* and Chabrol's *Madame Bovary* (1991). Meanwhile, though Western culture exhibits a long history of feminising dying it 'has never been overly hospitable to the female death icon', Guthke, *Gender*, p. 26.
37. Eugenides's emphasis falls on Cecilia's virginity instead.
38. Scott, '*Virgin*'.
39. Eugenides, *Virgin*, p. 3.
40. See Gates, *Victorian*.
41. Ibid., p. 141.
42. Brown, *Art*, p. 221.
43. See Shostak, 'A story', pp. 808–32.
44. Gates, *Victorian*, p. 141.

45. See Higonnet, 'Silences', p. 78.
46. Gates, *Victorian*, p. 142.
47. Eva Cantarella has remarked on the ancient association of femininity with swinging and 'the frequency of female hangings in Greek texts' and their magical import, see 'Dangling', p. 58.
48. In 2005, firearms accounted for 57.6 per cent of male suicides and 31 per cent of women's. See: http://www.suicide.org/suicide-statistics.html Accessed 18 August 2011.
49. Eugenidies, *Virgin*, pp. 36, 93.
50. See, for example, Bradshaw's review of the film.
51. Bronfen, *Over*, p. 356.
52. Aaron, *Spectatorship*, p. 26.
53. See Shostak, 'A story'.
54. Scott, *'Virgin'*. For Graham Fuller, in *Sight and Sound*, the film is a classic fairy tale demanding psychoanalytic reading; for others, its mythic, gothic and intertextual dimensions are the most compelling. See Fuller, 'Death'; and Winter, 'Mystery Girls', p. 144.
55. Cardullo, *Search*, p. 203.
56. As Shostak argues so well of the novel, the story is all about the relentless, consuming and even debilitating male quest for knowing woman. See 'A story'.
57. See, for example *Seventh Continent* or *Green Mile* (Frank Darabont, 1999). It is also, obviously, a heteronormative model.
58. Kay Dickinson makes the irony plain in her article, with its subheading 'vanishing points' ('Road', p. 150).
59. Mbembe, 'Necropolitics', p. 27.
60. Stam, 'Colonialism', p. 11. This kind of early film-making included anthropologists' films and, in far greater numbers, the 'native peoples' appearing in many commercial manufacturers' films, as well as their films of the Spanish-American and Philippine-American wars. See Abel, *Encyclopedia*, pp. 318, 453. I am grateful to John Horne for these examples.
61. Kaplan, *Looking*, p. 78.
62. Spivak, *Critique*.
63. Baucom, *Specters*, p. 155.
64. Gwendolyn Foster provides an interesting discussion of cinema 'capturing an/other' in *Captive*, p. 3. She equates all kinds of captives but it is worth not equating them as this chapter seeks to demonstrate.
65. The advantage of his living in Holland as an adult is to be duly noted too.
66. Like 'postcolonial' texts, it reveals the destructiveness and 'negation' at the heart of colonial impact. See Nayar, *PostColonial*.
67. Naficy, *Accented*, p. 26.
68. Wayne, *Political*.
69. Kira, 'Collective', p. 125.
70. Yaqub, 'Wedding', p. 77.

71. Dickinson, 'Road', p. 150. Dickinson, who addresses the repeated use of the car in Palestinian film, refers not only to Western exploitation, in general, but also to the Israeli highway through the territories which Palestinians are not allowed to use.
72. Pape, *Cutting*, pp. 10, 329, emphasis in original.
73. Spivak, '*Can the Subaltern Speak?*'
74. When one of the cab drivers mentions how the contaminated water is supposed to diminish men's sperm counts, the occupation is again shown to be responsible for this antigenerative state.
75. This 'no future' corresponds to the 'no-horizon' mentioned earlier and nods towards the radical antigenerative theme of Edelman's *No Future*.
76. I am using the male gaze here metonymically to stand for Western cinema's governing critical paradigms which prioritise objectification and narcissism but make invisible racial consciousness.
77. Brand, 'Identification', p. 172.
78. The resistance to first/dominant cinema's technical vocabulary, here, is not an 'imperfect cinema' as in the Cuban film-maker Julio García Espinoza's 1969 manifesto, 'For an Imperfect Cinema' which directs specific criticism against the credo of technical perfection, in Martin, *New*, pp. 71–82. *Paradise Now* is a highly accomplished, aesthetically wrought, product. Indeed, the 'amateurist' imperfect cinema of the terrorist film-maker is ridiculed within the film, where, in 'third cinema', according to Shohat and Stam, 'the lack of technical resources was metaphorically transmogrified into an expressive force', *Unthinking*, p. 256.
79. Khaled will similarly have a 'centred' scene in his 'unsuccessful' martyr video.
80. Brand, 'Identification', p. 170.
81. JanMohammed, *Death-Bound*, p. 298.
82. It remains to be seen what *Courier*, his next film for Hollywood, will be like.

Chapter 3

1. See Freud, 'Beyond', pp. 275–338 and 'Economic', pp. 413–25.
2. See Aaron, *Spectatorship*.
3. See, for example, Metz, *Imaginary* and Stam et al., *Vocabularies*, pp. 146–58.
4. Derrida in Borradori, *Terror*, p. 95.
5. Ibid., pp. 94, 95. For related discussions see Chomsky, *9-11*, Žižek, *Welcome*, and Butler, *Precarious*.
6. Statistics of casualties are available from the Defense Department of the United States at http://www.defense.gov
7. Derrida in Borradori, *Terror*, p. 151.
8. For the FBI's statistics on the increase in terrorist activity post-9/11, and their analysis, see O'Brien, 'Evolution'.

9. See King, 'Just Like', pp. 47–57.

10. Schneider, 'Architectural', p. 34.

11. Bradshaw, '*United 93*'.

12. Barker, *Toxic*, p. 4. Pierre Le Blavec notes how also in October 'the Institute for Creative Technologies (ICT) of the University of Southern California (USC) organized . . . with the support of the Pentagon, a series of seminars with Hollywood scriptwriters' ('International', p. 10).

13. For a more detailed list of its impact on television's film scheduling see Spigel, 'Entertainment', pp. 235–70.

14. See Markovitz, 'Reel', pp. 201–2.

15. Calvert, 'Ideology', p. 13.

16. Barker, *Toxic*, p. 1.

17. As well as Barker, see Birkenstein et al., *Reframing*; Hammond, *Screens*; and Prince, *Firestorm*.

18. See Aaron, *Perilous*; Brottman, *Crash*; Dixon, *Visions* and *After 9/11*; Grainge, *Memory*; Lewis, *End* and Sturken, *Tangled*.

19. Barker, *Toxic*, p. 1.

20. In a similar spirit one can gauge exactly how 'of the centre' anti-Iraq war feeling has become in the United States, through the 'blockbuster' status and odd reception accorded to *Lions for Lambs*.

21. Doherty, 'New', p. 4.

22. *Babel* also starts with, and leads on from, a terrorist act.

23. 'Spielberg', *Tonight*. Similarly, when some of the first words in *District 9* are 'Now to everyone's surprise the ship didn't come to a halt over Manhattan or Washington', the context is clear.

24. *War of the Worlds* is the exception here.

25. Žižek, commentary, *Children of Men*.

26. Chaudhuri, 'Unpeople', p. 198.

27. See production details for *Blood Diamond*, for example, on IMDb.

28. Marciniak et al., distinguish *Babel* as '[s]elf-consciously "global" and dedicated to the exploration of intercultural contrasts and conflicts' (p. 2). For further discussion of the film as transnational see their *Transnational*, pp. 1–20.

29. See Dixon, *Film and TV*.

30. Barker, *Toxic*, p. 6.

31. Kakoudaki, 'Spectacles', pp. 138, 121.

32. King, *Washed*, p. 3.

33. David Martin-Jones was similarly interested in how between 2003 and 2005 so many films would 'allegorically relive this trauma in order to work through national loss' (*Deleuze*, p. 156). But it is not trauma that I am interested in here or the 'unity' that might come from its processing.

34. Weber, *Imagining*, p. 4. According to Spigel this 'moral position ran through a number of television's "reality" genres' too ('Entertainment', p. 246).

35. Westwell, *War*, p. 113.

36. Ibid., p. 113.
37. Ibid., p. 113.
38. Ibid., p. 113.
39. The purchase of home security systems had boomed in the 1990s: see, for example, Lee, *Impact*, p. 33. According to Vanhala, '[f]rom 1980 through September 11, 2001, Hollywood produced sixteen films that used international terrorism as the film's central theme, and which were in the annual domestic top fifty box office' (*Depiction*, p. 6).
40. King, *Washed*, p. 4.
41. These films have ceased to be quite so peripheral or rare. More recent incarnations of this type of film would be the 'truth and reconcilation' films *Country of My Skull* (John Boorman, 2006) and *Red Dust* (Tom Hooper, 2004) which have an author and lawyer, respectively, in place of the journalist/photographer of the films from the 1980s. 'Human rights' films, such as *Even the Rain* (Iciar Bollain, 2010), increasingly with festivals dedicated to them, contribute to the contemporary expansion of this group too.
42. Thompson, *Apocalyptic*, p. 1. See also Dixon, *Visions* and Walliss, *End*. Films include *Outbreak* (Wolfgang Peterson, 1995), *Dante's Peak* (Roger Donaldson, 1997), *Volcano* (Mick Jackson, 1997), *Armageddon* (Michael Bay, 1998), and *Deep Impact* (Mimi Leder, 1998). According to Keane, the surge in the 1990s 'surpassed even the 1970s disaster cycle' (*Disaster*, p. 73).
43. There is a parallel argument here about the career of Zwick whose overblown focus on the American hero characterises all his films. Interestingly, *Blood Diamond* is one of only two of his films to make a hero of a non-American although Leo's star persona sustains the American identity. The other, *Defiance*, similarly emphasises heroism and in a decidedly and oddly anglicised manner.
44. See also, for example, Savran, *Taking it*.
45. See the film's website, http://blooddiamondmovie.warnerbros.com/main.html
46. Giroux, 'Democracy', p. 245.
47. Žižek, '9/11', p. 30.
48. Levinas, *Totality*.
49. Levinas, 'Ethics', p. 82. See my earlier discussion of this in Aaron, *Spectatorship*, pp. 111–13.
50. Aaron, *Spectatorship*, p. 111.
51. Butler, *Precarious*, p. 8.
52. Becker, *Surpassing*, p. x.
53. See Dyer's discussion of the male pin-up: 'Don't', pp. 61–73. *Hotel Rwanda*'s whitening of the West is evidenced further by the UN troops remaining after the Belgians leave who, as Hron notes, 'consisted of Ghaneans, Tunisians and Bangladeshi forces, so very few Whites' ('Genocide', p. 215).
54. Levinas is at the core of an emerging body of ethical film criticism: see Cooper, *Selfless*; Aaron, *Spectatorship*; Downing and Saxton, *Film*

and Ethics. Crucially, the issue of race is marginalised within these works.

55. A far more complex version of this 'white conscience' narrative is provided by the film *Even the Rain* (Iciar Bollain, 2010). This film wrestles with these issues explicitly and self-consciously. It still, however, centres the white experience at the expense of the indigenous Bolivians and raises, therefore, the question of whether mainstream film – that which aims for a mass audience – can ever avoid this neocolonialism. I revisit this question in the conclusion.

56. See, for example, Cameron, *Africa* and Bickford-Smith, *Black*.

57. Hron, 'Genocide', p. 215.

58. Ibid., p. 215. The film has been considered successful in offering an interactive 'working through', rather than voyeuristic spectacle, of the Rwandan atrocities; see Uraizee, *Jaws*.

59. For *Hotel Rwanda*'s historicisation see Harrow, '*Un train*', pp. 223–32.

60. Adhikari, 'Too Much', p. 281.

61. King, *African Americans*, p. 63. Writing of the 'counterhistorical dramatic film', Goldberg argues more broadly that 'the frame of this Western identity is built upon the spectacle of the tortured body of the national and cultural other' ('Splitting', p. 251).

62. Hornbuckle, 'Blood Diamond'.

63. Lee, 'Circling'.

64. Chaudhuri, 'Unpeople', p. 204.

65. Boyle, 'Disaster-capitalism'.

66. Chaudhary, 'Humanity', pp. 97, 98.

67. It was nominated and won various awards including an Oscar and Golden Globe for Rachel Weisz as best supporting actress.

68. Ebert, '*Constant Gardener*'.

69. Atkinson, 'Cold'.

70. Saxton, *Film and Ethics*, p. 56.

71. Härting, 'Global', pp.16–17.

72. Interestingly, the symbolic weight of the Canadian UN colonel, who Oliver is based on, has been more recently concretised in Spottiswoode's own Rwandan story: *Shake Hands with The Devil* (2007).

73. Moretti, *Signs*, p. 173.

74. Wade, 'Sublime', pp. 16–17.

75. For a discussion of the falsities of the film and Rusesbagina's role, see Ndahiro and Rutazibwa, *Tutsi*.

76. McKenna, 'Law's Delay', p. 201.

77. Horkheimer and Adorno, *Dialectic*, p. 39.

78. In her recent book, King also points to a continuance of what she calls Hollywood's 'sacrificial films' which '[e]specially since the 1970s . . . have emerged in correspondence with cycles of trauma culture'. While she similarly finds them to be 'regenerative and salvific', her argument is limited to

an internal American cultural politics and US-based and US-focused films (*Washed*, pp. 4–5, 6). I am pointing instead to something far more inherent and eternal to the Western condition which Hollywood is so central to.

79. Slocum, *Violence*, p. 13.
80. Derrida, *Gift*, p. 86.
81. Horkheimer, *Dialectic*, p. 39. Pahl's claim that '[a]ny screen death . . . might be sacrificial', suggests the pervasiveness of this political practice of substitution through cinema ('Sacrifice', p. 465).
82. Derrida in Borradori, *Terror*, p. 94.
83. See Wheatley, *Haneke*. She explicitly, and problematically, however, peripheralises race in the distinction of ethics. See also my distinction of dogma directors in *Spectatorship*.
84. *I am Legend* (Francis Lawrence, 2007) stands out here.
85. Rich, 'Back'.
86. Ibid.

Chapter 4

1. Scarry, *Body*, p. 4.
2. Ibid., p. 11.
3. Ibid., p. 16
4. Ibid., p. 16.
5. Schultz, 'Sensational!', pp. 137–49.
6. Tercier, *Contemporary*, p. 22.
7. McInerney, 'Cinematic', p. 211.
8. Burki, 'Film', pp. 103–4.
9. Kübler-Ross, *On Death*.
10. Sontag, *Metaphor*, p. 3.
11. See Richards, 'Rosetta' and Mackenna, 'Life'. Numerous online discussions testify to the informal use of film within the grieving process: see, for example, Dennis, 'Movies'. For a discussion of its for more formal use, see Hyler, 'Teaching'.
12. Bending, *Pain*, p. 109
13. The film is also unusual as a woman's film in 'encourag[ing] or facilitate[ing] spectatorial identification' with the 'diseased' protagonist, see Doane, 'Clinical', p. 224. Hollywood's privileging of strength and forbearance is not so different from what goes on in hospitals too; see Bond, 'Suffering'.
14. Typical of the distorted and underrepresentation of disability, blindness, so rarely represented in film, is merely a harbinger, if not the equivalent, of death here and a potentially inconspicuous one at that. This is also true of *Its My Party* (Randal Kleiser, 1996) and *Blue* (Derek Jarman, 1993) but, crucially, their AIDS-related blindness requires this equivalence.
15. Stacey, *Teratologies*, p. 2.
16. Ibid., p. 2.

17. Ibid., p. 13.
18. Fitzgerald, *Bette Davis*.
19. Holdstein, 'Dark Victory', pp. 22–4.
20. Sontag, *Metaphor*, p. 17.
21. Ibid., p. 17.
22. The original *Brian's Song* received various accolades. It gained an Emmy as well as various nominations in 1971. It is '[o]ften cited as the finest television movie ever made' (Niemi, *History*, p. 213). It was also considered the 'movie most likely to make men cry' (Didinger, *Ultimate*, p. 80).
23. Part of Pic's triumph was his anti-racism. The relationship between death and racism will be discussed fully in the next chapter.
24. Sontag, *Metaphor*, p. 31.
25. Wallace, *Dark*, p. 280.
26. Waites, 'Invisible', p. 483.
27. Ibid., pp. 488–9.
28. Ebert, 'Beaches'.
29. The narcissism of this surviving, replacement pair, of big and little C.C., should not be lost on anyone familiar with Midler's characterisation here or of divas elsewhere.
30. Though *Hilary and Jackie* returns to the girls as children at the film's close, its flash back is fantastical and, in featuring the elder Jackie, too, renders their innocence irrelevant.
31. Christmas as child-oriented and timeless event was part of the final words in *Boys on the Side* and integral to *Stepmom*'s final scene too.
32. *Stepmom* is also interesting for how it imagines 'after death' for the youngest child: fantasy of some form of afterlife.
33. See reviews by Ebert and Berardinelli.
34. Clark, 'Oncology'.
35. Gibran, *Prophet*, p. 35.
36. Feuer, 'Self-reflective', pp. 159–74.
37. Tanner, *Lost*, p. 221.
38. Bradbury, 'Good', pp. 60–1.
39. See Bradbury, *Representations*, p. 148.
40. Tanner, *Lost*, p. 23.
41. A different take on inexpressibility has also been noted by Allan Kellehear in his discussion of dementia and how it has 'silenced many of the voices' of the dying (*Social*, p. 253).
42. McInerney, 'Cinematic', p. 211.
43. Snyder et al., *Disability*, p. 2.
44. Scott, '*My Sister's Keeper*'.
45. See http://www.msif.org/en/about_ms/ms_by_topic/pain/index.html.
46. Sontag, *Metaphor*, p. 18.
47. And, as I argued above, the films about cancer manage to localise the disease to limit its impact within the body and therefore upon the body.

48. It is also no surprise that sex features within the protagonist's decline where it is absent in every other terminal illness film. The ill body remains desirous, and libidinal.
49. Gorbman, *Melodies*, p. 151.
50. There is a recurrence of performed music and singing in the terminal illness films too. The songs in *Beaches*, *Boys on the Side* and *Stepmom* provide pathos, enhance characterisation and, most importantly in the last two, familial bonds in their singalong sequences. In *Hilary and Jackie*, however, music serves not to exemplify joy and intimacy, as part of the fabric of the family that is being preserved, but rather the singularity of the individual. It is everyday.
51. Nowell-Smith, 'Melodrama', p. 194.
52. The Britishness of Fish's forecast was confirmed when an extract was shown during the opening ceremony of the London 2012 Olympic Games.
53. Tapia, *Pietas*, p. 19.
54. That the film is based on Hilary's memoir is, perhaps, an explanation for the 'slant' of the narrative.
55. Marks, *Skin*, p. xvi.
56. Tanner, *Lost*, p. 24.
57. See 'The Wit Film Project', 'a medical training programme' using the film. I'm grateful to John Horne for telling me how this film had been picked up in this way.
58. Bradbury, *Representations*, p. 162.
59. Prince, *Kurosawa*, p. 102.
60. Holden, '*Lazarescu*'.
61. Scarry, *Body*, p. 13
62. Mitchell, 'Narrative', p. 16.
63. Shildrick sees leakiness, in particular female leakiness, as radical, as 'the very ground for a postmodernist feminist ethic' (*Leaky*, p. 12).
64. For a discussion of dying as social exchange, see Kellehear, *Social*.
65. Tanner, *Lost*, p. 11.
66. Indeed, even Mioara has health problems.
67. McInerney, 'Cinematic', p. 211.

Chapter 5

1. Dyer discusses serial killing as a 'white thing' in *Matter*, p. 112.
2. For a fascinating discussion of the relationship between lynching and the tropes of melodrama on stage and then screen, see Wood, *Lynching*, pp. 113–46. Wood also traces the connections between lynching and elephant executions in the United States in the early 1900s, see 'Killing'.
3. McRuer, 'Compulsory', p. 89.
4. There are other ways in which gender has an impact on the representation of bodily dysfunction or disease. For example, for the 'strong gender

bias in the ways in which epilepsy is portrayed' see *Baxendale,* 'Epilepsy', p. 769.

5. For a discussion of this see, for example, Williams, 'Something', pp. 2–27.

6. Though this has been disputed statistically, it was commonly 'known' culturally, see Wilcox, 'Evolution'.

7. Children are still absent in the male-centred more art-house French films *Son frère* (Patrice Chéreau, 2003) and *Time to Leave* (François Ozon, 2005) but the topic is far from ignored.

8. It uses dying to explore more complex versions of relationships and of parenthood. The son will be recouped from a debauched and sexually unclear lifestyle and will give away his inheritance.

9. For a discussion of those African American traditions, see Bernier, *Characters.*

10. Gilroy, *Black*, p. 68.

11. Clark, 'Oncology'. The very rare film presence of African American physicians does not apply to television. The ensemble casts of the medical dramas and comedies since the 1990s (*Casualty, ER, Scrubs, Grey's Anatomy, House*) have been multiracial. Whoopi Goldberg's roles in *Boys on the Side* and *Clara's Heart* (Robert Mulligan, 1988), *Ghost* (Jerry Zucker, 1990) and *Corrina Corrina* (Jessie Nelson, 1994) are also mammy-like; see Bogle's discussion of her career in *Toms,* pp. 329–36.

12. Latifah's (closeted) status as lesbian supports this no doubt.

13. Not only have gay directors or screenwriters also been behind films viewed as confirming heteronormativity but queer radicalism is not the exclusive domain of LGBT film-makers either. Also, New Queer Cinema, especially as encapsulated here, was increasingly a 'white' movement. That said, its origins were not so normative, and, in fact, *Swoon* returned both homosexuality and, less so, Jewishness, (so homophobia and anti-Semitism) to the Leopold and Loeb story. For their more detailed return see Franklin, 'Jew Boys', pp. 121–48.

14. Edelman, *No Future*, p. 4.

15. I'm grateful to my PhD student Katie Barnett whose reading of *The Living End* as antireproductive futurism was instructive here.

16. The order of these also operates as a snapshot of gay Western history.

17. Burki, 'Film', pp. 103–4.

18. Bruhm, *Gothic*, p. 149 and Craig, 'Ontogenetic', p. 37. For broad discussions of the history of pain, see Morris, *Culture* and Hardcastle, *Myth.*

19. *Charlie's Angels* (McG, 2000) is the most obvious.

20. Arthur Laurents in *The Celluloid Closet* (Rob Epstein and Jeffrey Friedman, 1995).

21. Russo, *Celluloid*, pp.347–9.

22. For example, see Benshoff's *Monsters* and my ''Til Death', pp. 67–86.

23. Their scapegoated status is inflamed perhaps by the disproportionate number of lesbians on death row. See for example, Brownworth, 'Dykes', pp. 62–4.

24. See Shohat, *Unthinking* and Nadel, 'Whole', pp. 184–206. For a useful, if cursory, sense of the racial and national make-up of baddies in action films over various decades, see Leo, 'Action'. According to Shaheen, 'Arabs remains [*sic*] the most maligned group in the history of Hollywood' (*Guilty*, p. xi).
25. Gabbard calls the industry white Hollywood in *Magic*.
26. Taylor, 'Rebirth', p. 17.
27. Indeed, the least common baddie in the action film in the 1980s and 1990s was African American, see Leo, 'Action'. There are numerous studies of black stereotype in Hollywood: see Guerrero, 'New' and Bogle, *Toms*.
28. hooks, 'Sorrowful', pp. 10–14. These hood films' conventionality has been celebrated as 'strategic essentialism'; see Munby, *Under*, p. 8.
29. Ibid., p. 14.
30. *My Life without Me* also pivots on a bucket list.
31. Goldsby, *Spectacular*, p. 210.
32. For a detailed discussion of this, see Wood, *Lynching*, pp. 179–222.
33. Ebert, '*Bucket*'.
34. See Appiah, 'Blacks', pp. 77–90; Farley, 'Magic', p. 14; Entman, *Image*; Glenn, 'Power', pp. 135–52; Denzin, *Reading*; Okorafor-Mbachu, 'Stephen'. Kakoudaki locates 'color-blindness' within the heroics of action cinema too ('Spectacles', p. 121).
35. Hughey, 'Cinethetic', p. 544.
36. It does it less reductively. Altering the true story's Arab/Algerian protagonist, however, to a black African Frenchman confirms the enduring appeal of the mammy role.
37. Hughey, 'Cinethetic', p. 550. This racist post-racism, polite or 'passive racism' (Taylor, 'Rebirth', p. 17) is prevalent in film theory, too, in its doggedly solipsistic heartland but is especially troubling in so-called ethical criticism.
38. Glenn, 'Power'.
39. Interestingly this supernatural deathly dynamic does not stretch to the afterlife film. I elaborate on this in Chapter 7.
40. Farley, *Magic*, p. 14
41. Ibid., p. 14.
42. He has been positioned as fifth of the top ten 'total box office revenue' list. See: http://www.examiner.com/movie-in-baltimore/top-10-actors-morgan-freeman-5-on-total-box-office-revenue-list Accessed 25 January 2012.
43. Brooks, '*Bucket*'.
44. The film's odd combination of popular culture and pseudo-profundity was remarked upon by Burki who notes how 'the aesthetic of a Pizza Hut advert [was brought] to a film about mortality' ('Film', p. 104).
45. Bonilla-Silva, 'Linguistics', p. 63.
46. Edelman, *No Future*.
47. Wilderson, *Red*, p. 9.

48. The comedies are all set in the North: *Bucket List* in California, *Bruce Almighty* and *Evan Almighty* in Buffalo, NY. *Ghost* in New York City. The dramas in the South: *Legend of Baggar Vance* in South Carolina, *Green Mile* and *The Help* in Mississippi.

49. Holland, 'Death'.

50. King, *African Americans*, p. 50. Williams and Wiegman have made key contributions to the discussion of black suffering and American popular culture; see *Playing* and *Anatomies* respectively.

51. Ibid., p. 53.

52. Rowe, 'Feeling', p. 138.

53. King, *African Americans*, p. 50.

54. This points, unavoidably, to the relentless limitations to Hollywood's black images. Collins writes that, '[b]y suppressing the nurturing that African-American women might give their own children which would strengthen Black family networks, and by forcing Black women to work in the field, "wet nurse" White children, and emotionally nurture their White owners, slave owners effectively tied the controlling images of jezebel and mammy to the economic exploitation inherent in the institution of slavery' (*Feminist*, pp. 81–2).

55. Indeed, Leonard's influence from beyond the grave is rejected by Leticia.

56. That it said it's set in Georgia, but is actually filmed in Louisiana, reiterates the iconography of the South rather than the specifics of locales.

57. Meeropol, 'Strange'.

58. Holland, 'Death'.

59. Fleetwood, 'Failing', p. 777. See also Wailoo, *Imprint*.

60. Wilderson, *Red*, p. 332. See Marriott, *Men*.

61. See Wood, *Lynching*, pp. 179–222.

62. Similarly, while the title *Monster's Ball* refers to the night before execution, as Hank explains in the film, it connects more powerfully to immoral Hank getting his end away than Lawrence's deeds or death.

63. Berardinelli, '*Monster's*'.

64. Angelou, *Caged*. See cast and crew interviews in DVD of *Monster's Ball*.

65. Anyiwo, '*Monster's Ball*'.

66. This emphasis on legacy is made all the more stark through the sheer absence of kith and kin on the Musgrove side.

67. Wilderson, *Red*, p. 260.

68. Rowe, 'Feeling', p. 127.

69. Dreher, 'Eulogy', pp. 65–81.

70. Rowe, 'Feeling', p. 128.

71. Wilderson, *Red*, p. 340.

72. Ibid., p. 249.

73. Branigan, *Projecting*, p. 295, n. 95. See also Oudart, 'Suture'.

74. Rowe, 'Feeling', p. 124.

75. Ibid., p. 124.

76. Wilderson, *Red*, p. 339.
77. Dreher, 'Eulogy'.
78. Cutler's use of these two as the backdrop to her discussion of some African American documentaries on motherhood is indicative of the dearth of sites of comparison ('Don't', pp. 213–35).
79. Ibid., p. 219.
80. Pough, *Check it*, p. 131.
81. Ibid., p. 131. See also McCormick, 'Supermothers'. Wallace emphasises the primacy of the 'cultural phenomenon of invisibility, both racial and gendered' (*Dark*, p. 125).
82. Duncan, 'Women'.
83. For a discussion of the literary genre's relationship to women's, black and gay rights see, for example, Hampton, *Changing*; and, in terms of race and science fiction films, Nama, *Black Space*. For a discussion of *I am Legend*'s conservatism in contrast to 'other dystopian films that use racial "difference" to draw out the indecencies of the state', see Brayton, 'Racial'.
84. King, *African Americans*, p. 53.
85. Wilderson, *Red*, p. 23.

Chapter 6

1. Landsberg, *Prosthetic*, p. 150.
2. Chouliaraki, *Spectatorship*, p. 14.
3. In snuff a woman is 'really' murdered on screen for sexual gratification. In 'reaction videos' individuals upload amateur footage on to the web of their watching an uploaded film or media clip of graphic, usually obscene or violent, events. Most recently, reaction videos to filmed murders have proliferated online.
4. Mondo films include, most notably, *Mondo Cane* (Paolo Cavara, Gualtiero Jacopetti, Franco Prosperi, 1962) and John Alan Schwartz's *Faces of Death* (1978). For a recent discussion of their critical value, see Goodall, 'Real'.
5. Bruzzi, *New*, p. 1.
6. For example, *Near Death* won the FIPRESCI Prize at the Berlin International Film Festival in 1990; *Dying at Grace* won awards from the Phoenix Film Festival, Toronto's Gemini Film and the Directors Guild of Canada; *Silverlake Life* won many awards including at Berlin and Sundance. See International Movie Database online for more information. Roemer's *Dying* was shown on PBS, and King's *Dying at Grace* on CBC.
7. A list of these North American and British documentaries on death and dying can be found at http://www.programsforelderly.com/documentaries-death.php
8. There is a longer history of avant-garde films focusing on 'real' death, such as George Franju's *Le sang des bêtes* (1949). Though these films might chal-

lenge the hypocrisy of modern life's denial of death and violence they, too, sit outside my concerns in this chapter.

9. Grierson, 'Documentary', p. 8.
10. See, respectively, Horne, 'Screening' and Hallas, *Reframing*.
11. Arthur, 'Jargons', p. 108.
12. Sobchack, 'Inscribing'.
13. See Cooper, *Selfless* and 'Mortal', pp. 66–87; Saxton, *Haunted* and 'Fragile', pp. 1–14.
14. Noys, *Culture*, pp. 120–2.
15. Fleischer, 'Dying', p. 30.
16. Maslin, '*Near Death*'.
17. Koresky, 'Eclipse'.
18. Original review not available. Quoted in entry on *Dying at Grace* in the Canadian Film Encyclopedia.
19. Aaron, *Spectatorship*, p. 122.
20. As Noys warns in his own cultural study of death, 'writing of death must constantly challenge the fascination with death and the heroism that is often associated with "confronting" death. In fact, the whole language of confrontation, to which this study has not been immune, may need to be discarded' (*Culture*, p. 154).
21. Adams, '*How to*'.
22. Koresky, 'Eclipse'.
23. Canadian Film Encyclopedia.
24. Renoir wrote this is in a letter to King's New York publicist. The letter is reprinted in Feldman, *King*, p. 20.
25. Helwig, *Names*, p. 186.
26. For a sense of his various accomplishments see Guild, 'DGC'. See also Armstrong, 'Tribute'. For a full list of awards, see: http://www.imdb.com/name/nm0454437/awards
27. Breitinger, *Defining*, p. 206.
28. Koresky, 'Eclipse'.
29. King in Armstrong, 'Tribute'.
30. Lim, 'Second'.
31. Koresky, 'Eclipse'
32. Rosenthal, *New*, p. 12.
33. Block lambasted King's film ('Mixed-media', p. 21). King, a philosophy graduate, was clearly fascinated by ethics. His critics usually acknowledge its significance, rather than dismissal, in his work. It is no surprise, perhaps, that the film-makers distinguished for their ethical import are philosophically aware/trained; see Cooper's work on the The Dardenne Brothers and Saxton's on Claude Lanzmann.
34. Feldman, *King*, p. 19.
35. Nayman, 'Canada'.
36. Tercier, *Contemporary*, p. 22.

37. In contrast, Pond has argued that the film denies the dying true subjectivity and, instead, presents a fearful encounter with death. While there is merit in her discussion, it is too fixed on the lesson of dying for the dying, as a tool for palliative care only, where my interest lies with a broader context and finds the film not fearful at all ('Dying', p. 38).
38. In interview, King states that the lesson was intended for those dying, those in palliative care, but something broader makes it into the prologue. See 'Allan King', TVOntario.
39. Kellehear, *Social*, p. 253.
40. This 'surplus of representation' was the other side of the 'paucity of experience' of dying asserted by Tercier, *Contemporary*, p. 22.
41. See Levinas, 'Ethics'.
42. Aaron, *Spectatorship*, p. 111.
43. Cooper, *Selfless*, p. 8.
44. See Weber, *Drop Dead*, pp. 227–8.
45. Wiseman favoured 'reality fictions'; see Benson, *Reality*.
46. Within the direct cinema movement even editing is considered fictionalisation. See Platinga, *Rhetoric*, pp. 9–12.
47. Grant, *Voyages*, p. 230.
48. Jackson, 'Local'.
49. For King this was about our sheer insignificance in the enormity of the universe, about being humbled by life's passage. See 'Allan King', TVOntario.
50. Feldman, 'King', p. 3.
51. See Levinas, *Totality*, pp. 297, 299.
52. Townsend, *Art*, p. 13. Hallas also highlights witnessing in its significance to AIDS films; see *Reframing*.
53. Field, *Gender*, p. x.
54. Canada's public health care system is key here, as is the fact that the hospital is run by the Salvation Army and specialises in palliative care.
55. Carmella's neighbour speaks of her as like a grandmother; Eda's only visitor is her brother-in-law; and Richard seems to have chosen, rather than inherited, kin.
56. For an excellent discussion of the radical dialogue of queerness and disability, see McRuer, 'Compulsory'.
57. Jackson, 'Cadence'.
58. Allan, 'Interview'.
59. The critical import of art's negotiation of distance without indifference, proximity without appropriation, and feeling without self-indulgence, is an ongoing, as well as historical, theme. I'm thinking most immediately of feminist theory's 'passionate detachment'. Mulvey called for this in her seminal essay, 'Visual Pleasure and Narrative Cinema', in entreating women to sustain a critical distance within the lure of masculinist mass culture. This idea was picked up by various identity politics campaigns, though not enough according to Mayne, *Framed*, p. 176. It is little surprise, perhaps,

that a key text in apolitical cognitive theory would adapt this to *Passionate Views* thereby nullifying the personal urgencies that come with 'diverse' cultural life (Platinga, *Passionate Views*).

60. Koresky, 'Eclipse'
61. Landsberg, *Prosthetic*, p. 149.
62. Ibid., p. 2.
63. Ibid., p. 149.
64. Ibid., p. 3.
65. Chouliaraki, *Spectatorship*, p. 4.
66. For a discussion of the healthy gaze, see the first chapter of Tanner, *Lost*. King speaks of this audience in his discussion of the film on TVOntario.
67. Levinas, 'First', p. 82.
68. As Fanon reminds us: 'There is of course the moment of "being for others" of which Hegel speaks, but every ontology is made unattainable in a colonized and civilized society' (*Black Skin*, p. 109).
69. See Agamben's *Homo*, *Remnants* and *State of Exception*.
70. Agamben, *Homo*, p. 185.
71. Ibid., p. 137.
72. See Butler, *Frames*.
73. Various writers have challenged the generalities of Agamben's work; see for example, Schueller, 'Decolonizing', pp. 235–54.
74. Chouliaraki, *Spectatorship*. See Boltanski, *Distant*. This emphasis upon solidarity is similarly favoured within development theory.
75. As I argued in *Spectatorship*, and specifically in response to Butler's work, cross-disciplinary approaches, incorporating spectatorship theory, are critical for understanding mediated suffering (p. 113).
76. Chouliaraki, *Spectatorship*, p. 27.
77. Ibid., p. 215.
78. Pick, *Creaturely*.
79. Ibid., p. 3. Pick is referring specifically here to Weill, *Need*.
80. Tanner, *Lost*, p. 11
81. Pick, *Creaturely*, p. 160.
82. I'm distancing this film's intimate disinterest/corporeal detachment from the 'corporeal implication of witnessing' in Hallas's analysis of AIDS films (*Reframing*, p. 217), and its expressive non-literal 'face' from haptic preoccupations of desire-fuelled avant-garde films; see Marks, *Touch*.
83. It is worth noting that Butler favours the term 'touch' within her political discussion of 'common human vulnerability', though she uses it very differently from Marks, see *Precarious*, p. 30.
84. It can be thought of as decinematic in other ways too: in terms of its rejection of other film conventions especially as they pertain to depicting dying.
85. It is a journey that puts pressure on the technology, hence the past failures, and on ethics, which is why presumably *How to Die in Oregon* does not show it but remains deliberately outside the house.

86. Pick, *Creaturely*, p. 159.
87. Shklovsky, 'Art'.
88. Catsoulis, 'Difficulty'.
89. Metz, *Imaginary*, p. 94.
90. Ibid., p. 94
91. Sobchack, 'Inscribing', p. 244, emphasis in original.
92. Ibid., p. 252–3, emphasis in original.
93. Ibid., p. 253, emphasis in original.
94. Pick, *Creaturely*, p.159.
95. Ibid., p. 159. Pick is clear to trouble 'reciprocity', distinguishing this mainstream narcissism from a more creaturely connectivity.
96. See discussions of it in Phelan, *Mourning,* pp. 153–73, and Hallas, *Reframing.*
97. Derrida notes the extraordinary insight of the mythic/historical 'blind seer' (*Memoirs*, p. 127). For its more detailed application, see Saxton, *Haunted,* p. 95.
98. Pick, *Creaturely*, p. 159. In contrast, key to Sobchack's distinction of the two films is not only the complicity but even love between the film-maker and the dying individual; see 'Inscribing', p. 253.
99. Phelan, *Mourning*, p. 21.
100. Butler, *Precarious*, pp. xviii–xix.
101. Ibid., p. 32.
102. Scarry, 'Body', p. 14.
103. Canadian Film Encyclopedia.
104. Sobchack, 'Inscribing', p. 232.
105. Pick, *Creaturely*, p. 3.
106. In this way, it dovetails with Berlant's point about how '"trauma" has become the primary genre of the last eighty years for describing the historical present as the scene of an exception'; in *Cruel*, pp. 9–10.
107. Noys's distinction of a 'new aesthetic of bare life', via his reading of *Crash* (Cronenberg, 1996), makes an important, and complementary, case for a mainstream and fictional 'art of exposure to our exposure to death, which allows us no escape' (*Culture*, p. 121).

Chapter 7

1. Gunning, 'Attractions'.
2. See Brooke, *'How it Feels'*.
3. For a detailed discussion of the afterlife in early cinema, see Ruffles, *Ghost,* pp. 34–54.
4. Various writers have discussed the film's significance to the history of film and its theorisation. See, for example, Beckman, *Crash*, pp. 25–54.
5. For Tanner, this recuperation is 'the central project of a continuing impulse toward memorialization in American Culture' (*Lost*, p. 213).
6. Striner, *Supernatural*, p. 181, emphasis in original.

7. *Here Comes Mr Jordan* (Alexander Halls, 1941); *Heaven Can Wait* (Warren Beatty and Buck Henry, 1978); *Down to Earth* (Chris and Paul Weitz, 2001).

8. There is much more to be said about how other ethnic identities are excluded from the afterlife in film, on its pervasive whiteness and on the gendering of ghosts, though sadly not the space to pursue these here. On the latter, see Fowkes, *Giving*. For fascinating discussions of the former and, more particularly, on the intersection of citizenship and literal or figurative spectral figures, see del Pilar Blanco, *Popular.*

9. Ruffles, *Ghost*, p. 3.

10. See Clover, *Men*; Creed, *Monstrous-Feminine*; Benshoff, *Monsters*.

11. For recent discussions of the genre, of torture porn and of the contemporary rape-revenge film, see, for example Hantke, *Horror* and Henry, 'Rape-Revenge'.

12. Berlant, *Cruel*, pp. 9–10.

13. The attribution of 'fiction' is, of course, relative but Kitses et al. discuss *Three Burials*'s roots in real events, in particular how it represents 'Jones' own vow to honour the 1997 death of Esequiel Hernandez, an 18-year-old Mexican-American gunned down while tending sheep in Redford, Texas, by drug agents never charged with his killing' ('Days'). It is worth noting another film that breaks with these conditions but in a very different arena. The Chinese film *Getting Home* (Yang Zhang, 2007) tells a very similar, though more sentimental, story to *Three Burials*.

14. The productivity of melancholia has been a theme within recent queer theory; see, for example, David Eng and David Kazanjian's edited collection, *Loss: The Politics of Mourning*, and Monica B. Pearl's, *AIDS Literature and Gay Identity: The Literature of Loss*.

15. Such proximity is also distinctly Mexican: an enduring and everyday relationship with the dead is prevalent in Mexican culture; see, for example, Reyes-Cortez, 'Maintaining'. For a discussion of the dangerous reality of the American–Mexican borderland culture, see Vélez-Ibáñez, *Border* and Alonzo, *Badmen*.

16. Rainey, *Cowboy*, p. 4.

17. Skerry, 'Dances', p. 283.

18. Dixon, 'Film', p. 176.

19. The same has been said of revisionist westerns like *Dances With Wolves* (Kevin Costner, 1990) and even the broadly celebrated *Lone Star* (John Sayles, 1996). For a discussion of the latter's ultimate conformity, how its 'overture to multiculturalism is driven by a deeply colonial and phallocentric project' (p. 56), see Fregoso, *MeXicana*, pp. 48–70.

20. Kitses, 'Days', pp. 14–18.

21. Ibid., pp. 14–18.

22. Ibid., pp. 14–18.

23. Fojas, *Border*, pp. 194–5.

24. Anderson, 'Burning'.

25. Horkheimer, *Dialectic*, p.39.
26. Levinas, 'First', p. 82.
27. Kitses, 'Days', pp. 14–18.
28. Ibid., pp. 14–18.
29. Tanner, *Lost*, p. 11.
30. Ibid., p. 24. *Three Burials* contests the exceptionalism and privatisation of death by rendering it a shared, material or social experience. It is not just that Melquiades is present throughout the film but that we see his corpse, we hear the autopsy, we witness its burial(s). This persevering relationship with the dead loved one corresponds to Mexican practice too.
31. Waegner, 'Bodies', p. 52.
32. Eng and Han, 'Dialogue', p. 349. Jonathan Demme's *Beloved* (1998) is an imperfect exception as its translation into the trappings of horror further the failure of mainstream cinema to accommodate the 'politics of mourning' here.
33. Fuss, 'Corpse', p. 1.
34. Ibid., p.13.
35. Ibid., p. 15.
36. Butler, *Precarious*, p. 151.
37. Striner, *Supernatural*, p. 181, emphasis in original.
38. There is even an encounter with a blind man who generously provides food and water. Gesturing, knowingly, towards the evocativeness of this figure, as noted in Chapter 6, Jones undercuts its parabolic import through the scene's black humour.
39. Levinas, *Totality*, pp. 299, 297.
40. Agamben, *Homo*, p. 137.
41. Ibid., p. 137 and Butler, *Frames*.
42. Agamben, *Homo*, p. 185.
43. See Agamben, *Exception*.
44. Schueller, 'Decolonizing', p. 248. Schueller takes various 'postcolonial' critics from the American left, including Butler, to task for their own implicit equilibrations.
45. Warner, *Trouble*, p. 35.
46. Crimp, *Melancholia*, p. 16.
47. Eng, *Queer*, p. 15. With queer mired in its own limitations, the accented term 'quare' becomes preferable to queer.
48. Muñoz, *Cruising*.

Bibliography

Aaron, Michele (ed.), *The Body's Perilous Pleasures: Dangerous Desires and Contemporary Culture* (Edinburgh: Edinburgh University Press, 1999).

Aaron, Michele, *Spectatorship: The Power of Looking On* (London: Wallflower, 2007).

Aaron, Michele (ed.), *Envisaging Death: Dying and Visual Culture* (Newcastle: Cambridge Scholars Publishing, 2013).

Abel, Richard (ed.), *Encyclopedia of Early Film* (New York: Routledge, 2005).

Sam Adams, review of *How to Die in Oregon*, 'A devastating documentary on assisted suicide premieres on HBO'. http://timeoutchicago.com/arts-culture/movies-on-demand/14773693/how-to-die-in-oregon-tv-review (Accessed 10 May 2012).

Adhikari, Mohamed, '*Hotel Rwanda: too much Heroism, too Little History – or horror?*, in Vivian Bickford-Smith and Richard Mendelsohn (eds), *Black and White in Colour: African History on Screen* (Athens: Ohio University Press, 2006).

Agamben, Giorgio, *Homo Sacer: Sovereign Power and Bare Life*. Trans. Daniel Heller-Roazen (Palo Alto: Stanford University Press, 1998).

Agamben, Giorgio, *Remnants of Auschwitz: the Witness and the Archive*. Trans. Daniel Heller-Roazen (New York: Zone, 2002).

Agamben, Giorgio, *State of Exception*. Trans. Kevin Attell (Chicago: University of Chicago Press, 2005).

Akrami, Jamsheed, 'Rare Interview with Filmmaker Abbas Kiarostami', The Criterion Collection: *Taste of Cherry*.

Allan, Blaine et al., 'An Interview with Allan King', *Criterion*, first published *Brick* (winter 2010) http://www.criterion.com/current/posts/1737-an-interview-with-allan-king (Accessed 12 May 2012).

'Allan King – Awards', *IMDb*, available at: http://www.imdb.com/name/nm0454437/awards

'Allan King on *Dying at Grace*' on TVOntario's: http://www.youtube.com/watch?v=O2eYicTOHGA

Alonzo, Juan José, *Badmen, Bandits, and Folk Heroes: the Ambivalence of Mexican American Identity in Literature and Film* (Tuscon, AZ: University of Arizona Press, 2009).

Althusser, Louis, 'Ideology and Ideological State Apparatuses: Notes Towards an Investigation', *Lenin and Philosophy*. Trans. Ben Brewster (New York: Monthly Review Press, [1969] 1971), pp. 127–86.

Anderson, Melissa, review of 'The Burning Plain', *Film Comment*, 45.5 (September–October 2009), http://www.filmcomment.com/issue/september-october-2009 (Accessed 11 July 2012).

Angelou, Maya, *I Know Why the Caged Bird Sings* (New York: Random House, 1969).

Anyiwo, Melissa, review of *Monster's Ball*, *Scope*, 6 NS. http://www.scope.nottingham.ac.uk/filmreview.php?issue=6&id=176 (Accessed 2 November 2011).

Appiah, K. A., '"No bad nigger": Blacks as the Ethical Principle in the Movies', in Marjorie Garber et al. (eds), *Media Spectacles* (New York: Routledge, 1993), pp. 77–90.

Ariès, Philippe, *Western Attitudes toward Death*. Trans. Patricia M. Ranum (London: Marion Boyars, 1974).

Ariès, Philippe, *The Hour of our Death*. Trans. Helen Weaver (London: Allen Lane, 1981).

Armstrong, Mary Ellen, 'Tribute To Allan King: Truth, Fiction and the Issues in Between', *Playback*, 13 January 1997. http://playbackonline.ca/1997/01/13/5825-19970113/ixzz1vKkzlXdl (Accessed 12 May 2012).

Arroyo, José (ed.), *Action/Spectacle Cinema: A Sight and Sound Reader* (London: BFI Publishing, 2000).

Arthur, Paul, 'Jargons of authenticity (Three American Moments)', in Michael Renov (ed.), *Theorizing Documentary* (Los Angeles: AFI Film Readers, 1993), pp. 108–34.

Atkinson, Michael, 'Cold Comfort Pharm', review of *Children of Men*, *Village Voice*, 30 August (2005), http://www.villagevoice.com/film/0535,atkinson,67300,20.html (Accessed 17 September 2007)

Azoulay, Ariella, *Death's Showcase: the Power of the Image and Contemporary Democracy* (Cambridge, MA: MIT Press, 2001).

Azoulay, Ariella, *The Civil Contract of Photography* (New York: Zone Books, 2008).

Baechler, Jean, *Suicides* (New York: Basic Books, 1975).

Barthes, Roland, *Camera Lucida: Reflections on Photography*. Trans. Richard Howard (New York: Hill and Wang, 1981).

Barker, Martin, *A 'Toxic Genre': The Iraq War Films* (London: Pluto Press, 2011).

Batchelor, Bob (ed.), *Cult Pop Culture: How the Fringe Became Mainstream* (Santa Barbara, CA: Praeger, 2010).

Baucom, Ian, *Specters of the Altantic: Finance Capital, Slavery, and the Philosophy of History* (Durham, NC: Duke University Press, 2005).

Bauman, Zygmunt, *Mortality, Immortality & Other Life Strategies* (Stanford, CA: Stanford University Press: 1992).

Baxendale, Sallie, 'Epilepsy at the Movies: Possession to Presidential Assassination', *The Lancet Neurology*, 2 December (2003), pp. 764–70.

Bazin, André, 'Death Every Afternoon', in Ivone Margulies (ed.), *Rites of Realism: Essays on Corporeal Cinema*. Trans. Mark A. Cohen (Durham, NC: Duke University Press, [1958] 2003), pp. 27–31.

Bean, Jennifer M., '"Trauma Thrills": Notes on Early Action Film', in Tasker, *Action*, pp. 17–30.

Becker, Carol, *Surpassing the Spectacle: Global Transformations and the Changing Politics of Art* (Lanham, MD: Rowman and Littlefield Publishers, 2002).

Becker, Ernest, *The Denial of Death* (New York: The Free Press, 1973).

Beckman, Karen, *Crash: Cinema and the Politics of Speed and Stasis* (Durham, NC: Duke University Press, 2010).

Bending, Lucy, *The Representation of Bodily Pain in Late Nineteenth-Century English Culture* (Oxford: Clarendon Press, 2000).

Benshoff, Harry, *Monsters in the Closet* (Manchester: Manchester University Press, 1997).

Benson, Thomas W. and Carolyn Anderson, *Reality Fictions: the Films of Frederick Wiseman* (Carbondale, IL: Southern Illinois University Press, 1989).

Berardinelli, James, review of *My Life without Me*, http://www.reelviews.net/movies/m/my_life_without.html (Accessed 18 March 2011).

Berardinelli, James, review, available at: http://www.reelviews.net/php_review_template.php?identifier=1852 (Accessed 5 November 2011).

Berlant, Lauren, *Cruel Optimism* (Durham, NC: Duke University Press, 2011).

Bernier, Celeste, *Characters of Blood: Black Heroism in the Transatlantic Imagination* (Charlottesville, VA: University of Virginia Press, 2012).

Berns, Nancy, *Closure: The Rush to End Grief and What it Costs Us* (Philadelphia, PA: Temple University Press, 2011).

Bersani, Leo, *The Culture of Redemption* (Cambridge, MA: Harvard University Press, 1990).

Bickford-Smith, Vivian and Richard Mendlesohn (eds), *Black and White in Colour: African History on Screen* (Athens: Ohio University Press, 2006).

Birkenstein, Jeff, Karen Randell, and Anna Froula (eds), *Reframing 9/11: Film, Popular Culture and the "War on Terror"* (New York and London: Continuum, 2010).

Black, Joel, *Aesthetics of Murder* (Baltimore, MD: The Johns Hopkins University Press, 1991).

Block, Stephen, 'King of the mixed-media metaphor', *Cinema Canada*, 107 (May 1984), pp. 21–2.

'*Blood Diamond*', available at, http://blooddiamondmovie.warnerbros.com/main.html

Bloom, Mia, 'Female Suicide Bombers: a Global Trend', *Daedalus*, 136: 1 (winter 2007), pp. 94–102.

Bogle, Donald, *Toms, Coons, Mulattoes, Mammies, and Bucks: an Interpretive History of Blacks in American Film* (New York and London: Continuum, [1973] 2006).

Boltanski, Luc, *Distant Suffering: Morality, Media and Politics* (Cambridge: Cambridge University Press, 1999).

Bond, M. R., 'The Suffering of Severe Intractable Pain', in H. W Kosterlitz and L. Y Terenius (eds), *Pain and Society* (Weinheim: Verlag Chemie GmbH, 1980), pp. 53–62.

Bonilla-Silva, Eduardo, 'The Linguistics of Color Blind Racism: How to Talk Nasty about Blacks without Sounding "Racist"', *Critical Sociology*, 28: 1–2 (2002), pp. 41–68.

Bordwell, David and Kristin Thompson, *Film Art: An Introduction*, 4th ed. (New York: McGraw-Hill, [1979] 1993).

Borradori, Giovanna, *Philosophy in a Time of Terror: Dialogues with Jurgen Habermas and Jacques Derrida* (Chicago, IL: University of Chicago Press, 2004).

Boyle, Kirk, '*Children of Men* and *I Am Legend*: the disaster-capitalism complex hits Hollywood', *Jump Cut*, 51 (spring 2009).

Bradbury, Mary, *Representations of Death: A Social Psychological Perspective* (New York and London: Routledge, 1999).

Bradbury, Mary, 'The good death', in Donna Dickenson, Malcolm Johnson, Jeanne Samson Katz (eds), *Death Dying and Bereavement* (London: Sage, 2000), pp. 59–63.

Bradshaw, Peter, review of *Virgin Suicides*, *Guardian*, 19 May 2000, available at: http://www.guardian.co.uk/film/2000/may/19/culture.reviews (accessed 18 March 2010).

Bradshaw, Peter, review of *United 93*, *Guardian*, 2 June 2006, available at: http://www.guardian.co.uk/culture/2006/jun/02/1 (accessed 12 October 2011).

Brand, Roy, 'Identification with Victimhood in Recent Cinema', *Culture, Theory & Critique*, 49: 2 (October 2008), pp. 165–81.

Branigan, Edward, *Projecting a camera: language-games in film theory* (New York and London: Routledge, 2006).

Brayton, Sean, 'The Racial Politics of Disaster and Dystopia in *I Am Legend*', *The Velvet Light Trap*, 67 (spring 2011), pp. 66–76.

Breitinger, Eckhard, *Defining New Idioms and Alternative Forms of Expression: ASNEL Papers v. 1* (Amsterdam and Atlanta, GA: Rodopi B.V., 1996).

Breuer, Josef and Sigmund Freud, 'On the Psychical Mechanism of Hysterical Phenomena: Preliminary Communication', *Studies on Hysteria*, PFL vol. 3. Trans. James and Alix Strachey. Ed. Angela Richards (London: Penguin, [1893] 1991).

Bronfen, Elisabeth, *Over Her Dead Body* (Manchester: Manchester University Press, 1992).

Bronfen, Elizabeth and Sarah Webster Goodwin (eds), *Death and Representation* (Baltimore, MD: The Johns Hopkins University Press, 1993).

Brooke, Michael, *How it Feels to be hit by a Car*, *Screenonline*, available at: http://www.screenonline.org.uk/film/id/444674/index.html (accessed 25 January 2012).

Brooks, Xan, review of *Bucket List*, *Guardian*, 15 February 2008: http://www.guardian.co.uk/film/2008/feb/15/comedy.drama (accessed 1 January 2012).

Brottman, Mikita, *Offensive Films* (Westport, CT: Greenwood Press, 1997).

Brottman, Mikita, *Hollywood Hex: Death and Destiny in the Dream Factory* (Powder Springs, GA: Creation Books, 1999).

Brottman, Mikita (ed.), *Car Crash Culture* (New York: Palgrave Macmillan, 2002).

Brown, Ron M., *The Art of Suicide* (London: Reaktion Books, 2001)

Brownworth, Victoria, 'Dykes on Death Row', *Advocate*, 15 June 1992, pp. 62–4.

Bruhm, Steven, *Gothic Bodies: The Politics of Pain in Romantic Fiction* (Philadelphia, PA: University of Pennsylvania Press, 1994).

Brunette, Peter, *Michael Haneke* (Urbana and Chicago: University of Illinois Press, 2010).

Bruzzi, Stella, *The New Documentary*, 2nd ed. (London and New York: Routledge, 2006).

Burki, Talha, 'Film: *The Bucket List*', *Lancet Oncology*, 9: 2 (February 2008), pp. 103–4.

Butler, Judith, *Precarious Life: The Powers of Mourning and Violence* (London and New York: Verso, 2004).

Butler, Judith, *Frames of War: When is Life Grievable* (London and New York: Verso, 2009).

Calvert, Leon Saunders, 'Ideology & the Modern Historical Epic', *Film International*, 18 (2005), pp. 4–13.

Cameron, Kenneth, *Africa on Film: Beyond Black and White* (New York: Continuum, 1994).

Canadian Film Encyclopedia. http://tiff.net/CANADIANFILMENCYCLO PEDIA/content/films/dying-at-grace (accessed 25 January 2012).

Cantarella, Eva, 'Dangling Virgins: Myth, Ritual and the Place of Women in Ancient Greece', in Susan Rubin Suleiman (ed.), *The Female Body in Western Culture: Contemporary Perspectives* (Cambridge, MA: Harvard University Press, 1985), pp. 57–67.

Cardullo, Bert, *In Search of Cinema: Writings on International Film Art* (Montreal and Kingston: McGill-Queen's University Press, 2004).

Catsoulis, Jeannette, 'The Difficulty of Death Published', *The New York Times*, 23 May 2007, http://movies.nytimes.com/2007/05/23/movies/23dyin.html (accessed 2 January 2012).

Celik, Ipek A., '"I Wanted You to Be Present": Guilt and the History of Violence in Michael Haneke's *Caché*', *Cinema Journal*, 50: 1 (fall 2010), pp. 59–80.

Chaudhuri, Shohini, 'Unpeople: Postcolonial Reflections on Terror, Torture and Detention in *Children of Men*', in Marguerite Waller and Sandra Ponzanesi (eds), *Postcolonial Cinema Studies* (New York: Routledge, 2012), pp. 191–204.

Chaudhuri, Shohini and Howard Finn, 'The open image: Poetic realism and the New Iranian Cinema', *Screen*, 44: 1 (spring 2003), pp. 38–57.

Chaudhary, Zahid R., 'Humanity Adrift: Race, Materiality, and Allegory in Alfonso Cuarón's *Children of Men*', *Camera Obscura*, 24: 3 (2009), pp. 73–109.

Cheshire, Godfrey, 'How to read Kiarostami', *Cineaste*, 25: 4 (September 2000), pp. 8–15.

Chomsky, Noam, *9-11: Was there an Alternative?* (New York: Open Media Press, 2001).

Chopin, Kate, *The Awakening and Other Stories* (Oxford: Oxford University Press, [1899] 2000).

Chouliaraki, Lilie, *The Spectatorship of Suffering* (London: Sage, 2006).

Clark, Robert A., 'Reel Oncology: How Hollywood Films Portray Cancer', *Cancer Control: Journal of the Moffitt Cancer Centre*, 6: 5 (September/October 1999), http://www.moffitt.org/moffittapps/ccj/v6n5/dept7.htm (accessed 20 December 2011).

Clover, Carol J., *Men, Women, and Chain Saws: Gender in the Modern Horror Film* (Princeton: Princeton University Press, 1992).

Comentale, Edward P., Stephen Watt, and Skip Willman (eds), *Ian Fleming and James Bond: The Cultural Politics of 007* (Bloomington, IN: Indiana University Press, 2005).

Conlon, James, 'Making Love, Not War: The Soldier Male in Top Gun and Coming Home', *Journal of Popular Film and Television*, 18: 1 (spring 1990), pp. 18–27.

Cooper, Sarah, *Selfless Cinema? Ethics and French Documentary* (Oxford: Legenda, 2005).

Cooper, Sarah, 'Mortal Ethics: Reading Levinas with the Dardenne Brothers', *Film-Philosophy*, 11: 2 (2007), pp. 66–87.

Cowan, Michael, 'Between the Street and the Apartment: Disturbing the Space of Fortress Europe in Michael Haneke', *Studies in European Cinema*, 5: 2 (2009), pp.117–29.

Craig, K. D., 'Ontogenetic and Cultural Influences on the Expression of Pain in Man', in H. W Kosterlitz and L. Y Terenius (eds), *Pain and Society* (Weinheim: Verlag Chemie GmbH, 1980), pp. 37–52.

Creed, Barbara, *The Monstrous-Feminine: Film, Feminism, Psychoanalysis* (London: Routledge, 1993).

Crimp, Douglas, *Melancholia and Moralism: Essays on AIDS and Queer Politics* (Cambridge, MA: MIT Press, 2002).

Cutler, Janet, 'Don't say Mammy: Camille Bishop's meditations on Black Motherhood', in Heather Addison, Mary Kate Goodwin-Kelly, Elaine Roth (eds), *Motherhood Misconceived: Representing the Maternal in U.S. Films* (Albany, NY: State University of New York Press, 2009), pp. 213–35.

Deangelis, Michael, 'Mel Gibson and Tom Cruise: Rebellion and Conformity', in Robert Eberwein (ed.), *Acting for America: Movie Stars of the 1980s* (New Brunswick, NJ: Rutgers University Press, 2010), pp.77–98.

'Death & Dying Documentaries', *Programs for Elderly*, available at: http://www.programsforelderly.com/documentaries-death.php

Dennis, Jeanne, 'Movies That Help Parents and Children Understand Grief and Loss', The Blog, *Huffington Post*, 16 March 2012, http://www.huffington-post.com/jeanne-dennis/childrens-movies-discussing-grief_b_1340259.html (accessed 1 June 2011).

Denzin, Norman. K., *Reading Race* (London: Sage, 2002).

Derrida, Jacques, *Memoirs of the Blind: The Self-Portrait and Other Ruins*. Trans. P. A. Brault and M. Naas (Chicago: Chicago University Press, 1993).

Derrida, Jacques, *The Gift of Death* (Chicago and London: University of Chicago Press, 1995).

Diawara, Mantha (ed.), *Black American Cinema* (New York and London: Routledge, 1993).

Dickinson, Kay, 'The Palestinian Road (Block) Movie', in Dana Iodonova, Martin-Jones, Belen Vidal (eds), *Cinema at the Periphery* (Detroit: Wayne State University Press, 2010).

Dika, Vera, *Games of Terror* (Madison, NJ: Fairleigh Dickinson University Press, 1990).

Dika, Vera, *Recycled Culture in Contemporary Art and Film* (Cambridge: Cambridge University Press, 2003).

Didinger, Ray and Glen Macnow, *The Ultimate Book of Sports Movies: Featuring the 100 greatest Sports Films* (Philadelphia, PA: Running Press Book Publishers, 2009).

Directors Guild of Canada, 'DGC announces the Allan King Award for Excellence in Documentary'. http://www.dgc.ca/news.php?id=100&archives=true&main=false&news=1152 (accessed 1 June 2012).

Dixon, Simon, 'Film and Theater', in Rick Newby (ed.), *The Rocky Mountain Region: The Greenwood Encyclopedia of American Regional Cultures* (Westport, CT: Greenwood Press, 2004).

Dixon, Wheeler Winston, *Disaster and Memory* (New York: Columbia University Press, 1999).

Dixon, Wheeler Winston, *Visions of the Apocalypse* (London: Wallflower, 2003).

Dixon, Wheeler Winston (ed.), *Film and Television after 9/11* (Carbondale, IL: Southern Illinois University Press, 2004).

Doane, Mary Ann, 'The Clinical Eye: Medical Discourses in the "Woman's Film" of the 1940s', *Poetics Today*, 'The Female Body in Western Culture: Semiotic Perspectives', ed. Susan Rubin Suleiman, 6: 1/2 (1985), pp. 205–27.

Doherty, Thomas, 'The new war movies as moral rearmament', *Cineaste*, 27: 3 (summer 2002), pp. 4–8.

Dollimore, Jonathan, *Death, Desire and Loss in Western Culture* (London: Penguin, 1998).

Dönmez-Colin, Gönül, *Cinemas of the Other: A Personal Journey with Film-makers from the Middle East and Central Asia* (Bristol: Intellect Press, 2006).

Downing, Lisa and Libby Saxton, *Film and Ethics: Foreclosed Encounters* (London: Routledge, 2009).

Dreher, Kwakiutl, 'A Eulogy for Tyrell Musgrove: The Disremembered Child in Marc Forster's *Monster's Ball*', *Film Criticism*, 29: 1 (fall 2004), pp. 65–81. http://search.proquest.com.ezproxyd.bham.ac.uk/mlaib/docview/2059308/fulltext?accountid=8630 (accessed 5 November 2010).

Duncan, Carol B., 'Black Women and Motherhood in Contemporary Cinematic Science Fiction', *Journal of the Association for Research on Mothering*, 5: 1 (2003), pp. 45–52.

Durkheim, Émile, *Suicide* (London: Routledge, [1897] 2002).

Dyer, Richard, 'Don't Look Now – The Male Pin-Up', *Screen*, 23: 3–4 (September/October 1982), pp. 61–73.

Dyer, Richard, *Matter of Images: Essays on Representation* (London: Routledge, [1993] 2002).

Ebert, Robert, '*Beaches*', 13 January 1989, available at: http://rogerebert.suntimes.com/apps/pbcs.dll/article?AID=/19890113/REVIEWS/901130301/1023, (accessed 23 April 2010).

Ebert, Robert, '*My Life Without Me*', 17 October 2003, available at: http://rogerebert.suntimes.com/apps/pbcs.dll/article?AID=/20031017/REVIEWS/3101 70304/1023 (accessed 14 February 2010).

Ebert, Robert, review of *The Constant Gardener*, 1 September 2005. http://rogerebert.suntimes.com/apps/pbcs.dll/article?AID=/20050901/REVIEWS/5082 6001/1023/ (accessed 12 October 2008).

Ebert, Robert, '"The Bucket List" Thinks Dying of Cancer is a Laff Riot Followed by a Dime-store Epiphany', 10 January 2008, available at: http://rogerebert.suntimes.com/apps/pbcs.dll/article?AID=/20080110/REVIEWS/8011003 01/1023 (accessed 1 June 2009).

Edelman, Lee, *No Future: Queer Theory and The Death Drive* (Durham, NC: Duke University Press, 2004).

Eng, David and David Kazanjian (eds.), *Loss: The Politics of Mourning* (Berkeley: University of California Press, 2003).

Eng, David L. and Shinhee Han, 'A Dialogue on Racial Melancholia', in David Eng and David Kazanjian (eds), *Loss: The Politics of Mourning* (Berkeley: University of California Press, 2003), pp. 342–71.

Eng, David L., Judith Halberstam, José Estaban Muñoz (eds), *What's Queer about Queer Studies Now?* (Durham, NC: Duke University Press, 2005).

Entman, R. M. and A. Rojecki, *The Black Image in the White Mind: Media and Race in America* (Chicago: University of Chicago Press, 2001).

Espinoza, Julio García, 'For an Imperfect Cinema', in Michael T. Martin (ed.), *New Latin American Cinema*, Volume 1: *Theory, Practices, and Transcontinental Articulations*. Trans. Julianne Burton (Detroit: Wayne State University Press, [1969] 1997), pp. 71–82.

Eugenides, Jeffrey, *Virgin Suicides* (London: Bloomsbury, [1993] 2002).

Fanon, Franz, *Black Skin, White Masks*. Trans. Charles Lam Markmann (London: Pluto Press, [1952] 1986).

Farley, C. J., 'That old Black Magic: Hollywood is Still Bamboozled When it Comes to Race', *Time*, 27 November 2000, p. 14.

Farrell, Kirby, *Post-traumatic Culture: Injury and Interpretation in the Nineties* (Baltimore, MD: The Johns Hopkins University Press, 1998).

Feldman, Seth (ed.), *Allan King: Filmmaker* (Bloomington: Indiana University Press, 2003).

Feuer, Jane, 'The Self-reflective Musical and the Myth of Entertainment', in Rick Altman (ed.), *Genre: The Musical* (London: Routledge, 1981), pp. 159–74.

Field, David, Jenny Hockey and Neil Small (eds), *Death, Gender and Ethnicity* (London: Routledge, 1997).

Fiske, John, *Television Culture* (London: Routledge, 1987).

Fleetwood, Nicole R., 'Failing Narratives, Initiating Technologies: Hurricane Katrina and the Production of a Weather Media Event', *American Quarterly*, 58: 3 (2006), pp. 767–89.

Fleischer, Stefan, 'Dying to be on Television', *Film Quarterly*, 31: 4 (summer 1978), pp. 30–6.

Flaubert, Gustave, *Madame Bovary* (London: Wordsworth Editions, [1856] 2001).

Fojas, Camilla, *Border Bandits: Hollywood on the Southern Frontier* (Austin: University of Texas Press, 2008).

Foster, Gwendolyn, *Captive Bodies: Postcolonial Subjectivity in the Cinema* (Albany, NY: State University of New York Press, 1999).

Fowkes, Katherine A., *Giving Up the Ghost: Spirits, Ghosts, and Angels in Mainstream Comedy Films* (Detroit: Wayne State University Press, 1998).

Frank, Lucy E. (ed.), *Representations of Death in Nineteenth-Century US Writing and Culture* (Aldershot: Ashgate, 2007).

Franklin, Paul B., 'Jew Boys, Queer Boys: Rhetorics of Antisemitism and Homophobia in the Trial of Nathan "Babe" Leopold Jr. and Richard "Dickie" Loeb', in Daniel Boyarin, Daniel Itzkovitz, Ann Pellegrini (eds), *Queer Theory and the Jewish Question* (New York: Columbia University Press, 2003), pp. 121–148.

Fregoso, Rosa Linda, *MeXicana Encounters: The Making of Social Identities on the Borderlands* (Berkeley: University of California Press, 2003).

Freud, Sigmund, 'Remembering, Repeating and Working-Through', *The Standard Edition of the Complete Psychological Works of Sigmund Freud*, Vol. 12. Ed. and Trans. James Strachey (London: Hogarth Press, [1914] 1958), pp. 145–56.

Freud, Sigmund, 'Our Attitude Towards Death', *The Standard Edition of the Complete Psychological Works of Sigmund Freud*, Vol. 14. Ed. and Trans. James Strachey (London: The Hogarth Press, 1915), pp. 289–302.

Freud, Sigmund, 'Beyond the Pleasure Principle', *On Metapsychology: The Theory of Psychoanalysis*, Vol. 11. Ed. A. Richards, Trans. J. Strachey. (London: Penguin, [1920] 1991), pp. 275–338.

Freud, Sigmund, 'The Economic Problem of Masochism', *On Metapsychology: The Theory of Psychoanalysis*, Vol. 11. Ed. A. Richards, Trans. J. Strachey (London: Penguin, [1924] 1991), pp. 147–56.

Fuller, Graham, 'Death and the Maidens', *Sight & Sound*, X: 4 (April 2000), http://old.bfi.org.uk/sightandsound/feature/26 (accessed 20 March 2009).

Fuss, Diana, 'Corpse Poem', *Critical Inquiry*, 30 (autumn 2003), pp. 1–30.

Gabbard, Krin, *Black Magic: White Hollywood and African American Culture* (Rutgers, NJ: Rutgers University Press, 2004).

Gates, Barbara T., *Victorian Suicide: Mad Crimes and Sad Histories* (Princeton, NJ: Princeton University Press, 1988).

Gibran, Kahlil, *The Prophet* (Teddington: Echo Library, [1923] 2006).

Gibson, Margaret, 'Death and Mourning in Technologically Mediated Culture', *Health Sociology Review*, 16: 5 (2007), pp. 415–24.

Gilbert, Sandra M., *Death's Door: Modern Dying and the Ways we Grieve* (New York: W. W. Norton, 2006).

Gilroy, Paul, *The Black Atlantic: Modernity and the Double Consciousness* (London: Verso, 1993).

Giroux, Henry, 'Democracy and the Politics of Terrorism: Community, Fear and the Suppression of Dissent', in Norman K. Denzin and Yvonna S. Lincoln (eds), *9/11 in American Culture* (Walnut Creek, CA: AltaMira Press, 2003).

Glenn, Cerise L. and Landra J. Cunningham, 'The Power of Black Magic: The Magical Negro and White Salvation in Film', *Journal of Black Studies*, 40: 2 (2009), pp. 135–52.

Goldberg, Elizabeth Swanson, 'Splitting Difference: Global Identity Politics and the Representation of Torture in the Counterhistorical Dramatic Film', in J. David Slocum (ed.), *Violence and American Cinema* (New York: Routledge, 2001), pp. 245–70.

Goldsby, Jacqueline, *A Spectacular Secret: Lynching in American Life and Literature* (Chicago: University of Chicago Press, 2006).

Goodall, Mark, 'The Real Faces of Death: Art Shock in *Des Morts*', in J. Cline and R. G. Wiener (eds), *From the Grindhouse to the Arthouse* (Plymouth: Scarecrow Press, 2010).

Gorbman, Claudia, *Unheard Melodies: Narrative Film Music* (London: BFI Books, 1987).

Gorer, Geoffrey, 'The Pornography of Death', in John B. Williamson and Edwin S. Shneidman (eds), *Death: Current Perspectives* (London: Mayfield Publishing, [1955] 1995), pp. 71–6.

Grainge, Paul (ed.), *Memory and Popular Film* (Manchester: Manchester University Press, 2003).

Grant, Barry Keith, *Voyages of Discovery: The Cinema of Frederick Wiseman* (Champaign, IL: University of Illinois Press, 1992).

Green, James, *Beyond the Good Death: The Anthropology of Modern Dying* (Philadelphia, PA: University of Pennsylvania Press, 2008).

Grierson, John, 'The Documentary Producer', *Cinema Quarterly*, 2: 1 (autumn 1932).

Guererro, Ed, *Framing Blackness: The African American Image in Film* (Philadelphia, PA: Temple University Press, 1993).

Gunew, Sneja, 'Subaltern Empathy: Beyond European Categories in Affect Theory', *Concentric: Literary and Cultural Studies*, 35: 1 (March 2009), pp. 11–30.

Gunning, Tom, 'The Cinema of Attractions: Early Film, Its Spectator and the Avant-Garde', *Wide Angle*, 8: 3 and 4 (fall 1986), pp. 63–70.

Guthke, Karl S., *The Gender of Death: A Cultural History in Art and Literature* (Cambridge: Cambridge University Press, 1999).

Hagin, Boaz, *Death in Classical Holllywood Cinema* (Basingstoke: Palgrave Macmillan, 2010).

Hallas, Roger, *Reframing Bodies: AIDS, Bearing Witness, and the Queer Moving Image* (Durham, NC: Duke University Press, 2009).

Hammond, Philip (ed.), *Screens of Terror: representations of war and terrorism in film and television since 9/11* (Bury St Edmunds: Abramis Academic, 2011).

Hampton, Gregory Jerome, *Changing Bodies in the Fiction of Octavia Butler: Slaves, Aliens, and Vampires* (Lanham, MD: Lexington Books, 2010).

Hantke, Steffen (ed.), *American Horror Film: The Genre at the Turn of the Millennium* (Jackson, MS: University of Mississippi Press, 2010).

Hardcastle, Valerie Gray, *The Myth of Pain* (Cambridge, MA: MIT Press, 1999).

Harrow, Kenneth, '"*Un Train Peut en Cacher un Autre*": Narrating the Rwandan Genocide and *Hotel Rwanda*', *Research in African Literatures*, 36 (2005), pp. 223–32.

Härting, Heike, 'Global Humanitarianism, Race, and the Spectacle of the African Corpse in Current Western Representations of the Rwandan Genocide', *Comparative Studies of South Asia, Africa and the Middle East*, 28: 1 (2008), pp. 61–77.

Haynes, Jonathan (ed.), *Nigerian Video Films* (Athens, OH: Ohio University Press, 2000).

Helwig, David, *The Names of Things* (Ontario: The Porcupine's Quill, 2006).

Hemmings, Clare, 'Invoking Affect: Cultural Theory and the Ontological Turn', *Cultural Studies*, 19: 5 (September 2005), pp. 548–67.

Henry, Claire, 'Rape-Revenge Revisions: Case Studies in the Contemporary Film Genre', PhD thesis, Anglia Ruskin University, 2012.

Higonnet, Margaret, 'Speaking Silences: Women's Suicide', in Susan Rubin Suleiman (ed.), *The Female Body in Western Culture* (Cambridge, MA: Harvard University Press, 1985).

Hill Collins, Patricia, *Black Feminist Thought: Knowledge, Consciousness and the Politics of Empowerment* (London: Routledge, 2000).

Hirano, Kyoko, *Mr Smith Goes to Tokyo: Japanese Cinema Under the American*

Occupation 1945–1952 (Washington and London: Smithsonian Institution Press, 1992).

Holden, Stephen, '*The Death of Mr. Lazarescu* Tells a Modern Hospital Tale', *The New York Times*, 26 April 2006, available at: http://movies.nytimes.com/2006/04/26/movies/26deat.html (accessed 14 February 2011).

Holdstein, Deborah H., '*Dark Victory. Now Voyager. The Great Lie:* Women's Pictures and the Perfect Moment', *Jump Cut*, 32 (April 1987), pp. 22–4.

Holland, Sharon P., 'Death in Black and White: A Reading of Marc Forster's *Monster's Ball*', *Signs*, 31: 3 (spring 2006), pp. 785–813.

Holmlund, Chris (ed.), *American Cinema of the 1990s: Themes and Variations* (New Brunswick, NJ: Rutgers University Press, 2008).

Homicide and Suicide Rates – National Violent Death Reporting System, Six States, 2003 http://www.cdc.gov/MMWR/preview/mmwrhtml/mm5415a1.html; Leading causes of death, 91–106 http://www.cdc.gov/violenceprevention/suicide/statistics/leading_causes.html (accessed 1 July 2006).

hooks, bell, 'Sorrowful Black Death Is Not A Hot Ticket', *Sight and Sound*, 4: 8 (August 1994), pp. 10–14.

Horkheimer, Max and Theodor Adorno, *The Dialectic of Enlightenment.* Ed. Gunzelin Schmid Noerr. Trans. Edmund Jephcott (Stanford, CA: Stanford University Press, [1947] 2007)

Hornbuckle, Del, 'Blood Diamond . . . TIA (This is Africa)', review, *Pambazuka News*, 286 (17 January 2007), http://pambazuka.org/en/category/books/39192 (accessed 15 August 2008).

Horne, John, 'Screening the Dying Individual: Film, Mortality and the Ethics of Spectatorship', in Maria-José Blanco and Ricarda Vidal (eds), *The Power of Death: Perceptions of Death in the Western World* (Oxford: Berghahn Books, forthcoming).

Hron, Madeleine, '"But I find no place": Representations of the Genocide in Rwanda', in Colman Hogan and Marta Marín Dòmine (eds), *The Camp: Narratives of Internment and Exclusion* (Newcastle: Cambridge Scholars Publishing, 2007).

Hughey, Matthew, 'Cinethetic Racism: White Redemption and Black Stereotypes in "Magical Negro" Films', *Social Problems*, 56: 3 (August 2009), pp. 543–77.

Hyler, Steven E., and Jaime Moore, 'Teaching Psychiatry? Let Hollywood Help! Suicide in the Cinema', *Academic Psychiatry*, 20 (December 1996), pp. 212–19.

Jackson, Marni, 'The Local Cadence of Allan King's Filmmaking', *Brick* (winter 2010), http://www.criterion.com/current/posts/1739-the-local-cadence-of-allan-king-s-filmmaking (accessed 3 May 2012).

JanMohammed, Abdul R., *The Death-Bound Subject: Richard Wright's Archeology of Death* (Durham, NC: Duke University Press, 2005).

Jeffords, Susan, *Hard Bodies: Hollywood Masculinity in the Reagan Era* (New Brunswick, NJ: Rutgers University Press, 2004).

Jennings, Michael, Gary Smith and Howard Eiland (eds), *Walter Benjamin: Selected Writings*, Volume 3: *1935–1938* (Cambridge, MA: Harvard University Press, [1936] 2002).

Kakoudaki, Despina, 'Spectacles of History: Race Relations, Melodrama, and the Science Fiction/Disaster Film', *Camera Obscura*, 17: 2 (2002), pp. 109–53.

Kaplan, E. Ann, *Looking for the Other: Film, Feminism and the Imperial Gaze* (New York: Routledge, 1997).

Kawin, Bruce F., *Mindscreen: Bergman, Godard, and the First Person Film* (Princeton, NJ: Princeton University Press, 1978).

Keane, Stephen, *Disaster Movies: The Cinema of Catastrophe* (London: Wallflower, 2001).

Kellehear, Allan, *The Social History of Dying* (Cambridge: Cambridge University Press, 2007).

Kemp, Philip, *Fearless*, review, *Sight and Sound*, 4: 5 (1994), pp. 41–2.

Killilea, Alfred G., *The Politics of Being Mortal* (Lexington: University Press of Kentucky, 1988).

King, Claire Sisco, *Washed in Blood: Male Sacrifice, Trauma, and the Cinema* (New Brunswick, NJ: Rutgers University Press, 2012).

King, Debra Walker, *African Americans and the Culture of Pain* (Charlottesville, VA: University of Virginia Press, 2008).

King, Geoff, 'Just Like a Movie? 9/11 and Hollywood Spectacle', in Geoff King (ed.), *Spectacle of the Real: From Hollywood to 'Reality' TV and Beyond* (Bristol: Intellect, 2005), pp. 47–57.

Kitses, Jim, Marianne Gray and Edward Buscombe, 'Days of the Dead', *Sight and Sound*, 16: 4 (April 2006), pp. 14–18.

Kira, Ibrahim, 'Collective Identity Terror in the Israeli–Palestinian Conflict and Potential Solutions', in Judy Kuriansky (ed.), *Terror in the Holy Land: Inside the Anguish of the Israeli–Palestinian Conflict* (Westport, CT: Praeger Publishers Inc., 2006).

Koresky, Michael, Eclipse Series 24: 'The Actuality Dramas of Allan King', Criterion, http://www.criterion.com/current/posts/1599-eclipse-series-24-the-actuality-dramas-of-allan-king (accessed 5 May 2012).

Kramer, Peter D., 'The Anatomy of Melancholy', *The New York Times Book Review*, 7 April (1996), p. 27.

Kübler-Ross, Elisabeth, *On Death and Dying* (New York: Routledge, 1969).

Landsberg, Alison, *Prosthetic Culture: The Transformation of American Remembrance in the Age of Mass Culture* (New York: Columbia University Press, 2004).

Laplanche, Jean and Jean-Bertrand Pontalis, *The Language of Psycho-Analysis* (London: Karnac Books, 1988).

Le Blavec, Pierre, 'International Terrorism through Action & Disaster Movies', *France Amérique*, 1578 (7–13 September 2002), pp. 8–12.

Lee, Nathan, 'Circling the diamond industry, Zwick flick tackles nada',

Village Voice, 5 December 2006, http://www.villagevoice.com/film/0649,lee,75223,20.html (accessed 17 September 2007).

Lee, Seungmug, *The Impact of Home Burglar Alarm Systems on Residential Burglaries* unpublished thesis (Rutgers: State University of New York, 2008).

Leo, Alex, 'Action Movie Villains from the 80s to Today', http://alexleo.tumblr.com/post/2808000788/action-movie-villains-from-the-80s-to-today (accessed 25 January 2012).

Levinas, Emmanuel, *Totality and Infinity: An Essay on Exteriority*. Trans. A. Lingis (Pittsburgh: Duquesne University Press, 1969).

Levinas, Emmanuel, 'Ethics as First Philosophy', in S. Hand (ed.), *The Levinas Reader* (Cambridge, MA: Blackwell, 1989).

Levinas, Emmanuel, *God, Death, and Time*. Ed. Jacques Rolland. Trans. Bettina Bergo (Stanford, CA: Stanford University Press, 2000).

Lewis, Jon (ed.), *The End of Cinema as we know it: American Film in the Nineties* (New York: New York University Press, 2001).

Lim, Dennis, 'A Second Look: Allan King's "actuality dramas" get a new audience', *Los Angeles Times*, 19 September 2010, available at: http://articles.latimes.com/2010/sep/19/entertainment/la-ca-second-look-20100919 (accessed 5 May 2012).

Lindner, Christoph (ed.), *The James Bond Phenomenon: A Critical Reader* (Manchester: Manchester University Press, 2009).

Lippard, Chris, 'Disappearing into the Distance and Getting Closer All the Time: Vision, Position, and Thought in Kiarostami's *The Wind Will Carry Us*', *Journal of Film and Video*, 61: 4 (winter 2009), pp. 31–40.

McCormick, Adrienne, 'Supermothers on Film; or, Maternal Melodrama in the Twenty-first Century', in Andrea O'Reilly (ed.), *Twenty-First Century Motherhood: Experience, Identity, Policy, Agency* (New York: Columbia University Press, 2010), pp.140–57.

McInerney, Fran, 'Cinematic Visions of Dying', in Allan Kellehear (ed.), *The Study of Dying: From Autonomy to Transformation* (Cambridge: Cambridge University Press, 2009).

McKenna, Andrew, 'The Law's Delay: Cinema and Sacrifice', *Legal Studies Forum*, 15: 3 (1991), pp. 199–215, http://www.heinonline.org.ezproxye.bham.ac.uk/HOL/Page?handle=hein.journals/lstf15&div=29&collection=journals&set_as_cursor=0&men_tab=srchresults (accessed 24 March 2009).

Mackenna, Tracy, 'Life is Over! If you want it: mediating life and death', in Aaron, *Envisaging*.

Macnab, Geoffrey, review of *Mr Jones*, *Sight and Sound*, 4: 10 (1994), pp. 50–1.

McRuer, Robert, 'Compulsory Able-Bodiedness and Queer/Disabled Existence', in Snyder, *Disability*, pp. 88–99.

Marciniak, Katarzyna, Anikó Imre, Áine O'Healy, 'Introduction: Mapping Transnational Feminist Media Studies', in Marciniak, Imre and O'Healy (eds), *Transnational Feminism in Film and Media* (New York: Palgrave Macmillan, 2011), pp. 1–20.

Markovitz, Jonathan, 'Reel Terror Post 9/11', in Dixon, *Film*, pp. 201–25.

Marks, Laura U., *Skin of the Film: Intercultural Cinema, Embodiment, and the Senses* (Durham, NC: Duke University Press, 2000).

Marks, Laura U., *Touch: Sensuous Theory and Multisensory Media* (Minneapolis: University of Minnesota Press, 2002).

Marriott, David, *On Black Men* (New York: Columbia University Press, 2000).

Martin-Jones, David, *Deleuze, Cinema and National Identity: Narrative Time in National Contexts* (Edinburgh: Edinburgh University Press, 2008).

Maslin, Janet, 'Frederick Wiseman's "Near Death"', *New York Times*, 7 October 1989, available at: http://www.nytimes.com/1989/10/07/movies/frederick-wiseman-s-near-death.html?pagewanted=all&src=pm (accessed 18 March 2012).

Mayne, Judith. *Framed: Lesbians, Feminists and Media Culture* (Minneapolis: University of Minnesota Press, 2000).

Mbembe, Achille, 'Necropolitics', *Public Culture*, 15: 1 (2003), pp. 11–40.

Meeropol, Abel [Lewis Allen], 'Strange Fruit', *The New Masses* (1937).

Metz, Christian, *The Imaginary Signifier: Psychoanalysis and the Cinema*. Trans. Celia Britton, Annwyl Williams, Ben Brewster and Alfred Guzzetti (Bloomington: Indiana University Press, [1977] 1982).

Mitchell, David T., 'Narrative Prosthesis and the Materiality of Metaphor', in Snyder, *Disability*, pp. 15–30.

Modlinger, Martin and Philipp Sonntag (eds), *Other People's Pain: Narratives of Trauma and the Question of Ethics* (New York: Peter Lang, 2011).

Morag, Raya, 'The Living Body and the Corpse – Israeli Documentary Cinema and the *Intifadah*', *Journal of Film and Video*, 60: 3–4 (fall/winter 2008), pp. 3–24.

Moretti, Franco, *Signs Taken for Wonders*. Trans. S. Fischer, D. Forgacs and D. Miller (London: Verso, 1983).

Morris, David B., *The Culture of Pain* (Berkeley: University of California Press, 1991).

Morrison, Toni, *Playing in the Dark: Whiteness and the Literary Imagination* (Cambridge, MA: Harvard University Press, 1992).

Multiple Sclerosis International Federation, available at: http://www.msif.org/en/about_ms/ms_by_topic/pain/index.html.

Mulvey, Laura, 'Visual Pleasure and Narrative Cinema', *Screen*, 16: 3 (1975), pp. 6–18.

Munby, Jonathan, *Under a Bad Sign* (Chicago: University of Chicago Press, 2011).

Muñoz, José Esteban, *Cruising Utopia: The Then and There of Queer Futurity* (New York: New York University Press, 2009).

Nabokov, Vladimir, *Lolita* (London: Penguin, [1955] 2000).

Nadel, Alan, 'A Whole New (Disney) World Order: *Alladin*, Atomic Power, and the Muslim Middle East', in Matthew H. Bernstein and Gaylyn Studlar (eds), *Visions of the East: Orientalism in Film* (London: I. B. Tauris, 1997), pp. 184–206.

Naficy, Hamid, *An Accented Cinema: Exilic and Diasporic Filmmaking* (Princeton, NJ: Princeton University Press, 2001).

Nama, Adilifu, *Black Space: Imagining Race in Science Fiction Film* (Austin: TX: University of Texas Press, 2008).

Nayar, Pramod K., *PostColonial Literature: An Introduction* (Delhi: Pearson Education, 2008).

Nayman, Adam, 'King of Canada', *Criterion*, 16 September 2010, http://www.criterion.com/current/posts/1594-king-of-canada (accessed 6 May 2012).

Ndahiro, Alfred and Privat Rutazibwa, Hotel Rwanda *or the Tutsi Genocide as seen by Hollywood* (Paris: L'Harmattan, 2008).

Neupert, Richard, *The End: Narration and Closure in the Cinema* (Detroit: Wayne State University Press, 1995).

Niemi, Robert, *History in the Media: Film and Television* (Santa Barbara, CA: ABC-CLIO Inc., 2006).

Nowell-Smith, Geoffrey, 'Minnelli and Melodrama', in Bill Nicholls (ed.), *Movies and Methods: An Anthology*, Volume II (Berkeley: University of California Press, 1985), pp. 190–4.

Noys, Benjamin, *The Culture of Death* (Oxford and New York: Berg, 2005).

Nye, Joseph, *Bound to Lead: The Changing Nature of American Power* (New York: Basic Books, 1990).

O'Brien, Lauren B., 'The Evolution of Terrorism Since 9/11', http://www.fbi.gov/stats-services/publications/law-enforcement-bulletin/september-2011/the-evolution-of-terrorism-since-9-11 (accessed 11 July 2012).

Okorafor-Mbachu, Nnedi, 'Stephen King's Super-Duper Magical Negroes', *Strange Horizons*, 2004 http://www.strangehorizons.com/2004/20041025/kinga.shtml (accessed 14 February 2012).

Oudart, Jean-Pierre, 'Cinema and Suture', *Screen*, 18: 4 ([1969] 1977–78), pp. 35–47.

Pahl, John, 'Sacrifice', in *The Routledge Companion to Religion and Film*. Ed. John Lyden (New York: Routledge, 2009), pp. 465–81.

Pape, Robert A., and James K. Feldman, *Cutting the Fuse: The Explosion of Global Suicide Terrorism and How to Stop It* (Chicago: University of Chicago Press, 2010).

Pearl, Monica B., *AIDS Literature and Gay Identity: The Literature of Loss* (Abingdon and New York: Routledge, 2012).

Phelan, Peggy, *Mourning Sex: Performing Public Memories* (London and New York: Routledge, 1997).

Pick, Anat, *Creaturely Poetics: Animality and Vulnerability in Literature and Film* (New York: Columbia University Press, 2011).

del Pilar Blanco, Maria and Esther Peeren (eds), *Popular Ghosts: The Haunted Spaces of Everyday Culture* (London and New York: Continuum, 2010).

Pinquet, Maurice, *Voluntary Death in Japan*. Trans. Rosemary Morris (Cambridge: Polity Press, [1984] 1993).

Platinga, Carl, *Rhetoric and Representation in Non-Fiction Film* (Cambridge: Cambridge University Press, 1997).

Platinga, Carl and Greg Smith (eds), *Passionate Views: Film, Cognition, and Emotion* (Baltimore, MD: The Johns Hopkins University Press, 1999).

Pond, Jennifer Bennett, 'Dying & Death in North America through the Lens of *Dying at Grace*, *Kids care* & *Antonia's line*: Cause to Question our Fear', Canadian Theses, (Laurentian University, 2007).

Pough, Gwendolyn D., *Check it While I Wreck it: Black Motherhood, Hip-Hop Culture, and the Public Sphere* (Lebanon, NH: Northeastern University Press, 2004).

Prince, Stephen, *The Warrior's Camera: The Cinema of Akira Kurosawa* (Princeton: Princeton University Press, 1991).

Prince, Stephen, *Firestorm: American Film in the Age of Terrorism* (New York: Columbia University Press, 2009).

Propp, Vladimir, *Morphology of the Folktale*. Trans. Laurence Scott. Rev. and ed. Louis A. Wagner, 2nd ed. (Austin: University of Texas Press, 1986).

Radstone, Susannah (ed.), *Memory and Methodology* (London: Berg, 2000).

Radstone, Susannah, 'Trauma Theory: Contexts, Politics, Ethics', *Paragraph*, 30: 1 (March 2007), pp. 9–29.

Rainey, Buck, *The Reel Cowboy: Essays on the Myth in Movies and Literature* (Jefferson, NC: McFarland, 1996).

Ramazani, Vaheed, *Writing in Pain: Literature, History, and the Culture of Denial* (New York: Palgrave Macmillan, 2007).

Rank, Otto, *Will Therapy and Truth and Reality* (New York: Knopf, [1936] 1945).

Reyes-Cortez, Marcel, 'Maintaining the Dead in the Lives of the Living: Material Culture and Photography in the Cemeteries of Mexico City', in Aaron, *Envisaging*.

Ricciardi, Alessia, *The Ends of Mourning: Psychoanalysis, Literature, Film* (Stanford, CA: Stanford University Press, 2003).

Rich, B. Ruby, 'Back to the Future (Film after 9/11)', *The Nation*, 15 October 2001, available at: http://www.thenation.com/doc/20011015/rich/2 (accessed 12 October 2007).

Richards, Naomi, 'Rosetta Life: Using Film to Represent Experiences of Life-Limiting Illness', in Aaron, *Envisaging*.

Rosenthal, Alan, *The New Documentary in Action: A Casebook in Film Making* (Berkeley: University of California Press, 1971).

Rowe, Aimee Carrillo, 'Feeling in the Dark: Empathy, Whiteness, and Miscegenation in *Monster's Ball*', *Hypatia*, 22: 2 (2007), pp. 122–42.

Ruby, Jay, *Secure the Shadow: Death and Photography in America* (Cambridge, MA: The MIT Press, 1999).

Ruffles, Tom, *Ghost Images: Cinema of the Afterlife* (Jefferson, NC: McFarland, 2004).

Russell, Catherine, *Narrative Mortality: Death, Closure, and New Wave Cinemas* (Minneapolis: University of Minnesota Press, 1995).

Russo, Vito, *The Celluloid Closet: Homosexuality in the Movies* (New York: Harper and Row, 1987).

Savran, David, *Taking it Like a Man: White Masculinity, Masochism and Contemporary American Culture* (Princeton: Princeton University Press, 1998).

Saxton, Libby, 'Fragile Faces: Levinas and Lanzmann', *Film-Philosophy*, 11: 2 (2007), pp. 1–14.

Saxton, Libby, 'Close Encounters with Distant Suffering: Michael Haneke's Disarming Visions', in Kate Ince (ed.), *Five Directors* (Manchester: Manchester University Press, 2008).

Saxton, Libby, *Haunted Images* (London: Wallflower, 2008).

Scarry, Elaine, *The Body in Pain: The Making and Unmaking of the World* (Oxford: Oxford University Press, 1985).

Schneider, Steven Jay, 'Architectural Nostaligia and the New York City Skyline on Film', in Dixon, *Film*, pp. 29–41.

Schueller, Malini Johar, 'Decolonizing Global Theories Today: Hardt and Negri, Agamben, Butler', *Interventions*, 11: 2 (2009), pp. 235–54.

Schultz, Ned W. and Lisa M. Huet, 'Sensational! Violent! Popular! Death in American movies', *Omega: Journal of Death and Dying*, 42: 2 (2000–01), pp. 137–49.

Scott, A. O., '*The Virgin Suicides*: Evanescent Trees and Sisters in an Enchanted 1970's Suburb', *New York Times*, 21 April 21 2000, http://www.nytimes.com/library/film/042100virgin-film-review.html (accessed 20 August 2010).

Scott, A. O., 'My Kidney, My Life: Siblings in a Tough Spot', *New York Times*, 25 June 2009, http://movies.nytimes.com/2009/06/26/movies/26sister.html (accessed 13 October 2011).

Shah, Pannah, *The Indian Film* (Westport, CT: Greenwood Press, 1981).

Shaheen, Jack G., *Guilty: Hollywood's Verdict on Arabs after 9/11* (Northampton, MA: Olive Branch Press, 2008).

Sharrett, Christopher, 'The World that is Known: An Interview with Michael Haneke', *Cineaste*, 28: 3 (summer 2003), pp. 28–31.

Shildrick, Margrit, *Leaky Bodies and Boundaries: Feminism, Postmodernism and (Bio)ethics* (London: Routledge, 1997).

Shklovsky, Victor, 'Art as Device', *Theory or Prose*. Trans. Benjamin Sher. Intro. Gerald L. Bruns (Elmwood Park, IL: Dalkey Archive Press, [1925] 1990), pp. 1–14.

Shohat, Ella and Robert Stam, *Unthinking Eurocentrism: Multiculturalism and the Media* (London: Routledge, 1994).

Shostak, Debra, '"A story we could live with": Narrative Voice, the Reader, and Jeffrey Eugenides's *The Virgin Suicides*', *MFS: Modern Fiction Studies*, 55: 4 (winter 2009), pp. 808–32.

Skerry, Philip J., '*Dances with Wolves* and *Unforgiven*: Apocalyptic, Revisionist Westerns', in Paul Loukides and Linda K. Fuller (eds), *Beyond the stars:*

Studies in Popular Film (Bowling Green, OH; Bowling Green University Popular Press, 1996), pp. 281–91.

Slocum, John David (ed.), *Violence and American Cinema* (London and New York: Routledge, 2001).

Snyder, Sharon L., Brenda Jo Brueggemann, and Rosemarie Garland-Thomson (eds), *The Disability Reader: Enabling the Humanities* (New York: MLA, 2002).

Sobchack, Vivian, 'Inscribing Ethical Space: Ten Propositions on Death, Representation and Documentary', *Carnal Thoughts: Embodiment and Moving Image Culture* (Berkeley and Los Angeles: University of California Press, [1984] 2004), pp. 226–57.

Sontag, Susan, *Illness as Metaphor and AIDS and its Metaphors* (London: Penguin, [1977/1988] 1991).

'Spielberg says new movie reflects post-9/11 unease', *Tonight*, 13 June (2005), http://www.tonight.co.za/index.php?fArticleId=2556230 (accessed 10 October 2007).

Spigel, Lynn, 'Entertainment Wars: Television Culture after 9/11', in *American Quarterly*, 56: 2 (June 2004), pp. 235–70.

Spivak, Gayatri Chakravorty 'Can the Subaltern Speak?', in Cary Nelson and Lawrence Grossberg (eds), *Marxism and the Interpretation of Culture* (Urbana, IL: University of Illinois Press, 1988), pp. 271–313.

Spivak, Gayatri Chakravorty, *A Critique of Postcolonial Reason: Towards a History of the Vanishing Present* (Cambridge, MA: Harvard University Press, 1999).

Stacey, Jackie, *Teratologies: A Cultural Study of Cancer* (London: Routledge, 1997).

Stadler, Jane, *Pulling Focus: Intersubjective Experience, Narrative Film, and Ethics* (New York: Continuum, 2008).

Stam, Robert and Louise Spence, 'Colonialism, Racism and Representation', *Screen*, 24: 2 (1983), pp. 2–20.

Stam, Robert, Robert Burgoyne and Sandy Flitterman-Lewis (eds), *New Vocabularies in Film Semiotics: Structuralism, Post-structuralism and Beyond* (London: Routledge, 1992).

Stowe, Harriet Beecher, *Uncle Tom's Cabin* (San Francisco, CA: Ignatius Press, [1852] 2009).

Strange, Julie-Marie, *Death, Grief and Poverty in Britain, 1870–1914* (Cambridge, Cambridge University Press, 2005).

Striner, Richard, *Supernatural Romance in Film: Tales of Love, Death and the Afterlife* (Jefferson, NC: McFarland, 2011).

Stringer, Julian (ed.), *Movie Blockbusters* (London and New York: Routledge, 2003).

Sturken, Marita, *Tangled Memories: The Vietnam War, The AIDS Epidemic, and the Politics of Remembering* (Berkeley: University of California Press, 1997).

'Suicide Statistics', *Suicide.org*, http://www.suicide.org/suicide-statistics.html (accessed 18 August 2011).

Suleiman, Susan Rubin, *Risking Who One Is: Encounters with Contemporary Art and Literature* (Cambridge, MA: Harvard University Press, 1994).

Tanner, Laura E., *Lost Bodies: Inhabiting the Borders of Life and Death* (Ithaca, NY: Cornell University Press, 2006).

Tapia, Ruby C., *American Pietas: Visions of Race, Death and the Maternal* (Minneapolis and London: Minnesota University Press, 2011).

Tasker, Yvonne, *Spectacular Bodies: Gender, Genre and the Action Cinema* (London and New York: Routledge, 1993).

Tasker, Yvonne (ed.), *Action and Adventure Cinema* (Abingdon and New York: Routledge, 2004).

Taylor, Clyde, 'The Rebirth of the Aesthetic in Cinema', in Daniel Bernardi (ed.), *The Birth of Whiteness: Race and the Emergence of U.S. Cinema* (Rutgers: Rutgers University Press, 1996), pp. 15–37.

Taylor, Steve, *Durkheim and the Study of Suicide* (London: Macmillan, 1982).

Tercier, John Anthony, *The Contemporary Deathbed: The Ultimate Rush* (Basingstoke: Palgrave Macmillan, 2005).

Thompson, Kirsten Moana, *Apocalyptic Dead: American Film at the Turn of the Millennium* (Albany: State University of New York Press, 2007).

Todorov, Tzvetan, 'The Two Principles of Narrative', *Diacritics*, 1: 1 (fall 1971), pp. 37–44.

Tolstoy, Leo, *Anna Karenina* (London: Wordsworth Editions, [1877] 1999).

'Top 10 Actors', *Examiner.com*, available at: http://www.examiner.com/movie-in-baltimore/top-10-actors-morgan-freeman-5-on-total-box-office-revenue-list (accessed 25 January 2012).

Townsend, Chris, *Art and Death* (London: I. B. Tauris, 2008).

Usai, Paolo Cherchi, *The Death of Cinema* (London: BFI, 2001).

Uraizee, Joya, *In the Jaws of the Leviathan: Genocide Fiction and Film* (Newcastle: Cambridge Scholars Press, 2010).

US Department of Defense, available at: http://www.defense.gov

Vanhala, Helena, *The Depiction of Terrorists in Blockbuster Hollywood Films, 1980–2001* (Jefferson, NC: McFarland, 2011).

Vélez-Ibáñez, Carlos G., *Border Visions: Mexican Cultures of the Southwest United States* (Tuscon, AZ: University of Arizona Press, 1996).

Wade, Leslie A., 'Sublime Trauma: The Violence of Ethical Encounter', in Patrick Anderson and Jisha Menon (eds), *Violence Performed: Local Roots and Global Routes of Conflict* (Basingstoke: Palgrave Macmillan, 2011), pp. 15–30.

Waegner, Cathy Covell, 'Bodies and Hybrid Tropes: Border Crossings in Recent Films', in Rocío G. Davis, Dorothea Fischer-Hornung and Johanna C. Kardux Aro (eds), *Aesthetic Practices and Politics in Media, Music, and Art: Performing Migration* (New York and Abingdon: Routledge, 2011), pp. 48–65.

Wailoo, Keith, Karen O'Neill, Jeffrey Dowd and Roland Anglin (eds), *Katrina's Imprint: Race and Vulnerability in America* (New Brunswick, NJ: Rutgers University Press, 2010).

Waites, Kathleen J., 'Invisible Woman: Herbert Ross' *Boys on the Side* Puts HIV/

AIDS and Women in Their Place', *The Journal of Popular Culture*, 39: 3 (June 2006), pp. 479–92.

Wallace, Michele, *Dark Designs and Visual Culture* (Durham, NC: Duke University Press, 2004).

Walliss, John and Kenneth G. C. Newport (eds), *The End all Around Us: Apocalyptic Texts and Popular Culture* (London: Equinox, 2009).

Warner, Michael, *The Trouble with Normal: Sex, Politics, and the Ethics of Queer Life* (Cambridge, MA: Harvard University Press, 1999).

Wayne, Mike, *Political Film: the Dialectics of Third Cinema* (London: Pluto Press, 2001)

Weber, Cynthia, *Imagining America at War* (London: Routledge, 2006).

Weber, Tina, *Drop Dead Gorgeous: Representations of Corpses on American TV Shows* (Chicago, IL: University of Chicago Press, 2012).

Weigman, Robin, *American Anatomies: Theorizing Race and Gender* (Durham, NC: Duke University Press, 1995).

West, Cornel, 'A Matter of Life and Death', *October*, 61 (summer, 1992), pp. 20–3.

Westwell, Guy, *War Cinema: Hollywood on the Front Line* (London: Wallflower, 2006).

Wheatley, Catherine, *Michael Haneke: The Ethic of the Image* (Oxford: Berghahn Books, 2009).

Wilcox, W. Bradford, 'The Evolution of Divorce', *National Affairs*, 1 (fall 2009), http://www.nationalaffairs.com/publications/detail/the-evolution-of-divorce. (accessed 3 July 2012).

Wilderson III, Frank B., *Red White and Black: Cinema and the Structure of U.S Antagonisms* (Durham, NC: Duke University Press, 2010).

Williams, Linda, 'Something Else Besides a Mother: *Stella Dallas* and the Maternal Melodrama', *Cinema Journal*, 24: 1 (autumn, 1984), pp. 2–27.

Williams, Linda, *Hard Core: Power, Pleasure and the 'Frenzy of the Visible'* (Berkeley: University of California Press, 1989).

Williams, Linda, *Playing the Race Card: Melodramas of Black and White from Uncle Tom to O. J. Simpson* (Princeton and Oxford: Princeton University Press, 2001).

Williams, Tony, '*The Dirty Dozen*: the Contradictory Nature of Screen Violence', in Tasker, *Action*, pp. 345–57.

Wilson, Emma, *Love, Mortality and the Moving Image* (Basingstoke: Palgrave Macmillan, 2012).

Winter, Jessica, 'Sofia Coppola's mystery girls', *The Village Voice*, 45: 15 (2000), p. 144.

'The Wit Film Project: Innovative Medical Education for End-of-Life Care', available at: http://www.growthhouse.org/witfilmproject/index.html (accessed 11 July 2011).

Wood, Amy Louise, *Lynching and Spectacle: Witnessing Racial Violence in*

America, 1890–1940 (Chapel Hill, NC: University of North Carolina Press, 2009).

Wood, Amy Louise, '"Killing the Elephant": Murderous Beasts and the Thrill of Retribution, 1885–1930', *The Journal of the Gilded Age and Progressive Era,* 11: 3 (July 2012), pp. 405–44.

Wood, Robin, *Hollywood: From Vietnam to Reagan* (New York: Columbia University Press, 1986).

Yaqub, Nadia, 'The Palestinian Cinematic Wedding', *Journal of Middle East Women's Studies,* 3: 2 (spring 2007), pp. 56–85.

Žižek, Slavoj, *Welcome to the Desert of the Real* (London: Verso, 2002).

Žižek, Slavoj, 'On 9/11, New Yorkers Faced the Fire in the Minds of Men', *Guardian,* 11 September (2006), p. 30.

Žižek, Slavoj, commentary, *Children of Men,* DVD (Universal City, CA: Universal Studios, 2007).

Filmography

After Life (Hirokazu Koreeda, 1998)

Alexander (Oliver Stone, 2004)

All That Jazz (Bob Fosse, 1979)

All Things Fall Apart (Mario Van Peebles, 2011)

Always (Steven Spielberg, 1989)

Amour (Michael Haneke, 2012)

And Life Goes On (a.k.a. *Life, and Nothing More*, Abbas Kiarostami, 1992)

The Antagonists (Universal TV Series, 1981)

Apocalypto (Mel Gibson, 2006)

Armageddon (Michael Bay, 1998)

Babel (Alejandro González Iñárritu, 2006)

Bambi (James Algar et al.,1942)

Basic Instinct (Paul Verhoeven, 1992)

Batman Begins (Christopher Nolan, 2005)

Beloved (Jonathan Demme, 1998)

Beaches (Garry Marshall, 1988)

Bette Davis: A Basically Benevolent Volcano (BBC, 1983)

Birth of a Nation (D. W. Griffith, 1915)

Biutiful (Alejandro González Iñárritu, 2010)

Black Hawk Down (Ridley Scott, 2001)

Blood Diamond (Edward Zwick, 2006)

Blue (Derek Jarman, 1993)

Body of Evidence (Uli Edel, 1992)

Bonnie and Clyde (Arthur Penn, 1967)

Bound (Andy and Gary Wachowski, 1996)

The Bourne Identity (Doug Liman, 2002)

The Bourne Supremacy (Paul Greengrass, 2004)

The Bourne Ultimatum (Paul Greengrass, 2007)

Boys on the Side (Herbert Ross, 1995)

Brian's Song (Buzz Kulik, 1971)

Brian's Song (John Gray, 2001)

The Bridge (Eric Steel, 2005)

Bruce Almighty (Tom Shadyac, 2003)

The Bucket List (Rob Reiner, 2007)

Butch Cassidy and the Sundance Kid (George Roy Hill, 1969)

Caché (Michael Haneke, 2005)

Casino Royale (Martin Campbell, 2006)

Catch a Fire (Phillip Noyce, 2006)

The Celluloid Closet (Rob Epstein and Jeffrey Friedman, 1995)

Charlie's Angels (McG, 2000)

Children of Men (Alfonso Cuarón, 2006)

The Children's Hour (William Wyler, 1961)

Clara's Heart (Robert Mulligan, 1988)

Collateral Damage (Andrew Davis, 2002)

The Constant Gardener (Fernando Meirelles, 2005)

Corrina Corrina (Jessie Nelson, 1994)

*Country of my Skull (*John Boorman, 2006)

The Courier (Hany Abu-Assad, 2012)

Cruising (William Friedkin, 1980)

Dances with Wolves (Kevin Costner, 1990)

Danger Zone: The Making of Top Gun (2004), *Top Gun* 2-Disc Special Collector's Edition DVD, 2007.

The Dark Knight (Christopher Nolan, 2008)

The Dark Knight Rises (Christopher Nolan, 2012)

Dante's Peak (Roger Donaldson, 1997)

Dark Victory (Edmund Goulding, 1939)

The Death of Mr Lazarescu/ Moartea domnului Lazarescu (Cristi Puiu, 2005)

Deep Impact (Mimi Leder, 1998).

The Dirty Dozen (Robert Aldrich, 1967)

District 9 (Neill Blomkamp, 2009)

The Diving Bell and the Butterfly (Julian Schnabel, 2007)

Dogville (Lars Von Trier, 2003)

Don't Look Now (Nicolas Roeg, 1973)

Double Indemnity (Billy Wilder, 1944)

Downfall (Oliver Hirschbiegel, 2004)

Down to Earth (Chris and Paul Weitz, 2001)

Dr No (Terence Young, 1962)

Dying (Michael Roemer, 1976)

Dying at Grace (Allan King, 2003)

Electrocuting an Elephant (Thomas Edison, 1903)

Evan Almighty (Tom Shadyac, 2007)

Evening (Lajos Koltai, 2007)

Even the Rain (Iciar Bollain, 2010)

The Event (Thom Fitzgerald, 2003)

Faces of Death (John Alan Schwartz, 1978)

Fearless (Peter Weir, 1993)

Le Feu Follet (Louis Malle, 1963)

50/50 (Jonathan Levine, 2011)

Flag of Our Fathers (Clint Eastwood, 2006)

Four Lions (Chris Morris, 2010)
Freebie and the Bean (Richard Rush, 1974)
Getting Home (Yang Zhang, 2007)
Ghost (Jerry Zucker, 1990)
Girl Interrupted (James Mangold, 1999)
The Godfather: Part II (Francis Ford Coppola, 1974)
Gone with the Wind (Victor Fleming, 1939)
Glory (Edward Zwick, 1989)
Goldfinger (Guy Hamilton, 1964)
The Great Escape (John Sturges, 1963)
The Green Mile (Frank Darabont, 1999)
Grumpy Old Men (Donald Petrie, 1993)
La Guelle Ouverte (Maurice Pialat, 1974)
Harold and Maude (Hal Ashby, 1971)
Harry Potter and the Philosopher's Stone (Chris Columbus, 2001)
Harry Potter and the Chamber of Secrets (Chris Columbus, 2002)
Harry Potter and the Prisoner of Azkaban (Alfonso Cuarón, 2004)
Harry Potter and the Goblet of Fire (Mike Newell, 2005)
Harry Potter and the Order of the Phoenix (David Yates, 2007)
Harry Potter and the Half-Blood Prince (David Yates, 2009)
Harry Potter and the Deathly Hallows – Part 1 (David Yates, 2010)
Harry Potter and the Deathly Hallows – Part 2 (David Yates, 2011)
Heaven Can Wait (Warren Beatty and Buck Henry, 1978)
The Help (Tate Taylor, 2011)
Here Comes Mr Jordan (Alexander Halls, 1941)
Hilary and Jackie (Anand Tucker, 1998)
Hotel Rwanda (Terry George, 2004)
The Hours (Stephen Daldry, 2002)
The House of Mirth (Terence Davies, 2000)
How it Feels to be Run Over (Cecil Hepworth, 1900)
How to Die in Oregon (Peter Richardson, 2011)
I am Khan (Karan Johar, 2010)
I am Legend (Francis Lawrence, 2007)
Ich Klage an (I Accuse) (Wolfgang Liebeneiner, 1941)
Ikiru (Akira Kurosawa, 1952)
Imitation of Life (John M. Stahl, 1934)
Imitation of Life (Douglas Sirk, 1959)
In Bruges (Martin McDonagh, 2008)
Inception (Christopher Nolan, 2010)
Independence Day (Roland Emmerich, 1996)
In the Valley of Ellah (Paul Haggis, 2007)
Intouchables (Oliver Nakache and Eric Toledano, 2011)
Iris (Richard Eyre, 2001)
The Iron Lady (Phyllida Lloyd, 2011)

It's my Party (Randal Kleiser, 1996)
Jonestown: The Life and Death of Peoples Temple (Stanley Nelson, 2006)
Jonestown: Paradise Lost (Tim Wolochatiuk, 2007)
The Killers (Robert Siodmak, 1946)
King Arthur (Antoine Fuqua, 2004)
The Kingdom (Peter Berg, 2007)
Lara Croft: Tomb Raider (Simon West, 2001)
Last Days (Gus Van Sant, 2005)
Last Holiday (Wayne Wang, 2006)
The Last King of Scotland (Kevin MacDonald, 2006)
The Last Samurai (Edward Zwick, 2003)
The Last Seduction (John Dahl, 1994)
Leaving Las Vegas (Mike Figgis, 1995)
Legend of Baggar Vance (Robert Redford, 2000)
Lethal Weapon (Richard Donner, 1987)
Letters from Iwo Jima (Clint Eastwood, 2006)
The Life of David Gale (Alan Parker, 2003)
Life as a House (Irwin Winkler, 2001)
Lightning Over Water (Wim Wenders, 1980)
Lions for Lambs (Robert Redford, 2007)
The Living End (Gregg Araki, 1992)
Lolita (Stanley Kubrick, 1962)
Lone Star (John Sayles, 1996)
Longtime Companion (Norman René, 1989)
Love Story (Arthur Hiller, 1970)
The Lord of the Rings: The Fellowship of the Ring (Peter Jackson, 2001)
The Lord of the Rings: The Two Towers (Peter Jackson, 2002)
The Lord of the Rings: The Return of the King (Peter Jackson, 2003)
Madame Bovary (Claude Chabrol, 1991)
Manderlay (Lars Von Trier, 2005)
The Manual (Osamu Fukutani, 2003)
Masada (Craig Haffner, television documentary, 2002)
The Matrix (Wachowski brothers, 1999)
A Matter of Life and Death (Michael Powell and Emeric Pressburger, 1946)
Million Dollar Baby (Clint Eastwood, 2004)
Mr Jones (Mike Figgis, 1993)
Mondo Cane (Paolo Cavara, Gualtiero Jacopetti, Franco Prosperi, 1962)
Monster's Ball (Marc Forster, 2001)
My Life (Bruce Joel Rubin, 1993)
My Life without Me (Isabel Coixet, 2003)
My Sister's Keeper (Nick Cassavetes, 2009)
National Geographic: Inside 9/11 (2005)
Near Death (Frederick Wiseman, 1989)
The New World (Terence Malick, 2005)

New York (Kabir Khan, 2009)

The Next Best Thing (John Schlesinger, 2000)

9/11 (James Hanlon et al., 2002)

The Notebook (Nick Cassavetes, 2004)

The Object of My Affection (Nicholas Hytner, 1998)

One Flew over the Cuckoo's Nest (Milos Forman, 1975)

On Her Majesty's Secret Service (Peter R. Hunt, 1969)

Outbreak (Wolfgang Peterson, 1995)

Out of the Past (Jacques Tournier, 1947)

Paradise Now (Hany Abu-Assad, 2005)

Peter's Friends (Kenneth Branagh, 1992)

Philadelphia (Jonathan Demme, 1993)

The Poseidon Adventure (Ronald Neame, 1972)

Quantum of Solace (Marc Forster, 2008)

Rear Window (Alfred Hitchcock, 1954)

Redacted (Brian de Palma, 2007)

Red Dust (Tom Hooper, 2004)

Rendition (Gavin Hood, 2007)

Rope (Alfred Hitchcock, 1948)

Salvador (Oliver Stone, 1986)

Le Sang des Bêtes (George Franju, 1949)

Saving Private Ryan (Steven Spielberg, 1998)

Schindler's List (Steven Spielberg, 1993)

The Sea Inside (Alejandro Amenábar, 2004)

The Sergeant (John Flynn, 1968)

Set it Off (F. Gary Gray, 1996)

Seven Samurai/Shichinin no Samurai (Akira Kurosawa, 1954)

The Seventh Continent (Michael Haneke, 1989)

Shake Hands with The Devil (Roger Spottiswoode, 2007)

'Shooting Stars', *CSI: Crime Scene Investigation*, season 4, episode 6, first screened 13 October 2005.

The Siege (Edward Zwick, 1998)

Silverlake Life: The View from Here (Peter Friedman and Tom Joslin, 2003)

Son frère (Patrice Chéreau, 2003)

Soylent Green (Richard Fleischer, 1973)

Star Trek: First Contact (Jonathan Frakes, 1996)

Stepmom (Chris Columbus, 1998)

Strange Days (Kathryn Bigelow, 1995)

Swoon (Tom Kalin, 1992)

Tabu (Miguel Gomes, Mexico, 2012)

Taste of Cherry (Abbas Kiarostami, 1997)

Terms of Endearment (James L. Brooks, 1983)

Theeviravaathi: The Terrorist (Santosh Sivan, India, 1998)

Thelma and Louise (Ridley Scott, 1991)

Third Star (Hattie Dalton, 2010)
The Three Burials of Melquidas Estrada (Tommy Lee Jones, 2005)
300 (Zack Snyder, 2006)
Through the Olive Trees (Abbas Kiarostami, 1994)
Time to Leave (François Ozon, 2005)
Titicut Follies (Frederick Wiseman, 1967)
Top Gun (Tony Scott, 1988)
Train Pulling into a Station (Lumière brothers, 1895)
Troy (Wolfgang Peterson, 2004)
True Lies (James Cameron, 1994)
2012 (Roland Emmerich, 2009)
Uncle Tom's Cabin (Edwin S. Porter, 1903)
Under Fire (Roger Spottiswoode, 1983)
United 93 (Paul Greengrass, 2006)
Vantage Point (Pete Travis, 2008)
Vertigo (Alfred Hitchcock, 1958)
The Virgin Suicides (Sofia Coppola, 1999)
Volcano (Mick Jackson, 1997)
War of the Worlds (Steven Spielberg, 2005)
Warrendale (Allan King, 1967)
The War Within (Joseph Castelo, 2005)
We Were Soldiers (Randall Wallace, 2002)
What Dreams May Come (Vincent Ward, 1998)
White Material (Claire Denis, 2009)
Who's in Charge (Allan King, 1983)
Wit (Mike Nichols, 2001)
Witness to Jonestown (Stephen Stept, 2008)
World Trade Center (Oliver Stone, 2006)
Wristcutters: A Love Story (Goran Dukic, 2006)
Zero Patience (John Greyson, 1993)

Index